The Strange and Terrible Visions
of Wilhelm Friess

Cultures of Knowledge in the Early Modern World
Edited by Ann Blair, Anthony Grafton, and Jacob Soll

The series Cultures of Knowledge in the Early Modern World examines the intersection of encyclopedic, natural, historical, and literary knowledge in the early modern world, incorporating both theory (philosophies of knowledge and authority) and practice (collection, observation, information handling, travel, experiment, and their social and political contexts). Interdisciplinary in nature, the goal of the series is to promote works that illustrate international and inter-religious intellectual exchange and the intersections of different fields and traditions of knowledge.

History, Medicine, and the Traditions of Renaissance Learning
Nancy G. Siraisi

The Information Master: Jean-Baptiste Colbert's Secret State Intelligence System
Jacob Soll

Printing and Prophecy: Prognostication and Media Change 1450–1550
Jonathan Green

The Strange and Terrible Visions of Wilhelm Friess
Jonathan Green

The Strange and Terrible Visions of Wilhelm Friess

*The Paths of Prophecy in
Reformation Europe*

JONATHAN GREEN

The University of Michigan Press
Ann Arbor

Published in the United States of America by
The University of Michigan Press
Manufactured in the United States of America
⊗ Printed on acid-free paper

2017   2016   2015   2014   4   3   2   1

A CIP catalog record for this book is available from the British Library.

Library of Congress Cataloging-in-Publication Data

Green, Jonathan, 1970–

The strange and terrible visions of Wilhelm Friess : the paths of prophecy in
Reformation Europe / Jonathan Green.
        pages cm.   (Cultures of knowledge in the early modern world)
    Includes Dutch and German versions of Willem de Vriese's prophecies
from the years 1558 and 1577 respectively, adaptation of a French version
of the Vademecum of Johannes de Rupescissa.
    Includes bibliographical references and index.
    ISBN 978-0-472-11921-9 (hardcover : alk. paper)—ISBN 978-0-472-
12007-9 (e-book)
    1. Prophecy—Christianity—History.   2. Vriese, Willem de—
Appreciation.   3. Predictive astrology—Europe, German-speaking—
History.   4. Books—Europe, German-speaking—History—1450–1600.
5. Apocalyptic literature—History and criticism. I. Vriese, Willem de. II.
Title.
BR115.P8G745   2014
261.5'130940909031—dc23

                                                    2013048766

Preface

As anyone who has gone through the process can attest, the latter stages of publishing a book involve periodic bursts of intense effort under tight deadlines, interspersed with lengthy periods of waiting on all the things that are not under the author's control. During one of those waiting periods while *Printing and Prophecy* was making its way toward publication, it occurred to me that I would soon have to work on something else. Looking for the next project has always been a process of false starts as one idea proves unworkable and another turns out to have been sitting on the library shelves for the last decade or more, so I thought I would start small. I had limited the scope of *Printing and Prophecy* to the century following the invention of print, roughly 1450–1550, so I decided to find out which of the most popular prophetic pamphlets of the later sixteenth century had the least scholarly literature devoted to them. As it turns out, no secondary literature addressed any of them in any depth, including what turned out to be the most popular of them: the prophecies of Wilhelm Friess of Maastricht. I had touched on Wilhelm Friess in *Printing and Prophecy*, but not at any length, as all its editions were published after 1550. I resolved to write a quick, short article while I tried to figure out what my next major project would be.

As you already know, as you are reading a book rather than a short article, none of that worked out as planned. In the middle of leaving one town and academic position for another, I realized that the Wilhelm Friess pamphlets represented not one text but two (as Robin Barnes had noticed long ago), with no obvious relationship between them. I began tracking down editions and gathering facsimiles. There were many of them.

Within a few months, I had written the article I had planned. I even worked up a cover page and formatted the article for submission, but I could not escape the nagging feeling that I had not yet entirely solved the riddle of Wilhelm Friess and his strange and terrible prophecies. I redoubled my search for new sources, and my tidy little German project soon turned into a Dutch-German-Swiss project that was straining the word-count limits of a journal article. I decided to start writing again to discover if there might just be enough material for a short book, something like the scholarly equivalent of a novella. Ellen Bauerle, the editor who had acquired *Printing and Prophecy* for the University of Michigan Press (and to whom I am grateful for her early support and continual encouragement), was willing to look at a draft that I thought was nearly complete, and she responded positively.

As you already know, as you are not reading an academic novella, I was actually much farther from completing my research on Wilhelm Friess than I thought at the time. I still could not escape the nagging feeling that I had overlooked something, so I went back to prophecies printed in the fifteenth and sixteenth centuries to see if I had overlooked potential sources. Eventually I found them, but not in the century I had expected, so my manageable Dutch-German-Swiss research project added French and Latin sources and another century to its scope.

While *Printing and Prophecy* mostly examined prophecy from the remote, bird's-eye view that media studies often require, working on the prophecies of Wilhelm Friess has entailed a tightly focused examination of a few texts associated with one authorial name, so that the placement of one letter or alteration of one word can become a highly significant detail. The required approach falls toward the mustier side of traditional research methods in the humanities. Yet the methods of textual history and bibliographic inquiry were able to uncover a story that I found to be utterly fascinating and sometimes marked by drama, tragedy, duplicity, and stubborn resistance in the face of overwhelming force. The reader may take comfort in knowing that I am no longer troubled by the feeling that I have overlooked something important: while I have no doubt that I have not discovered every significant connection or relevant contextual fact, the nagging sensation that there is yet more to say is now the responsibility of those who will read this book, uncover and improve on its flaws, and extend—or reject—its conclusions.

As this project required me to engage with what were new areas of research for me, I was only able to complete it with the generous assistance of many people and institutions. My thanks go first to the libraries that made their material available for inspection or provided facsimiles, including the Museum Plantin-Moretus in Antwerp, the Erfgoedbibliotheek Hendrik Conscience in Antwerp, the Staatsbibliothek Preußischer Kulturbesitz in Berlin, the Lehrerbibliothek des Görres-Gymnasiums in Düsseldorf, the Eichstätt Universitätsbibliothek, the Forschungsbibliothek in Gotha, the Universitäts- und Landesbibliothek Halle, the Universiteitsbibliotheek Leiden, the Leipzig Universitätsbibliothek, the Bayerische Staatsbibliothek in Munich, die Württembergische Landesbibliothek in Stuttgart, the Universiteetsbibliotheek Utrecht, the Herzogin Anna Amalia Bibliothek in Weimar, and the Herzog August Bibliothek in Wolfenbüttel. In addition to the gratitude I owe their institutions, several librarians and archivists deserve special mention for their personal assistance in locating editions and obtaining facsimiles, including Dr. Karl-Ferdinand Besselmann of the Universitäts- und Stadtbibliothek in Cologne, Frank Aurich of the Sächsische Landesbibliothek/Staats- und Universitätsbibliothek Dresden, Uwe Kahl of the Christian-Weise-Bibliothek Zittau, and Prof. Dr. Christoph Eggenberger and Dr.phil. Alexa Renggli of the Zentralbibliothek Zürich. Several other individuals deserve special thanks for answering inquiries from the other side of the world on obscure topics, including Prof. Dr. Ulrich Seelbach of the Universität Bielefeld, Prof. Dr. Willem Frijhoff of the Vrije Universiteit in Amsterdam, Dr. Annelies van Gijsen of the Ruusbroecgenootschap in Antwerp, Dr. L. Wiggers of the Regionaal Historisch Centrum Limburg, and Dr. Wilhelm Klare of the Landeshauptarchiv Sachsen-Anhalt. I especially thank Dr. Oliver Duntze of the Gesamtkatalog der Wiegendrucke for his repeated willingness to answer inquiries and for pulling needles from haystacks on a number of occasions. I owe the interlibrary loan librarians of Brigham Young University my thanks as well for their assistance in locating microfilm facsimiles that would have normally been unobtainable, in which they were rivaled only by the personal efforts of my friend Bill Atkinson. I am grateful for the support that Brigham Young University–Idaho provided for my research and for its providing a place to conduct that research among friendly and supportive colleagues. I also thank all those who read early drafts of this work, including Dr. David Neville, Dr. Francien Markx, Dr. Wilfried Decoo, and the students in my German literature course in fall 2011. Finally, I am grateful most of all for my children's enduring patience and for the unwavering support and editorial acumen of my wife, Rose, to whom this book is dedicated.

Contents

⚓

Abbreviations

———— ✦ ————

NB   Pettegree, Andrew, and Malcolm Walsby. *Netherlandish Books: Books Published in the Low Countries and Dutch Books Published Abroad before 1601.* 2 vols. Leiden: Brill, 2011.

STCN   Short Title Catalogue Netherlands. http://picarta.pica.nl/DB=3.11/

USTC   Universal Short Title Catalogue. http://ustc.ac.uk/index.php/search

VD16   Verzeichnis der im deutschen Sprachbereich erschienenen Drucke des 16. Jahrhunderts. http://gateway-bayern.bib-bvb.de/aleph-cgi/bvb_suche?sid=VD16.

VD17   Verzeichnis der im deutschen Sprachbereich erschienenen Drucke des 17. Jahrhunderts. http://gso.gbv.de/DB=1.28/.

VL²   *Die deutsche Literatur des Mittelalters: Verfasserlexikon.* Ed. Kurt Ruh et al. 2nd ed. 14 vols. Berlin: de Gruyter, 1978–2008.

Introduction

As I write this, several devout students of holy scripture have just seen their careful calculations for the date of the Rapture come to naught, while budget and debt projections for the next seventy-five years continue to dominate the headlines. No matter how unpredictable the future might be, we remain obsessed with what tomorrow holds. Whether full harvests or foul weather, the dawn of a golden age or the advent of the Antichrist, divining the future has been a feature of human civilization since the time of its earliest written records, when a few scratches on clay or tortoiseshell might record the sale of grain or reveal the will of the gods.

How a culture imagines its future reveals as much about it as how it memorializes its past. Methods change; once, the brightest lights and guiding minds of civilization parsed each letter of the Bible, pondered the worth of prophetic utterances, or charted the course of the planets in order to discern how the world would change and when it would end. Predicting the future based on fluctuations in the royal treasury or birthrates in the hinterlands would have been dismissed as quackery. Today, horoscopes are relegated to the back pages of newspapers, and foreseeing the world's imminent end is consigned to the religious fringe, while economists, climate scientists, and other experts are the trusted oracles about the calamities that face us. As for tomorrow, I am reluctant to venture a prediction, but we can be confident that whatever human society exists centuries from now will still struggle over the meaning of the future.

To know the history of how the future has been imagined is to understand the course of human society. As Robin Barnes observes, "The history of eschatology lies at the heart of the history of culture and of civilization itself, for in beliefs concerning ends are reflected the most basic assumptions about meaning and purpose."[1] For many decades, scholars have studied the "powerful symbols in which apocalypticism has expressed its sense of the universal meaning of history," to borrow a phrase from Bernard McGinn.[2] Studying apocalypticism, or how people have related their present moment to the world's expected end, is a necessary part of investigating how people have understood themselves.

In the late Middle Ages, prophecies of the end of the world involved a cast of characters and a series of established scenes whose conventionality is reminiscent of the Commedia dell'Arte. Today, we are dimly aware that Harlequin, Columbine, and Scaramouche all inhabit the same fictional world and have various relationships with each other, although they would have been familiar to many Europeans in the sixteenth and seventeenth centuries. In the same way, by the late Middle Ages, over a thousand years of study and speculation had produced an elaborate end-time drama involving several stock figures, including false prophets and Angelic Popes or preachers, diabolical tyrants and a righteous Last Emperor, the invasion of the heathens and the conversion of the unbelievers, and, most prominently, the advent of the Antichrist.[3] Thanks to periodic resurrections in popular culture, we have a vague notion even today that all these characters belong to the same story. The narrative was not fixed, however: as in the Commedia dell'Arte, different retellings might involve different members of the cast or emphasize different events. In the late Middle Ages, there were several points of controversy, such as whether the advent of the Antichrist could be determined by astrology or other natural means. Many theologians saw this as an illegitimate attempt to know the hour of the Second Coming, but others disagreed, such as Cardinal Pierre d'Ailly (ca. 1350–1420), who drew on the planetary conjunction theories of Arabic astronomers to predict the advent of the Antichrist for the year 1789.[4] Other disputed points focused on the identities of the false tyrants and the pious Last Emperor: was the current Holy Roman Emperor the divinely appointed Last Emperor, with the king of France serving as Satan's servant, or vice versa? Arguments for either side appeared frequently, such as the late fourteenth-century "Gamaleon" prophecy or Telesphorus of Cosenza's commentary on the Cyrilline oracle.

In the history of prophetic texts and apocalyptic thought, the subsequent early modern period, extending roughly from 1500 to 1700, is a critical and complex time of transitions. It is neither satisfyingly medieval nor comfortably modern. This was the age of exploration that filled in most of the remaining blank places on the globe, but if we hope to discover an early blooming of enlightenment during these centuries, we will often find the embarrassing and tenacious grip of superstition instead. Just when one thinks that a medieval tradition has finally been extinguished, one often finds it rekindled a century or two later.

The end of history, whose rich religious narrative enjoyed considerable theological support, was not the only future that people in the sixteenth and seventeenth centuries sought to know. The heritage of Greek and Arabic astrologers provided the most common theoretical framework for predicting the course of the next few years or decades. Although astrology was subject to suspicion from some scholars and theologians, there was also considerable overlap between the practitioners and concepts of astrology and religious eschatology.[5] Just as meteorologists and climatologists both try to model weather patterns that differ only in time scale, and just as the opening prices on the New York Stock Exchange cannot entirely be separated from the expectations for a nation's long-term financial health, there was constant interaction between astrological prognostication and eschatological expectation in the early modern period. A theologian describing the Antichrist's career might point with concern to a recent comet or planetary conjunction, while an astrologer describing the ominous configuration of the heavens in the upcoming year might remind readers not to delay their repentance until it was too late.

The early modern period is also a time in which those who predicted the world's end could see their predictions fulfilled without needing to cross their eyes more than a little. The early sixteenth century witnessed nearly everything that a medieval prophet of doom could hope for or fear, save only the Resurrection and Last Judgment. As Johannes Virdung, prince of the German astrologers, wrote around 1524, "Therefore when we see that these things occur, as many of them unfortunately do now, namely, with the Turks and the clergy and the sacraments and offices of the church and so on, then we know that the Antichrist and the Last Day is near."[6] Christian apocalypticism of the preceding thousand years had created an end-time drama featuring a cast of characters whose arrival was expected before long, and many of them seemed to be actually taking their turns on stage. The Turkish invasions that stopped only at the gates of Vienna could be seen as a sign that Gog and Magog had been unleashed on the world from their long captivity, while Martin Luther could easily serve as the false prophet of the Antichrist in the orthodox imagination (of course, the popes took on that role for many Protestants). Charles V, the last Holy Roman Emperor to be crowned by the pope, began his reign with the sack of Rome, just as many of those hoping for the arrival of the Last Emperor had predicted, and Charles even relinquished his crown in 1556, as the fabled emperor of the end-time was expected to do (although the true Last Emperor was supposed to reconquer the Holy Land first).

As tumultuous as these events were, slower developments and quieter changes spelled the true end for the order of the world that had prevailed during the Middle Ages. The religious contention and ensuing wars of religion that followed the Protestant Reformation were provisionally resolved in 1555, not with final victory for either side, but with the Peace of Augsburg, which established the principle that each principality would follow its sovereign's faith (*cuius regio, eius religio*); the solidifying of confessional boundaries over the following decades put a final end to hopes for a united Christendom. Slowly but surely, the heliocentric model of Nicolas Copernicus, first published in the 1540s, displaced the cosmology that had prevailed since antiquity; eventually, a generation of astronomers came along who neither cast horoscopes nor dabbled in theology. The inferno of the Thirty Years' War between 1618 and 1648 upended the political order of Central Europe and left the Holy Roman Empire a mere husk, hardly a vehicle for the fulfillment of eschatological hopes, to which Napoleon Bonaparte administered the coup de grâce in 1806.

If expectations of future progress or calamity reveal much about human culture, and if the early modern period is a critical transitional time in how the end of the world was viewed, then these centuries hold one additional advantage over earlier times for the study of popular imagination: the invention of the printing press. While printing with movable type did not immediately revolutionize all forms of literacy following its invention by Johannes Gutenberg and his associates in Mainz shortly after 1450, the printing press slowly but fundamentally changed reading and writing over the following decades and centuries. The press did not just make possible the distribution of inexpensive texts to new classes of readers: the economics of print *required* it, as Gutenberg had already learned before he undertook his monumental Bible edition. Before a single copy of a printed work could be sold, a printer had to invest substantial amounts of specialized labor and equipment in preparing the press and had to acquire paper and ink in considerable quantities. Printing only a few copies would not justify the expense. Selling only a few dozen copies of a large scholarly book was financially ruinous, as more than a few overambitious printers discovered after their distribution networks proved to be less capable than they had thought. Smaller printers and larger operations in search of a quick profit had to target the audiences they could reach with a product that was shorter and written in the vernacular and that addressed the concerns of urban readers outside the professional and clerical classes that had long dominated readership.

What printers required was the pamphlet. Small booklets of a few dozen leaves or less, which had been the earliest products of Gutenberg's workshop in Mainz, remained a popular format for the following decades and came into their own after 1517, during the early Reformation, as the leading medium for religious polemic. Along with broadsides, pamphlets were an ideal vehicle for quickly reproducing a text, distributing it widely, and selling it inexpensively. For individual study or reading aloud to others, pamphlets had the advantage over broadsides that they were easier to hold in the hand. In addition, they structured the text into pages. While a pamphlet required a few more steps in its production compared to a broadside, it was more economical in its use of paper (the single largest expense for printers), as the pages of a pamphlet could be printed on both sides.[7]

For the history of popular imagination, pamphlets offer rich and invaluable evidence. Any scribbler with a bit of spare parchment could jot down his or her own pronouncements on the end of the world or copy a prophecy that struck his or her fancy, but printers had to strike the nerve of hundreds or thousands of customers. This makes pamphlets—and printed works in general—a different kind of evidence than manuscripts. Only a small fraction of the manuscripts written during the Middle Ages have survived, and we can only speculate as to whether a text known today from a single manuscript copy ever circulated more widely among the intellectual elites that comprised the readers and writers of the Middle Ages. A single copy of a printed pamphlet, however, is strong evidence that someone intended to distribute the work to thousands of people among a much broader spectrum of society. While a work printed just once may well have failed to find customers, the appearance of further editions is a sure sign that a printer had hit on a formula for success.

Pamphlet editions tell us something that manuscripts and learned treatises do not about the tastes and imaginations of a broad reading public. For the discussion we are engaged in here, "history of popular imagination" is perhaps a better description than "Renaissance history," "Reformation history," or "literary history," although we will engage with all of those fields. Few would confuse the texts printed in most pamphlets with great works of literature, which did not stop their production by some writers who are today acknowledged as the most important of their time. Most of the seminal works that propelled the Reformation or drove the Renaissance are lengthy treatises rather than short tracts, but when scholars and theologians engaged a wider public or when a broader audience grappled with their ideas, the pamphlet was often the preferred medium. Our focus will be fixed on the popular literature of urban readers in the later sixteenth century, but that, too, will illuminate the intellectual and religious currents of the time.

Printed works addressing the near or distant future for a popular audience in early modern Germany included astrological booklets (called "practicas") that offered one astrologer's prognostications for the following year or for longer periods. When practicas were at their height of popularity, editions from up to thirty different authors might appear each year. The Leipzig professor Wenzel Faber von Budweis, the teacher of Johannes Virdung, dominated the field before 1501. Virdung achieved even greater popularity through the late 1530s; a younger astrologer, Johann Carion, rose to a similar stature around the same time.[8]

Until recently, one could only give an impressionistic opinion about the relative popularity of early printed works. Only in the last twenty years, with the development of searchable databases of fifteenth-, sixteenth-, and seventeenth-century printing, has comparing the actual number of recorded editions become practical, and it remains a cumbersome process. Among the centers of early modern European printing in France, Germany, Italy, and the Low Countries, the state of bibliographic cataloging is still the most advanced in Germany (I will here use the name *Germany* as a shorthand designation for the politically fractured German-language region in the sixteenth century). Census projects of long standing, including the Verzeichnis der im deutschen Sprachbereich erschienenen Drucke des 16. Jahrhunderts (VD16, which does not include broadsides) and Verzeichnis der im deutschen Sprachraum erschienenen Drucke des 17. Jahrhunderts (VD17), provide access to reliable information about printed editions and are now available online. Projects underway elsewhere in Europe are quickly catching up, and continent-spanning projects will soon provide an even more comprehensive account of early printing, as seen in the recent appearance of the Universal Short Title Catalog (USTC).

Prophetic books and pamphlets were elements in a public conversation that included astrological, religious, political, and literary dialogues. Thanks to modern bibliographic databases, these conversations can now be reconstructed—if not completely, then with a previously unmatchable depth and specificity. Today, it is much easier not only to discover and count the editions of a given work but also to determine the textual environment within which that work was situated by identifying the texts that informed public debate in a particular city or region. Rather than tracing the influence of only one or a few major works, we can re-create much more of the discursive context in which a book was written and received.

Centuries before the establishment of legal copyright or of a unified nation-state to enforce it, competing printers in several cities rapidly reprinted any work that promised to be profitable. Consequently, the history of prognostication and prophecy in print consists of a series of eruptions of numerous editions of a single work within a few years. Johannes Lichtenberger's *Prognosticatio*, a prophetic compilation first printed in 1488, appeared in seven editions by 1497 and in sixteen in 1500–1501. The *Extract of Various Prophecies*, a pamphlet composed of selections from Lichtenberger and from his younger colleague Joseph Grünpeck, went through ten editions between 1516 and 1518. Several familiar names appear in the list of best-selling works that succeeded until midcentury: Johannes Virdung's prognostication for 1524–63 (ten editions between 1521 and 1524); a resurgence of Lichtenberger's *Prognosticatio* (thirteen editions between 1525 and 1530); Johann Carion's *Interpretation and Revelation*, with prognostications for the years to 1540 or 1550 (fourteen editions from 1526 to 1531 and eleven more from 1539 to 1543); the *Practica for Europe* of Paracelsus (eight editions of 1529–30); the *Onus ecclesiae*, a prophetic compilation attributed to Berthold Pürstinger (eight editions in 1531); Joseph Grünpeck's *Prognosticum* (eleven editions in 1532); and, finally, the interpretation of Johann Carion's "Hidden Prophecy" (fifteen editions in 1546–47).

The picture changes dramatically in the latter half of the century: Lichtenberger's name was less frequently mentioned, and his work was rarely published.[9] The most popular prophetic pamphlets in Germany during this time (apart from the posthumous compilations of Martin Luther's sayings, which formed a whole industry unto itself), with over forty-five total editions between 1558 and 1590, were instead those attributed to Wilhelm Friess of Maastricht.[10] These booklets first appeared in a burst of seventeen German editions in 1558–59, followed by a few more as late as 1568. Then the name of Wilhelm Friess reappeared in thirteen editions published between 1577 and 1580, with twelve more published by 1590. The editions of Wilhelm Friess were the first of several highly popular prophetic pamphlets that appeared in intermittent bursts over the rest of the century, none of which were quite able to match the prophecies of Wilhelm Friess in popularity.

While nearly all the popular prophetic works in the first half of the century were written by historical figures whose names were well known to their contemporaries, the most popular pamphlets that appeared after 1550 are mostly attributed to virtual unknowns or to long-dead authors. Prophetic books that followed in the wake of Wilhelm Friess included that of Paul Severus, with fifteen editions in 1560–63 and two more before 1570; Caspar Füger's translation of an extract from Lactantius (a Roman writer of the third and fourth centuries), with fourteen editions of 1584–88 and a total of twenty-three between 1566 and 1591, including ten printed together with a prophecy attributed to Luther's teacher Johann Hilten; and the compilation of prophecies by Gregor Jordan that appeared in fourteen editions in 1591–92.[11] Each of these take different approaches to describing the future: the prophecy attributed to Hilten is primarily an attempt to reckon the years of the end-time, the prophecy of Lactantius emphasizes sin and disorder, and that of Gregor Jordan is primarily concerned with the role of the Ottoman Turks as the Antichrist's standard-bearers. The prophecy of Paul Severus touches on several different aspects of the near future, which is unsurprising for a work that is simply the conclusion of an astrological prognostication that was roughly separated from its astronomical foundations. The prophecies of Wilhelm Friess not only appeared in more editions but also present a more concise and coherent narrative of the last days than any of their rivals. If prophecies of the future provide insights about a culture, and if pamphlets provide a glimpse of the popular imagination, then the prophecies of Wilhelm Friess are singularly important evidence for a critical moment in European cultural history following the Peace of Augsburg.

Despite the manifest popularity of Friess's pamphlets, his name is all but unknown today, even among specialists. While books and articles have been written about the lives and works of Grünpeck, Lichtenberger, Carion, Virdung, and Faber, the scholarly record on Friess is slight.[12] Pamphlets are easily overlooked, of course, and the sheer number of editions has only recently become discoverable. The pamphlets' insistence that they contain prophecies found with Friess after his recent death moreover invites suspicion that we are dealing with a pseudonym rather than a historically tangible human being. Equally disconcerting is the discovery that, despite their common claim to be prophecies found with Friess, the booklets in fact represent two quite different texts, each attested in different versions.

While this may be disconcerting, it is also extraordinary. Among the prophetic best sellers of early modern Germany, the reappearance of Wilhelm Friess as the author of a second prophecy almost twenty years after the appearance of the first is without parallel. Johann Carion's "Hidden Prophecy" was merely an excerpt of his first great success, the *Interpretation and Revelation*. Joseph Grünpeck's brief *Prognosticum* enjoyed a burst of popularity at the end of his career (with nine editions in 1532) that his major work, the *Speculum*, had not enjoyed (with only two editions in 1508 and just four more between 1510 and 1540). Carion and Grünpeck were, moreover, well-known individuals quite capable of writing multiple works. For a pseudonym like "Wilhelm Friess," there is no precedent for the name to be pressed into service decades after an initial success for an entirely different work. Wilhelm Friess's appearance as the author of a second prophecy is a highly unusual event that requires explanation.

The popularity of Wilhelm Friess's prophecies may have gone unrecognized because they ricocheted across national, religious, and linguistic boundaries, often in ways that run contrary to how we expect things to work in the sixteenth century. The pamphlets were published in leading centers of German printing, such as Nuremberg; in the far south of the German-speaking lands, in Basel; in Lübeck, in the far north; and in the Dutch-speaking Low Countries. Following their trail thus involves the bibliographies of several nations and languages. The pamphlets attributed to Wilhelm Friess also underwent a genre migration—from astrological prognostications, to a recapitulation of the medieval end-time drama, to a terrifying vision of future desolation. Over the decades of their greatest popularity, the pamphlets were found in contexts ranging from embattled Dutch Protestantism to German Lutheranism to Swiss and German Calvinism. More than mere products of various national and religious identities, the prophecies of Wilhelm Friess were among the narratives through which not only Lutherans and Calvinists but also German, Swiss, and Dutch citizens were coming to define themselves.

In the following chapters, I will argue that the prophecies of Wilhelm Friess, the most popular German prophetic pamphlets of the later sixteenth century, were a reworking of Johannes de Rupescissa's *Vademecum* of 1356. While "Wilhelm Friess" was a pseudonym, the prophecies' alleged origin in the Netherlands is authentic. (I will use the names *Low Countries* and *Netherlands* interchangeably here, keeping in mind the complicated and shifting circumstances of this region during the sixteenth century, rather than modern political boundaries.) The popular German prophecy of Wilhelm Friess began as a seditious anti-Habsburg tract disguised as prophecy that was printed by Frans Fraet, the most prolific publisher of forbidden Protestant literature in Antwerp. In Nuremberg, the prophecy came to be understood as supporting the Holy Roman Emperor, while the prophecy took on a distinctly Lutheran form in the Netherlands during the early years of the Dutch Revolt. The second version of the prophecy then arose as a Calvinist reaction to the Lutheran prophecy, appropriating the name but reversing the confessional polarity. It used the prophetic form to address events from the perspective of Strasbourg in the year 1574. A compelling candidate for the author of the second version is Johann Fischart, one of the most important German writers of the sixteenth century and the most accomplished satirist of that time.

The story of these strange and terrible prophecies might be said to start in 1545. In that year, a decade before the first booklet attributed to Friess appeared, a printer was beheaded on the market square in Antwerp. He was the first of two who would meet that fate in the print history of the prophecies of Wilhelm Friess, and it is with his story that I will begin in chapter 1.

CHAPTER 1

A Strange Prognostication

———— ᨑᨑ ————

The prophecies of Wilhelm Friess, the most popular German prophetic pamphlets of the later sixteenth century, were the writings of a dead man: the title pages of these booklets insist that the prophecies were found with their ostensible author after his death. Their story begins, however, not in Germany but in the Low Countries, not in Friess's native Maastricht but in Antwerp, with Friess not yet dead, and with a printer being led to his execution.

On 28 November 1545, Jacob van Liesvelt was beheaded on the Great Market Square in Antwerp as the sudden conclusion to a lengthy and halting trial.[1] He had been accused, not for the first time, of printing heretical works that had not received official approval and ecclesiastic endorsement, at a time when the Protestant Reformation was facing increasingly severe resistance. In some of the German principalities and imperial cities to the east, the Reformation had enjoyed decades of sovereign or civic support following its first stirrings in 1517, but in their hereditary lands in the Netherlands, the Habsburg rulers were vigorous and intolerant champions of orthodoxy.[2]

At the time, Antwerp was approaching the height of its prosperity as the center of world trade, and with around one hundred thousand residents, it was second only to Paris among cities north of the Alps.[3] Antwerp was home to around a thousand foreign merchants, with many more foreigners passing through the city at any given moment. Antwerp's economic preeminence was matched by its importance in printing and the book trade. The city was nominally subject to the dukes of

Burgundy, but the dukes' other royal titles and more pressing matters elsewhere required the appointment of governors. Rule over the Netherlands remained a Habsburg family affair, however. Until 1556, the reigning Duke of Burgundy was the Holy Roman Emperor Charles V, succeeded on his abdication by his son Philip II, king of Spain. Until 1555, the Habsburg governor was Mary of Austria, the queen of Hungary and Charles's sister, followed by Emmanuel Philibert, the Duke of Savoy and Charles's nephew, who was, in turn, succeeded in 1559 by Margaret of Austria, the Duchess of Parma and Charles's illegitimate daughter. Antwerp's ruling magistrates took pains to preserve the city's privileges against the Habsburg royal court in Brussels, however. The struggle became more acute with the outbreak of the Reformation, as Antwerp's continued prosperity depended on the willingness of foreign merchants, including Protestants, to live and work in a Habsburg territory. Citizens of Antwerp who sympathized with the Reformation in the second half of the century were divided between Lutherans; adherents of various Anabaptist groups, who were subject to the most intense persecution; and, increasingly, Calvinists.

Jacob van Liesvelt, born into a family of printers around 1489 and with over three decades of his own experience in the profession by 1545, would have known where the boundaries of the unprintable lay in sixteenth-century Antwerp. Some of these boundaries were economic. The entrepreneurial nature of printing required van Liesvelt to produce books for which there was sufficient demand to justify the investment in paper, ink, and type, as well as the expertise of the laborers in his workshop. Politics also played a role, as state officials were wary of the press and its ability to quickly produce heretical or seditious works in hundreds or thousands of copies. As a medium for distributing texts, print was vulnerable to official sanctions at a number of pressure points. Unlike the slow and dispersed process of copying manuscripts, the printing of books was usually centralized in a single workshop, and many workshops were often located within the walls of a single city, so that all could be kept under the watchful eye of the local government. As the production of several hundred or a thousand copies of a given book required a great deal of specialized equipment and raw material, printers had a strong economic incentive to avoid official sanctions. Local and state governments could also offer rewards in the form of lucrative commissions for printing official proclamations, which prudent printers would not jeopardize. Jacob van Liesvelt was well aware that new regulations had stipulated the penalty of death for the unauthorized printing of religious works in 1540, as he had printed those regulations himself.[4]

Yet the shifting demands for prepublication approval had caused legal troubles for van Liesvelt before and would be his eventual undoing. He had published the first complete Bible printed in Dutch in 1526, based in part on Martin Luther's translation, and some of van Liesvelt's later Bible editions included marginal notes and other material influenced by Luther. Van Liesvelt was denounced to local authorities in 1533 for printing a "very evil Bible" influenced by the German heresies; around the same time, the Antwerp executioner had burned a Bible and other books from van Liesvelt's workshop for promoting Lutheranism.[5] In 1536, van Liesvelt was accused of printing a book that contained a false claim of official approval; in 1542, he was again charged with printing an unapproved and heretical work entitled *Consolations of Divine Scripture.*[6] While another Antwerp printer, Adrian van Berghen, was executed in 1542, Jacob van Liesvelt was able to defend himself against the charges by arguing that the controversial work he had been accused of printing without approval was only a series of excerpts from other, previously approved books.

In late 1544, however, the edicts on printing began to be enforced with renewed harshness, and Jacob van Liesvelt again found himself in legal jeopardy for his edition of *Consolations of Divine Scripture.* Although Jacob van Liesvelt obtained the services of two professional advocates who made the same argument that had previously led to his exoneration, van Liesvelt's frequently postponed trial ended in November 1545 with his condemnation and execution.

The van Liesvelt family remained in Antwerp and continued printing, however. Jacob's widow, Maria Ancxt, published over eighty editions between 1546 and 1565, identifying herself both by her own name and as the widow of Jacob van Liesvelt.[7] At first, Maria Ancxt printed primarily devotional works and portions of the Bible in Dutch and, to a lesser extent, in French, along with a few works of well-known humanists, including Erasmus and Sebastian Brant. In 1551, Maria Ancxt began printing secular popular literature. Hans van Liesvelt, the son of Jacob van Liesvelt and Maria Ancxt, also took up printing in that year, although on a smaller scale, with eighteen known editions until 1563. Mother and son cooperated on a number of projects, including the publication of Virgil's *Aeneid* in Dutch translation.[8] The true sympathies of Maria Ancxt and Hans van Liesvelt may well have lain with the cause of Dutch Protestantism: literacy rates tended to be highest among the groups that were receptive to the Reformation, and printers were among the most literate of all professions.[9] The conditions of the time made it impossible to express such views openly, however. Maria Ancxt and Hans van Liesvelt both understood only too well what the consequences were for appearing to flout the law at a time when persecution of religious dissent in the Netherlands had reached an unprecedented severity, and their editions were published with the required approval of local clergy and the countersignatures of government officials.

Protestant devotion in the Netherlands of the 1550s provides an example of what James C. Scott has termed a "hidden transcript," a discourse that must take place outside the view of those in power. That would seem to preclude the possibility of Protestant printing, as it would have been all but impossible to distribute books for sale to a dispersed audience and, at the same time, to avoid official scrutiny that could easily end in severe punishment. By their nature, printed books belong to the "public transcript," or the visible interactions of the subordinate and the dominating classes.[10] One way out of this impasse lay in anonymous publication. As Scott notes, anonymity is a common strategy for stating prohibited opinions or taking forbidden actions, and some Dutch printers with a zeal for the new religion did choose to print Protestant works clandestinely under false names.[11] Anonymous publication was specifically prohibited by the edicts on printing, however, and the risk of being caught was substantial. Other printers chose exile, attempting to export their forbidden books back into the Netherlands from Dutch émigré communities in England and Germany.[12]

The difficulty of anonymous printing and the inefficiency of relying on imported books opened a gap between what Dutch readers wanted to read and what the book market offered. In 1562, a monk was said to have called for Antwerp to be burned, as the people were entirely Lutheran apart from the Italians and Spaniards living there. This overstated the case considerably: even more than twenty years later, Catholics remained the largest religious bloc in nearly all of the city's wards.[13] Yet interest in the Reformation was quite substantial: Protestant and dissident works together constituted a quarter of all titles printed in the Netherlands at the outbreak of the Dutch Revolt in 1566.[14] For printers still under Habsburg rule, the considerable market opportunities presented by the popularity of these works could not be exploited without risking one's life and livelihood. In matters of religion, an immense distance lay between what many of their customers wanted to read and purchase and what printers were allowed to print and sell. Those who continued printing despite their Protestant affinities were forced to seek other strategies.

One such strategy, which Scott calls "euphemism," involved disguising prohibited expression just enough to avoid punishment. For Antwerp in the sixteenth century, this often entailed publishing ostensibly Catholic works with a hidden Protestant message.[15] The combination of heightened devotion and an environment of intense persecution that existed in Antwerp and other Dutch printing centers in the mid-sixteenth century provides a classic example of communication under censorship, in which any message may be a multilayered statement meant both for its intended recipient and for the scrutinizing eye of the censor.[16] One of the very few ways for printers to profit from public interest in the Reformation was to provide the Dutch reading public with doubled messages that were comprehensible to those sympathetic with the Reformation but that were opaque or unobjectionable to censors and civic authorities. The results of censorship include not only silencing or banality but also a redoubling of ingenuity. The full meaning of texts created under these conditions may not lie on the surface, but we can attempt to discover it through application of cultural knowledge and comparison with later, more open expressions of previously forbidden sentiments.[17]

Read with an eye open for messages between the lines of type, some of Maria Ancxt's editions appear in a new light. In 1548, she published Savonarola's explications of Psalms 30 and 50 in a Dutch version based on a prohibited German translation. Savonarola had written these two commentaries while he was in prison awaiting execution.[18] Around 1548 and again in 1555, Maria Ancxt published two editions of *Histories and Prophecies from the Holy Scriptures Decorated with Pure Images and Devout Prayers*, a devotional work consisting of prayers and Bible stories. An almanac was printed with both editions. The Bible stories would have been unobjectionable, but the prayers should have raised a few eyebrows by their exclusive focus on God's grace without mention of the church, by referring to clerical abuses, and by their decrying of the persecution that Christians were suffering.[19] "Those who oppress Christ in his members are gaining the upper hand," one prayer complains, while another laments, "For now they persecute those who dare to tell people the truth and they cast them out and despise them where they can. Others they arrest and hang, and so much grief is done to them that almost no one dares to speak." Yet another prayer asks the Lord to witness how "no one dares risk his neck[!] for the glory of your name."[20] Although the intent of these prayers should have been clear, the 1548 edition of the *Histories and Prophecies* was approved by Jan Goossens, parish priest of the Church of St. Jacob in Antwerp, and countersigned by Philips de Lens, secretary at the royal court of Brabant in Brussels. Maria Ancxt's second edition of the *Histories and Prophecies*, printed around 1555, was inspected and approved by Nicolaus Coppijn, dean of St. Peter's and chancellor of the university in Louvain.

Perhaps the censors willfully ignored the heretical religiosity of Maria Ancxt's edition of the *Histories and Prophecies*. While there is no evidence that Goossens secretly supported the Reformation, many of the clergy who declared for the new faith after 1566 (by which time Goossens had died) had no record of previous involvement.[21] As for de Lens, later chroniclers report (without citing their evidence) that he was suspected of sympathizing with the Reformation as early as 1525.[22] Franciscus van der Haer's 1623 annals of Brabant surmised that de Lens was the anonymous author of the "Compromise of the Nobility," a petition calling for the end of the Inquisition and the laws against heresy, which was issued by an alliance of Dutch noblemen in the winter of 1565–66, around the time of de Lens's death.[23] The true allegiance of de Lens and Goossens may be beyond recovery, but they exemplify the environment of Antwerp in the 1550s, where not even priests and court officials were above suspicion, where a careless word might lead to denunciation and arrest, and where censorship, rather than simply preventing communication, was a constitutive element of a mode of reading and writing that was always alert for meanings below the surface. It was an environment where "fervent protestations of loyalty"—and, one might add, many other kinds of speech acts and written texts—"could not be taken at their face value."[24] Despite the dual approbation, the heretical nature of the *Histories and Prophecies* was eventually recognized, and it was placed on the index of prohibited books in 1570. By then, however, Maria Ancxt was beyond the reach of any inquisitor.

In the 1550s, as Dutch Protestants were facing persecution of increasing severity, printers in the Low Countries began publishing astrological prognostications with increasing frequency, principally in Antwerp.[25] Although Maria Ancxt was the earlier and more prolific printer of the two, her son, Hans van Liesvelt, was the first to print prophecies and prognostications. In fact, that type of literature comprises over half of his known output. For the years 1551 and 1552, Hans van Liesvelt printed three prognostications in French, two by Jacques Sauvages and one by Pierre de Goorle. Maria Ancxt took over the printing of de Goorle's prognostications by 1556, with six of his prognostications coming from her press by 1565. These short booklets containing astrological predictions for the upcoming year comprised an important and annually renewable market segment for early modern printers.[26]

As much as astrological prognostications were marketed as learned experts' sober pronouncements based solely on careful observation of the planets and time-honored interpretive principles, the publication of astrological hocus-pocus gave authors broad leeway to comment on and critique the society in which they lived. The criticism was usually directed at any who might disrupt the established order, but times of upheaval also saw astrology enlisted in the cause of reform. The early days of the Reformation provide an example of astrological agitation— and also of its limits, even under a sympathetic sovereign. Johann Copp dedicated his prognostication for 1521 to Martin Luther and published another one a year later concerning the ominous planetary conjunctions of 1524. In this pamphlet, Copp, claiming to merely report what the stars ordained, predicted "much spilling of blood, burning, disunity and uproar between the common man and the clergy" and tried to sound sincere in expressing his fear of an "uprising against the bishops and all priests."[27] Even though Copp insisted that the rebellion was unjust, this was more upheaval in an astrological prognostication than Prince-elector Frederick III of Saxony would tolerate, despite the prince's strong support for Martin Luther. The next year, Copp tried to walk back his prediction with a new pamphlet that examined the course of the heavens "more clearly than a year ago," but he soon found it advantageous to leave Saxony.[28]

The Habsburg rulers of the Netherlands decreed punishments much worse than exile for supporting the Reformation, and yet Hans van Liesvelt published two annual prognostications, for 1555 and 1556, that are, in many ways, reminiscent of the anticlerical prognostications of Johann Copp. According to the title block on their first pages, they were the work of the "famous and highly learned Master Willem de Vriese, doctor of medicine and the liberal arts."[29]

The pamphlet for 1555 opens with de Vriese's statement that because astrology had fallen into such disrepute among theologians and the unlearned common people (to which he promised to soon publish a definitive rebuttal), he had intended to stop publishing annual prognostications, but some powerful noblemen and other good friends had convinced him to continue, as several of his predictions for the previous year had turned out to be accurate. No prognostication for 1554 by Willem de Vriese is known, but that does not mean that none ever existed. For a genre as ephemeral as astrological booklets, it is likely that many editions have entirely disappeared, and the careers of several practitioners are known today only from a single work or from the incomplete fragments of a few editions.

The organization of de Vriese's prognostication for 1555 is quite conventional. Following the opening statement, de Vriese presented the astronomical facts for the year (including a lunar eclipse and various planetary conjunctions), determined the governing planets, and noted the days on which each season would begin. Subsequent sections also followed their conventional order in describing the influence of the heavens on agricultural fertility, disease, war, and human society (consisting of the clergy, nobility, and common people). The prognostication concluded with the fortunes of various nations, regions, and cities, which suggest the author's political alignment: the planets conferred good fortune on the Habsburg emperor and the cities of the Netherlands, while the picture for other European nations was decidedly mixed, particularly for the king of France, who could expect setbacks at every turn.

De Vriese's pronouncement concerning the common people comes as a surprise: "They will want to carry out amazing things against their rulers and regents. They will complain of burdens and troubles that they cannot bear. They will seek new policies and statutes according to their own will, indeed seek them by force. They will murmur, mumble, whisper, and talk back against their rulers and, if it were possible, eagerly bring them into hate and envy. So the lord regents and superiors of the lands and cities should use wise council and peaceably rule their communities, as they may justify it before God and the entire world." As Hinke van Kampen has recognized, this was not a prediction but a threat.[30]

At a time when Emperor Charles V was determined not to permit the German heresies to take hold in the Netherlands, de Vriese's prognostication for 1555 had a dangerous focus on Germany, which occupies nearly the entire chapter on war and peace: "Germany will not be at peace in any way, but rather armies, cavalry, and soldiers will be gathered here and there and no one will know where they should go. One army will not trust another, nor one city the other, but instead they will rise up against and destroy each other. In the same way there will be war and contention in all of Europe, for everyone will fear to be attacked and brought into greater subjection and servitude. Therefore everyone will try to defend their liberty and obtain freedom until at last they will entirely erupt and burn so violently that all of Europe will feel the sparks and also the coals."[31] Less than a decade earlier, the German princes had sought to assert their authority in matters of religion against the emperor in the Schmalkaldic War. The most recent violent confrontation had occurred just a few years prior, and the Peace of Augsburg was still months away. The inflaming of all of Europe by sparks from Germany was precisely what Charles V would do anything to prevent.

De Vriese's predictions for the clergy, again focusing on Germany, dispel any remaining doubt about the intentions of his prognostication. The retrograde motion of Jupiter will not be able to protect the clergy from the furies of Saturn and Mars, de Vriese states, and so the clergy will experience a great humiliation: "Their prelates and greatest leaders will be renounced, chased away, and driven out in some lands toward the west. In Germany some bishops will give up and abandon secular rule on their own. Some clerics and religious men will leave and abandon their places and residences, not because they know of anyone who will persecute or threaten them, but only out of fear and doubt. Some will pretend that they are not clerics, disguising and changing their lives. The others will think that they have secure, free, and reliable places in some lands, but that will be far from the case. They will have to depart quickly from their anticipated places. In sum, great oppression, fear, and suffering will befall them." De Vriese is careful to add that he does not know whether this will occur because of the evil of other people or because of the clergy's own guilt, but he warns that, in any case, the clergy should be sure to lead exemplary lives and teach God's word, so that God will turn away his wrath "from them and from us."[32]

De Vriese's predictions can be read as a comment on clerical poverty and usurpation of secular rule, two issues that had excited reformers for centuries prior to the Protestant Reformation. Claiming to make predictions based only on the motions of the planets was a form of euphemism that allowed—barely—for the expression of such sentiments at a time when similar thoughts could hardly be uttered without serious repercussions. Moreover, the genre of astrological prognostication already involved looking for arcane importance in readily apparent signs. The highly stereotyped and formulaic nature of astrological prognostications made it easy for a censor to quickly skim the surface without noticing anything disturbing, while the discerning reader under censorship would be alert for hidden messages. The prognostication for 1555 of Willem de Vriese stated as astrological prediction something that could not be expressed directly.

But the prediction of trouble for the clergy also raises doubts about whether the author was only consulting astronomical tables and astrological treatises, as the image of clerics scurrying in search of a safe corner had long been found in reform-minded prophecies about the clergy.

Fifteenth- and sixteenth-century editions of the *Onus mundi* (Burden of the world), a fifteenth-century compilation of Birgitta of Sweden's fourteenth-century revelations, supplemented with additional material, attribute a similar prophecy to the thirteenth-century *Super Hieremiam* in the tradition of Joachim of Fiore, as well as to the twelfth-century Benedictine abbess Hildegard of Bingen: "Also Abbot Joachim of Calabria, founder of a monastery in Florence, who lived around the same time, wrote in his gloss on Jeremiah the prophet that a great tribulation will come upon Christendom from the heretics, pagans, and evil Christians, and that the goods of the clerics will be taken away and many cities and castles destroyed, just as St. Hildegard predicted, and they will be hunted from one land into another. Because of this many of them will go into the wilderness and lead a life of poverty."[33] The prediction of a clergy purified by enforced exile and poverty is made even more clearly in the tract *On the End of the World* attributed to Vincent Ferrer, published fourteen times between 1475 and 1550, in Latin and four independent German translations.[34] In response to the third chapter of Daniel, the tract foresees a persecution of the clergy by the Antichrist, which will lead some priests to "flee to the wilderness and live in great misery and poverty. They will disguise their clerical robes, wear no tonsure, lead no clerical life, and conceal the fact that they can read. They will have no chapels, houses of prayer, or altars, but instead hurriedly read mass in the early morning upon a stone or stump." According to pseudo-Vincent Ferrer, the persecution by the Antichrist would be imposed by God in order to purify the clergy from their sins.[35]

Willem de Vriese's prognostication for 1556 was, if anything, even more transparent in its calls for reform. For Antwerp, de Vriese predicted strife and discord among the citizens and inhabitants, sometimes because they desired new policies and sometimes "in the matter of religion."[36] De Vriese foresaw rebellion among the common people concerning religion and dissatisfaction with their pastors ("perhaps not without cause or reason") because the clergy did not give the people the "bread of the divine word." The clergy's sins would blind the people to their own shortcomings, and as punishment, they would have hypocrites as rulers and unlearned evil men as teachers.[37] Because of the clergy's sins, the common people and the secular rulers would despise them. De Vriese called on the clergy to repent and foresaw a great reformation taking place among them. The clergy's treasure and dominions are again predicted to pass into the hands of worldly princes, for the highest ruler does not wish to be served in the temple of Mammon.[38] The prognostication for the clergy ends on a strikingly unastrological note: "For many things that were prophesied long ago will be fulfilled this year."[39]

Willem de Vriese's prognostications employed several strategies to survive official scrutiny. Much of their discussion of ecclesiastic issues used double language that was liable to contrary interpretations depending on the position of the reader. The prognostication for 1556 claims that a secret conspiracy among the clergy was causing mutiny against the rulers and sowing enmity among Christian princes, an assertion that would have struck both orthodox and Protestant readers as all too true, as it could be read as a reference either to inquisitors or to reformers.[40] So, too, references to the "Apostolic church," the Lord's "elect little band," or the Lord's "chosen Bride," were not on their face heretical, but these ecclesiological terms were widespread among Anabaptist and Reformed groups.[41] Willem de Vriese's prognostications pair religious agitation with unwavering loyalty to the emperor, and they are quick to flatter any Habsburg who might tolerate the Reformation. Shortly after the Peace of Augsburg had been negotiated, de Vriese predicted peace for Germany and prosperity for Ferdinand (the heir apparent to the Holy Roman Emperor as "King of the Romans" since 1531, later Emperor Ferdinand I from 1558–64), and he saw favorable prospects for a union between the house of Habsburg and the German nation. De Vriese likewise saw the planets aligning for Maximilian (Ferdinand's son and king of Bohemia at the time, later reigning as Emperor Maximilian II from 1564–76) to "bring about reform and renovation in the Christian religion" and to make a great treaty with the German princes.[42]

The Peace of Augsburg had no effect in the Habsburg hereditary lands in the Netherlands, however, where de Vriese's prognostications appeared just as religious persecution, more severe in Antwerp than in other Dutch cities, was approaching a new peak of intensity.[43] To avoid criticizing the Habsburgs directly, de Vriese introduced a different bloodthirsty tyrant on which to project its disapproval, a "prince of the Slavs named Esau Pharmona," who waged war against "Suleiman, Ottoman the Turkish emperor, the Great Khan, the Lord of Muscovy, and the Shah of Persia"; de Vriese had heard about him from Byelorussians and other Slavs when he had traveled with his lord to Poland.[44] In addition to usurping authority and territory and persecuting Christians for the sake of power and prestige, de Vriese's particular accusation against "Esau Pharmona" was that he holds the people in such servitude "that no one in the land can speak against his tyranny without losing his life."[45] De Vriese saw the planets working against "Esau Pharmona" in 1556 and hoped for the tyrant's downfall, whereupon the treachery of evil Christians who had made secret alliances with him would be exposed. The figure of "Esau Pharmona" may be a distorted rendition of people and events among the khanates bordering Russia to the south, as there were contemporary Begs of the Nogai Horde with the names *Ismael* and *Yusef*—both names, like *Esau*, known from the book of Genesis. Like Esau, Ishmael fares rather better in the Koran than in the Hebrew scriptures.[46] Whatever the historical basis of "Esau Pharmona" may be, he serves in de Vriese's prognostications as a cruel and censorious tyrant in league with false Christians who can be safely criticized and whose downfall can be safely predicted, unlike the Habsburg oppressors closer to home.

While the pro-Reformation intent of the prognostications seems apparent, it remains unclear who—or what—Willem de Vriese was. Although the prognostications of Willem de Vriese call their author a famous and learned doctor of medicine and the liberal arts, no aspect of his life is attested outside of these two pamphlets. It is possible that de Vriese was a real human being whose biographical reality remains to be discovered, but there are also reasons to suspect that the name is nothing more than a pseudonym. I will return to the uncertain status of Willem de Vriese in the next chapter.

It does not seem difficult to detect pro-Reformation propaganda just barely concealed by the pretense of objective prognostication in de Vriese's pamphlets, but censors approved Hans van Liesvelt's printing of both editions. The censors of Willem de Vriese's prognostication for 1555 are already familiar names: Jan Goossens and Philips de Lens. The prognostication for 1556 was approved by de Lens again and by a "Master Strick," another secretary to the royal court.[47] How could a parish priest and an imperial official have overlooked such obvious sedition? To a modern observer, and perhaps to any careful contemporary as well, the censors' work appears to be either incompetent or duplicitous. Whatever the case may be, many people associated with the Dutch publishing industry in the mid-1550s, by no means only the printers themselves, would have wanted to avoid close scrutiny of their work.

So it must have caused considerable consternation in several quarters in late 1557 when an anonymously printed "evil and seditious prognostication" by a "Master Willem de Vriese" appeared for sale.[48] An Antwerp printer was soon arrested, convicted, and executed on the Great Market Square of Antwerp for printing it and other seditious books. But the beheaded printer, the second in our story, was not Hans van Liesvelt.

CHAPTER 2

A Seditious Prophecy

On 4 January 1558, the printer Frans Fraet was executed in Antwerp for publishing seditious books. Until quite recently, Fraet's martyrdom was the only thing anyone knew about him as a printer, as there were no known copies of any book from his press.[1] Instead, Fraet was known as an author and poet and as the translator and editor of the first Dutch emblem book, which had been printed twice by Maria Ancxt, in 1554 and 1556, and once more by her son, Hans van Liesvelt, in 1564.[2] Fraet had been a member of one of Antwerp's rhetorician's guilds, which were centers of Protestant agitation.[3] Today, at least two pamphlets are known that bear the imprint of Frans Fraet, one praising the emperor's power and the other praising his military victories. As with the prognostications of Willem de Vriese, however, the unwavering devotion to the emperor camouflaged a much different publication agenda. By carefully scrutinizing the type material of Antwerp printers, the Dutch scholar Paul Valkema Blouw was able to uncover many more editions that Fraet had printed under fictitious names, dates, and places of publication, which Valkema Blouw described in a 1992 article subtitled "Why Frans Fraet Had to Die."[4] Much of Fraet's life and work remains obscure, but one thing is clear: during much of the 1550s, Fraet led a double life as the most important printer of forbidden Protestant works in Antwerp.[5]

As the legal records concerning Fraet's arrest and trial attest, the matter drew the attention of the highest levels of government and threatened to upset Antwerp's precarious civic affairs. From a response by Philip II to Jan van Immerseel, the Margrave of Antwerp, we know that van Immerseel had first reported Fraet's arrest to Emmanuel Philibert, the Duke of Savoy and governor of the Habsburg Netherlands, in a letter (no longer extant) of 6 December 1557, and he sent another letter (also lost) on 31 December.[6] Van Immerseel was also Antwerp's *schout*, an office that simultaneously gave him the functions of both chief of police and prosecutor. He earned an evil reputation among adherents of the Reformation in the Netherlands by vigorously enforcing imperial decrees concerning heresy; the *Martyrs' History* calls him a "bloodthirsty person."[7]

According to city archival records, Fraet was charged with having "printed, sold, and distributed various seditious books such as prognostications and others under embellished and fictive names," and his trial before the high tribunal began on 30 December 1557.[8] Van Immerseel moved to strip Fraet of his citizenship and subject him to torture in order to discover who had commissioned the work or assisted Fraet. According to the report of the city council's secretary and legal advisor, when the trial was continued the next day, the mayors and magistrates agreed with van Immerseel's motion, but, as was often the case, the representatives of Antwerp's citizenry rejected it.[9] By 4 January 1558, Philip II, the king of Spain and lord of the Dutch provinces since 1556, had heard of the affair. While agreeing that there was more than enough evidence to warrant Fraet's torture, the king had also heard of the "difficulties" that the third estate might cause, and he asked Jan van Immerseel, his margrave, to keep him informed of further developments.[10]

By then, however, the trial had reached its conclusion. Fraet was not tortured, but he was quickly found guilty of violating the imperial decrees against heresy, and Fraet's argument that his prognostications were not seditious and therefore did not merit the death penalty was rejected.[11] Fraet was beheaded the next day, on 4 January 1558. Jan van Immerseel reported to Philip II on 6 January that Fraet's "article of death publicly declared that he had no evil intentions, so that he died willingly and as a good Christian for the works that he said to have made in order to support his wife and children."[12] Fraet left no inheritance, and his widow, Tanneken, who had been involved in the trial, was left destitute.[13]

Why did Frans Fraet have to die? Valkema Blouw's implicit answer to that question is that Fraet had been discovered to be the anonymous printer of forbidden religious works, a view shared by Hofman.[14] Yet there are several unusual aspects of Fraet's case. Most printers found guilty of publishing heretical works escaped with modest punishments instead of execution, and leniency could be shown to defendants with children or to those who printed heretical works only to earn a living, rather than out of conviction. Both to avoid worrying foreign merchants and to maintain Antwerp's privileges against the central government, the city magistrates exercised caution in repressing religious dissent. As Habsburg regent, Margaret of Parma often complained that the edicts against printing heretical works were unenthusiastically enforced. Beginning in 1558, most executions for heresy were not conducted in public (unlike Fraet's beheading), in order to avoid the occasion for public unrest.[15]

So there are several reasons to suspect that what led to Fraet's execution was not the printing of Protestant works but, rather, the publication of seditious ones, which the magistrates of Antwerp were more likely to answer with unmitigated severity.[16] In fact, the documents of Fraet's trial do not refer to the printing of religious works. While the law Fraet had violated was the imperial edict against heresy, the specific crime of which Fraet was accused was the anonymous and unauthorized printing of scandalous and seditious books. The only work specifically mentioned—one that is noted several times in the archival records—is a "very evil rebellious prognostication under the name of a Master Willem de Vriese."[17]

Although this prognostication, as a central piece of evidence against Friess, was read by all members of Antwerp's Great Council, the documents say little about its content. The primary complaint was that the prognostication printed by Fraet stirred up trouble between the common people and their rulers. The "prognostication or prophecy" contained "many grievous things against the secular and also the clerical rulers" and intruded in the affairs of "all clerical and secular princes and potentates and also the common people, arousing the same to sedition or desperation."[18]

Frans Fraet and Hans van Liesvelt both printed works ascribed to Willem de Vriese. Fraet was beheaded, however, while Hans van Liesvelt continued to print prognostications for several more years. What can explain the disparity between their fates? We can assume that Frans Fraet, as the most prolific printer of forbidden Protestant literature in Antwerp under the Habsburgs in the 1550s, had learned to exercise the proper amount of caution, especially since he had had prior brushes with the law.[19] Why had printing a prognostication by "Master Willem de Vriese" led to his swift arrest and execution? The evidence against Fraet must have been incontrovertible. Valkema Blouw surmised that copies of forbidden works were found in Fraet's own workshop or that the proof was of a similarly incriminating nature.[20] The documents related to the trial are conspicuously silent on the events that led to Fraet's arrest, however. The letter of Philip II to the Margrave of Antwerp refers to Fraet as a prisoner but also mentions another person, a witness. The letter offers few details but does note that the "above-mentioned witness cannot have done that thing alone, but undoubtedly helped him with evil, false, and seditious spirits, perhaps having a secret agreement with our enemies."[21] But no witness is named previously in the letter or elsewhere. Who was this witness, and what could he not have done without Fraet? Or, as the document is ambiguous, what could Fraet not have done without the aid of the witness? Without additional documentary evidence, there is no way to be sure.

The circumstantial evidence does suggest, however, that Hans van Liesvelt likely found himself in vexing circumstances. Not only had his press, as the producer of de Vriese's annual prognostications, been brought into connection with the alleged author of a subversive tract, but the seditious subtext of de Vriese's earlier pamphlets had now been made explicit for all to see. The appearance of the new prophecy would have made Hans van Liesvelt a suspect, and the subversive potential of the prognostications bearing van Liesvelt's name and workshop address would have given the magistrates of Antwerp significant leverage over him. In 1566, when the magistrates of Antwerp wanted to identify the publisher of a subversive pamphlet, they were forced to rely on the expertise of a type cutter, whose unhelpful testimony blocked their inquiry, while investigations of anonymous pamphlets that secured the cooperation of the printing community were often successful.[22] The publication of a seditious prophecy attributed to Willem de Vriese left Hans van Liesvelt in a compromised position. As a fellow Antwerp printer and as the son and sometimes partner of the publisher of Frans Fraet's literary work, he almost certainly would have been able to identify products of Fraet's workshop. Hans van Liesvelt had the means to identify Fraet as the printer, likely had an opportunity to do so, and undoubtedly had the motivation of seeing his own neck at risk. It is possible, of course, that Frans Fraet's arrest resulted simply from an exceedingly poor choice of accomplices or from the efforts of a zealous government agent. Given the precarious situation into which Fraet's publication of a seditious prophecy attributed to Willem de Vriese would have placed Hans van Liesvelt, it would be surprising if van Liesvelt had done nothing to preserve his life and livelihood. If Hans van Liesvelt did guide civic authorities to the real printer, however, it would have meant sending Frans Fraet to the same martyr's death on the Great Market Square of Antwerp that van Liesvelt's own father had suffered a decade earlier.

According to Hofman, the prognostication of Willem de Vriese has never been found, and Valkema Blouw points only to a reprint from 1566, of which no trace has been seen in over two hundred years.[23] As no copies of Fraet's edition of the prophecy are known to survive, one more mystery arises. What could Fraet have printed that could plausibly connect the name of Willem de Vriese, whose earlier prognostications were dutifully loyal to the Habsburg emperor, with a work said to instigate popular rebellion against both ecclesiastic and secular authorities? Without an extant copy to consult, this question would likely remain insoluble. However, soon after Fraet's execution, the prophecies of Willem de Vriese—or "Wilhelm Friess," as he was called in Germany—were on their way to becoming a minor publishing sensation, with at least nineteen German editions issued by 1568 that preserve the prophecies of Wilhelm Friess in four different versions.

The German prophecies that appeared beginning in 1558 treat "Wilhelm Friess of Maastricht" as recently deceased. Curiously, however, a calendar and prognostication by Willem de Vries, a medical doctor of Maastricht, were published in 1581, and another calendar by him was published in 1596 (see the list of editions in appendix 3). One way to resolve this mystery is to consider Willem de Vriese as having not only a real biography but also a son: "Meester Willem de Vriese den ouden" would then be not just aged but "Willem de Vriese Sr." The pamphlets and broadsides published in 1581 and 1596 are illustrated by the same crest that is found on the prognostication for 1556, although they were printed decades later and by a different printer. The name *Wilhelmus Phrisius Buscoducensis* is attested for a student at Louvain in 1552, although any connection to Willem de Vriese remains uncertain.[24] If we suppose that a junior Willem de Vriese followed his father into the medical profession and into publishing astrological prognostications—and there are certainly several contemporary examples of father-son pairs authoring astrological prognostications—then the younger de Vriese also seems to have shared his father's religious tendencies. The uncensored calendar for 1581, published during Antwerp's period as a Calvinist republic, supplements its notes about the upcoming weather with anniversaries of important events in the Dutch Revolt, while the prognostication intersperses its predictions for wind and weather with disasters (particularly war and sedition) and with pointed observations concerning the fates of monks, bishops, princes, and the state of religion in Spain. The calendar for 1596, published when Antwerp was once more under Habsburg rule and again subject to the approval of clerical and secular authorities, largely confines itself to noting the weather, planetary movements, and feast days, although it was likely also printed along with a prognostic booklet whose contents and tenor remains unknown.

Yet there are reasons to suspect that *Willem de Vriese* was not the name of a father and son duo of prognosticating Protestant physicians from Maastricht but, instead, a pseudonym that was identified with a particular kind of political and religious agitation. For all his alleged fame, the name of Willem de Vriese does not appear anywhere in the city records of Maastricht.[25] The legal documents from the trial of Frans Fraet treat Fraet as the author who had both invented and printed the seditious prophecy.[26] *Willem de Vriese* appears as Fraet's pseudonym, not as the name of an author whose rights had been infringed or who might be suspected of authoring other seditious tracts. Fraet published several of his editions under the pseudonym "Niclaes van Oldenborch," which was used by as many as eight Dutch printers for forbidden works of Protestant literature.[27] It is quite possible that Fraet, in similar fashion, did not associate the name *Willem de Vriese* with any living person but, rather, saw in it a pseudonym available to anyone writing something of similar purpose. In this analysis, the name *Willem de Vriese* combines one of the most common given names of the time with a reference to the province of Friesland, while the alleged age and medical profession of the bearer of that name merely serve to increase the text's perceived authority.[28] That Fraet published a combination of prophecy and protest under the name *Willem de Vriese* suggests that Fraet recognized the subversive message and prophetic undercurrent in de Vriese's prognostications. Rather than a historical person and author, "Willem de Vriese" would be an authorial identity that was associated with anti-Habsburg polemics disguised as prophecy or astrology, which is how the name *Willem de Vriese* functioned again in 1581. In either case, German readers knew nothing about "Wilhelm Friess" beyond the few details offered on the pamphlets' title pages.

The Strange Prophecy of Wilhelm Friess

The publication history of the strange prophecy of Wilhelm Friess opens, as we have now seen, with a tale of duplicity, betrayal, sedition, and covert resistance to political and religious oppression. To fully understand the severity of the sentence handed down on Frans Fraet, we need to look away from historical events for a moment and into the text printed by Fraet. As the text of Fraet's edition is not available directly, we will have to draw on the extant German pamphlets and determine how Fraet's edition fits into the textual history of the prophecies. While the German pamphlets differ considerably among themselves, all versions of the prophecy provide a concise summary of the medieval Christian end-time drama, with all the disasters and conflicts on a cosmic scale that the end of the world entails. In the following pages, I provide an English rendition of the most popular German version of the "unusual prophecies prophesied by the old Master Wilhelm Friess of Maastricht, recently deceased, which were found with him after his death, extending from 1558 to 1563, in which very unusual and horrible changes are prophesied" (an edition of the German text is found in appendix 1).[29]

I consider nothing more wicked and unfortunate than when someone lives forever in joy and has never borne suffering or faced opposition, for he cannot understand himself. I consider that person unhappy who is without persecution, for human life is (as Job says) nothing but a constant war with the devil. Therefore I advise you, my dear friends, that you yield yourselves willingly to affliction, for there has never been such suffering as will fall upon all Christendom in the next five years since God created the world. Or, if God will turn aside his righteous judgment, we must be reconciled to God in his anger. God will have mercy on us if we turn from our sins to him during this time, which will be very evil for five years, and then after that everything will become better.

The entire clergy will be brought low, oppressed, and terrified by great hunger. The monasteries will be destroyed and the monks and priests in them will be driven into severe poverty and find no place where they are safe. The prelates of the Church will not clothe themselves with velvet, scarlet, or colorful cloaks, for in that time the Roman Curia will be assailed everywhere. Neither pope nor cardinal, neither legate nor bishop, nor any of the great prelates (who live in all kinds of blasphemy and disgusting depravity) will retain their positions. They will lose all their riches, worldly power, and great palaces because of their pride, greed, and other grievous sins. All great lords, princes, and kings will heap scorn and disgrace upon them and rob them of all their majesty, splendor, power, arrogance, and indeed of all ecclesiastic estates both large and small that they have acquired by lying and murder, and leave them so utterly naked that they will barely have a little cloak or cloth to cover their bodies. After that, their persecutors will regard them favorably.

They will be driven out and mocked, and they will run from one corner to the other to seek a place where they can hide. When they see and experience these things and are unable to avoid them but rather must suffer them, these things will give them understanding so that they will humbly confess their sins and failings and will call upon the Lord with crying eyes and hot tears and say: "O Lord, it is just that we endure suffering and sore persecution, for we have sinned grievously against you in our tremendous greed, pride, debauchery, and sloth, and in countless other grievous sins." When the clergy confess and are sorry for their sin, God will return them to their original condition as they were in the beginning of the apostolic church. They will be provided with a suitable income so that they can lead an honest and God-fearing life, but they will not receive excessive benefices and pensions again, and they will not be allowed to exercise control or tyranny over their people.

Such a plague and misfortune will come over the clergy that it cannot be spoken or written. You should diligently read and consider the ninth chapter of Ezekiel, where you will find unusual prophecies that will come upon the clergy.

In addition, dear friends, do not think that such fear and persecution will only come upon the clergy. Every person will likely receive his portion, so that no one will be able to mock anyone else. For so much suffering, wailing, and misfortune will come upon all Christendom in 1560 and 1561 and the following years that no one could truly believe it, no matter how great his intelligence and wisdom. Unbearable and unspeakable signs will appear in order to bring the world to repentance.

First, worms will come that look as if they could easily be destroyed, but they will gain such power and strength that they will attack and almost kill lions, wolves, leopards, dragons, bears and oxen. The little birds like titmice, finches, sparrows, larks, thrushes, and starlings will attack and kill sparrow hawks, falcons, hawks, and griffins in great numbers. This sign is certain proof that all people will be in great sorrow because of their afflictions and suffering during these five years.

Among the common people a great uproar will arise against the lords. The nobility will uncover the traitors, deliver them to the sword, take from them all their goods and riches, and permit them to have no protection or peace any longer. In sum, no person can in any way imagine in their hearts or speak with their mouths the evil, persecution, and sorrow that will come upon princes and the nobility in those days. For in truth, before these five years come to an end, disloyalty and betrayal will be so rampant among the people that no one will find a friend or companion that can be trusted. Many great and terrible plagues will come over the entire world from the unbelieving Saracens and Turks. All who follow Mohammed will attack the Christians and destroy many lands and places, especially Italy, Hungary, and a large part of Germany. In addition, many unbearable plagues will come upon the entire world. Turn your hearts to God, for between 1558 and 1559 a great and grievous pestilence much worse than anyone could imagine will occur everywhere.

First of all, I proclaim to you a great famine, and after that such a terrible storm that no one born from mother's womb has ever seen greater. The waters will rise so high in many places that all people will be horrified. Lands and cities will be in discord and disagreement and suffer such great fear, especially in Italy and France and also in other lands, that many people will fall into bitter poverty and deprivation because of it. Food will disappear. No one will have mercy on others, which will cause great sorrow.

This plague of discord, war, storm, and death will come upon the whole world until the year 1562. It will begin between Italy and France. Let those who desire grace from the Lord turn their hearts to God, for beginning in 1559, insomuch as our Lord God does not turn aside his wrath, France will be in such a dire state and all princes, counts, heralds, knights, and noblemen of that kingdom will be brought so low and weakened during this time that they will not be able to defend or protect themselves or others, for the French will have a large and powerful people as their enemy. The oppression is beyond my power to describe. Read the fifth chapter of Ezekiel, where you will find the great affliction mentioned above that will come upon France and the French in these five years.

After that a false heathen emperor from the west will join with those in the east and come down upon the entire land. He will persecute and torment the Christians with utmost cruelty and spare nothing, but rather devastate and destroy everything over which he gains power. All suffering and persecution since the beginning of the world cannot be compared with the plagues that will occur during the reign of this emperor, for no city or fortress, no matter how large or strong it may be, will be able to stand before him. When one writes the year 1561, whatever has survived until then will be destroyed.

The world will be in such great suffering from the tempests and warfare that will traverse the entire earth until the year 1563 that every person should be clothed with the clothes and weapons of virtue and patience so that they do not fall into despair.

Now that you have heard how the Christians will be plagued with persecution, fear, hunger, and war, you will also hear and learn the first remedy or teaching concerning how one can flee from this persecution.

God teaches in the Gospels that one should call on him with humility and true faith and cease all evil acts so that he would forgive our sins and give us patience in suffering and distress. The second teaching is that everyone who is able should acquire provisions for five years so that they can stave off hunger in the coming five years. For you should know (as was said above) that from 1558 to 1563 there will be such awful distress and deficiency because of famine and hunger in all lands that many people will likely die because of hunger and famine, and all people will be frightened because of the famine's severity. Whoever is wise and truly prudent will prepare supplies until the year 1564, for then all misfortune will be past. You should also know that great earthquakes will occur in Germany, Burgundy, and Spain. When we are in such great suffering, false prophets will arise who will convince the people of incredible things through their false teaching. Do not rely on your own reason and wisdom when you come to hear them or to see the signs and miracles that they will perform, for God will permit them to do many things because of our sins. The devil will act very cunningly through them in order to deceive the people and turn them away from God. I would therefore advise that the people who do not want to be poisoned by false teaching should avoid them and seek secret places and corners wherever they can to escape from such evil.

The third teaching to escape such misfortune is that we must avoid all lust and repent of all sins according to our ability and with sincere remorse and penitence, for all stubborn and unrepentant people who remain in their sins will die in great fear and distress. The supplies that they have hoarded will not help them, because not all people will die from hunger, the sword, or war, but rather many will leave this life through various accidents such as tempests, flooding, and earthquake, which will not spare people of any station.

At the time when the unchristian emperor and tyrant reigns, the Lord will awaken two pious and holy men who will be clothed with virtue and holiness. They will preach the true and pure word of God against the false teachers and will have great power from God over good and evil. They cannot be killed by any mortal creature or human being. They will also have great power from God to strike and plague the unbelieving and stiff-necked people wherever they want, but no one will feel or be aware of it. They will have force and power from the Lord God to work whatever signs they choose here on earth in order to awaken people to virtue. They will preach throughout the lands and proclaim the day of the Lord against the many false teachers. Afterwards one of the two will be chosen as the highest bishop by the true Christians. He will restore the holy apostolic church to its proper order, which has lain ruined for so long. He will lead a life of great holiness. He will ordain talented and worthy people to the preacher's office. After that, human power will not be considered important and no one will possess great benefices or bishoprics for the sake of money. Only those who are worthy and can proclaim the word of the Lord will be chosen, even if the world regards them as the lowest of all people, as in the beginning of the holy apostolic church. Indulgences, requiems, and other things like that will wither away. Everyone will conduct his church office in his own place. They will receive only the appropriate sustenance.

At the same time, an emperor will arise whose power will extend throughout the whole world. He will fear God and be so pious that he will be loved by young and old and by rich and poor. He will wear no crown on his head for the sake of Christ, who was crowned with sharp thorns because of our sins. He will also be loyal to the holy apostolic church and do everything in his power for God's honor. It is certainly true that the world, which before was in great fear and anxiety, will be brought to honor and peace through these two persons, the emperor and the bishop. They will eradicate the sects of the unbelievers unless they are converted and thereby return to grace. Most will deny their false opinions. The unbelievers will deny the false religion of Mohammed and receive holy baptism from the Christians.

Afterward, in the year 1564, there will be one religion and faith, and it will no longer be necessary to carry any kind of weapons. The bishop and emperor will make a law that no one should bear any kind of weapon that can be used for killing, and whoever violates it will be killed with the same weapons that are found with him without a lengthy trial or appeal.

The entire world will strive for unity, for people will remain in proper order and in harmony forever after. Indeed it will be such a unity as has not existed since the creation of the world.

After that the emperor will travel over the ocean, conquer the Promised Land, and have the Christian faith proclaimed there. After that has been done, he will return and take leave of the world and his empire and lead a holy life. He will leave someone after him who will rule the land wisely, but it will not last long. His rule will last five years. The highest bishop will not survive the emperor by five years, which will trouble the holy apostolic church greatly. Then after that the entire world will enjoy wonderful peace and joy without any discord or contention. People will live forever after in true and sincere love for one another. Every person will be filled with virtue, and everyone will have understanding and wisdom like the apostles at the beginning of the apostolic church. They will be illuminated by the Spirit of God in holy scripture, which had previously long been dark. They will also understand all prophecies and predictions that the prophets have prophesied and foretold. There will also be many who will not only understand the prophets but will themselves also proclaim future things by the Holy Spirit.

No one will have power to deceive others or to lead them into false doctrine or down to Hell. But to proclaim the time, hour, and day when the Son of Man will come—Christ speaks in Matthew chapter 24 that no one knows of the day and hour, not even the angels in heaven, but only the Father. Therefore let us ask with humble hearts our Lord Jesus Christ, who suffered the most ignominious death for the human race, that he might be our advocate before his Heavenly Father so that we receive a merciful judgment. Amen.

Conclusion

Wake up, you Christians, from the sleep of sin! Open your ears, sharpen your senses, and hear my words! For you have cast God's word from you into the puddles of disunity, forgetfulness, and disdain, and have begun to make use of vice, and you are also very wise in doing evil, and cunning and crafty. You pervert all honor and you drink yourselves drunken in the blood and sweat of the miserable widows and orphans. There are few days remaining until the Christian cities will be destroyed. Therefore put on the clothing of sorrow and penance, and run to the Lord with wailing and lamentation. If you do not do this, the days of tribulation will come very quickly, from which you will flee to the ends of the sea. You will call on them to help end your life quickly and gently.

There will be such lamentation and wailing among the Christians that one will say to another, "Would it not have been better if we had died in our mother's womb?" Therefore let us ask the Lord humbly for his grace with remorse for our sins so that he might turn away all of this from us. But if God has called us to suffering, let us bear it patiently and willingly as punishment for our sins so that we might be rewarded by the Lord with eternal life, which eternal life our dear Lord Jesus Christ (whether it be after a fortunate or unfortunate time) may in his mercy grant to us, to whom be honor and praise throughout all eternity. Amen.

This is the prophecy of Wilhelm Friess, at least in the version that became most popular in Germany. What Frans Fraet printed in Antwerp was certainly different in some ways. The precise wording of Fraet's edition is beyond recovery, but we can establish certain facts about his text with some degree of confidence, and these facts will help answer the question of why Frans Fraet had to die.

While the legal documents treat Fraet as the author of a pseudonymous prophecy, this was certainly not the case. Although Fraet had considerable talent as a writer and likely edited the text he published, he was not its creator. Perhaps Fraet recognized the subversive message or believed that he recognized the source of the prophetic undercurrent in de Vriese's astrological prognostications and chose to attribute the text to Willem de Vriese to stave off accusations toward himself of seditious publication. Or perhaps the prophecy of "Wilhelm Friess" is precisely what it claims to be, a text found with Willem de Vriese of Maastricht after his death, which Frans Fraet then edited and published. One way or the other, Fraet seems to have come into possession of an old prophecy in late 1557. He should have expected trouble to follow its publication, however, as the text he chose to print and distribute to the citizens of Antwerp was one that, almost exactly two centuries earlier, had earned its author a life spent mostly in prison.

CHAPTER 3

From Avignon to Antwerp and from Antwerp to Nuremberg

—— ⚭ ——

The ways in which the text attributed to Wilhelm Friess changed from edition to edition run parallel to changes in who was reading it and where it was being printed. Those who published and redacted the prophecy left their marks on the text. By piecing together the history of the text (which will be referred to in quotation marks as "Wilhelm Friess" to distinguish the text from Wilhelm Friess, its alleged author), we will be able to trace how the prophecy entered Germany and understand how a text that was suppressed with the severest penalties in Antwerp could become a popular and openly printed pamphlet in Nuremberg. The textual history of "Wilhelm Friess" provides an example of how texts changed in the context of censorship, in the genre of early modern prophecy, and in the medium of print. By focusing on the details of textual history, we will later be able to attempt an answer to more fundamental questions: where do prophecies come from, and more broadly, how were texts made in the late Middle Ages and early modern period?

From Avignon to Antwerp:
Johannes de Rupescissa and "Wilhelm Friess"

That Frans Fraet was printing something incendiary should have been apparent from the fact that the text he printed was first written by an

author who spent most of his adult life in prison.[1] In the 1330s, Johannes
de Rupescissa, a young man of knightly heritage in southern France,
began to have visions. Rupescissa described his visions as sudden illumi-
nations of his mind that helped him understand scripture and extrabib-
lical prophecies, informed him of the Antichrist's birth and impending
appearance, and inspired him to become a Franciscan. Prophesying of
things to come was a hazardous undertaking at that time in southern
France, which had recently seen several lay and clerical prophesying religious enthusiasts denounced—and, in some cases, burned—as heretics.
Rupescissa denied that he was a prophet in the same way that Jeremiah
or Isaiah had been, but he did so by quoting the biblical prophet Amos.[2]
Rupescissa's disavowal of the title of prophet did not prevent him from
claiming that part of one of his works had been revealed to him by the
Virgin Mary.[3] Rupescissa was arrested in late 1344 and imprisoned until
his trial in 1346. The inquiry found Rupescissa to be not a heretic but a
fantast, and he remained confined for most of the remainder of his life.
In 1349, during the Great Schism, Rupescissa was allowed to make his
case before the papal court in Avignon. While Rupescissa's imprisonment prevented him from preaching openly, his superiors respected his
prophetic claims enough that he was allowed access to books and writing materials and allowed to work, although often under appalling conditions, and some interested observers began copying and circulating
Rupescissa's writings. Despite his imprisonment, Rupescissa read widely
and composed an impressive list of his own prophetic commentaries and
interpretations before his death in 1366.

In 1356, Rupescissa summarized his prior prophetic work in a short
tract entitled *Vademecum in tribulatione* (Walk with me in tribulation). The
Vademecum was soon known to readers in and beyond Avignon, and it
eventually dispersed throughout Europe in various forms and in both
Latin and several vernacular languages. Rupescissa divided his work
into twenty sections or "intentions" that sketch out the primary events
and actors of the end-time, including the rise of false prophets and
Antichrists of the east and west, the purification of the clergy through
poverty, and then the overthrow of heresy and other diabolical powers
through the actions of righteous preachers and a final virtuous emperor.
The *Vademecum* is unusually specific in its predictions: Rupescissa foresaw
all these events occurring between 1356 and 1370.

The prophecy of "Wilhelm Friess" is considerably shorter than the
Vademecum, and the material is treated in a somewhat different order,
with many sections being omitted entirely. Comparing the two texts is

made more difficult by the lack of a modern edition of the *Vademecum*. Considering the numerous manuscripts of the original version and many later adaptations in Latin and other languages, preparing a critical edition would be an enormously difficult undertaking. Yet without a critical edition of the *Vademecum*, one of the most well-known and influential prophetic texts of the later Middle Ages, we are left in the scandalous situation of relying on an edition from 1690 edited by Edward Brown. Even worse, the marginal notes in the printed edition rudely mock Rupescissa, the poor quality of the manuscript consulted, and the incompetence of the scribe who copied it: "All of these things are confused, partly because of the scribe's flaws, and partly because of the author's faulty discernment and coarse ignorance," reads one of Brown's notes. In another, the editor remarks, "The text is miserably corrupted here because of the exceptional ignorance of the copyist or transcriber: if anyone can make sense of these mangled words, well and good. Reader, take note of how much damage authors suffer when foolish copyists who don't know how to read old manuscripts try to transcribe their works. The sweetest music of the ass upon the lyre!"[4]

Despite the inexact correspondences and the unsatisfactory state of the edition, the origin of "Wilhelm Friess" in the *Vademecum* is beyond doubt, as the numerous parallel passages demonstrate. To give one example, both texts predict an uprising of worms and small birds against larger creatures (134–48, here and in the following discussion, parenthetical references indicate lines from the edition in appendix 1).[5] The changes to this passage are similar to the transformation of the text as a whole between the *Vademecum* and "Wilhelm Friess," where some sections are reduced to a summary or omitted, others are expanded or have new material added, and entire sections are rearranged. The influence of Johannes de Rupescissa's prophetic works in Germany is a topic still awaiting intensive study. Until now, the spread of the *Vademecum* in Germany was only known from a handful of fifteenth-century manuscripts and its inclusion in a number of Latin compilations in the sixteenth century as well as one rendition into German verse.[6] By virtue of its appearance in print in nearly twenty vernacular editions by 1570, "Wilhelm Friess" was the most significant route by which the ideas of the *Vademecum* spread throughout Germany in the sixteenth century.

But the author of "Wilhelm Friess" was not working from the original *Vademecum*. The author was not even working with a Latin text. Much of the language not found in the *Vademecum* that shows up in "Wilhelm Friess" reflects a French redaction that is preserved in one manuscript now found in the Vatican library (BAV Reg. lat. 1728). The opening of "Wilhelm Friess," with its disdain for those who do not experience trials, follows a preface added to the original *Vademecum*: "I consider nothing more wicked and unfortunate than when someone lives forever in joy and has never borne suffering or faced opposition," or as the French manuscript begins, "*Ha creature qui tousjours vivre vouldroies en ce monde en prosperité, riche aise, habundant en biens temporeulz et en sa voulenté, sans avoir point de tribulation, encombrement, ne nul meschief ne desolation . . . livré a dampnation.*"[7]

While the *Vademecum* was highly influential, it was not well organized, and it treats several topics multiple times in various disconnected sections. The French redaction rationalizes the organization by bringing together into the same section material that the *Vademecum* mentions in disparate chapters, resulting in a more linear narration. In comparison to the Latin *Vademecum*, Barbara Ferrari calls this French redaction a "true rewriting, characterized not only by additions, deletions, and significant modifications compared to the source, but also by a profound reorganization of the material."[8]

"Wilhelm Friess" continued the process of rationalization begun in the French redaction by bringing together all predictions of woe for the clergy into a single section at the beginning of the prophecy. It also omitted long sections while adding its own new material. Despite the differences, the similarity in wording between "Wilhelm Friess" and the French redaction is so close that there is little doubt that they both belong to the same tradition of the *Vademecum*. Striking verbal echoes are found in the Low German 1558 edition of "Wilhelm Friess," where the word *tribulation* is found twice as the rendering of French *tribulascion*, a correspondence not found in other editions (219, 310). Another remarkable case concerns the clergy's frantic searching for a place of refuge, which the French text says they will hardly find: "ce que a paine trouveront." The same Low German edition and two later ones read "a paine" literally and instead foresee the clergy seeking refuge in great pain ("mit groter pyne" or "mit groter smarten," 67).

The manuscript now found in the Vatican was written around 1470–75 on paper bearing a watermark that can be localized to the Champagne and Île-de-France regions of northeastern France.[9] Geographically, chronologically, and textually, the manuscript represents a middle step between the Avignon of the 1350s and the Antwerp of the 1550s. The manuscript was not the direct ancestor of "Wilhelm Friess," however, as the German pamphlets preserve a few passages found in the

Latin *Vademecum* but missing in the French manuscript. The prediction in "Wilhelm Friess" of terrible earthquakes in Germany, Burgundy, and Spain (276–79) corresponds quite closely to the Latin of the *Vademecum*, for example, but no equivalent can be found where it would be expected in the French redaction.

Compared to its source, "Wilhelm Friess" often briefly summarizes material that the French *Vademecum* redaction treats in considerable detail. Beyond this tendency to summarize, "Wilhelm Friess" systematically omits references to Johannes de Rupescissa. The French redaction describes Rupescissa's life in Avignon and mentions his name, but it usually refers to him as "le Cordelier" (the Franciscan). Other versions of the *Vademecum* tend to suppress the author's name in a similar fashion.[10] In "Wilhelm Friess," this was done so rigorously that Wilhelm Friess shifted from the owner of a book of prophecies to their implicit author. The religious battlefield of the mid-sixteenth century was much changed compared to the fourteenth or fifteenth centuries, and the antagonists of "Wilhelm Friess" are different. Unlike the *Vademecum* in its original Latin or in the French redaction, "Wilhelm Friess" nowhere mentions Jews or faithless Christians. Although "Wilhelm Friess" has nothing good to say about monks or the French, it omits the disasters foretold for specific French and Italian cities and for each monastic order.

"Wilhelm Friess" contains many conventional elements of the standard end-time drama, with some notable exceptions. The rebellion of the common people against their lords begins a series of disasters, including an invasion of Saracens and Turks, pestilence, famine, storm, earthquake, war, and flood that are found in many end-time narratives of the late Middle Ages, as are the false prophets and false heathen emperor who persecute Christians with unspeakable harshness. The two holy men who preach against false prophets and restore the offices and sacraments of the church, as well as the righteous Last Emperor who joins them in establishing peace and extinguishing heresy, were similarly well known. However, the prophecy of "Wilhelm Friess" omitted several other elements that most readers would have expected. Compared to the original *Vademecum* or to its French redaction, Frans Fraet committed a number of striking sins of omission. "Wilhelm Friess" leaves out some material so consistently that it would seem to reflect the redactor's agenda. The prophecy omits all mention of Gog and Magog, Enoch and Elias, Lucifer's fall, the Second Coming of Christ, and the resurrection of the dead. The *Vademecum* has two Antichrists; "Wilhelm Friess" has none. Instead of Antichrists, the German prophecy describes false prophets and a tyrant from the west with allies in the east. A bishop and emperor bring peace and unity to the world as in the *Vademecum,* but "Wilhelm Friess" sees the future golden age continuing on indefinitely past the death of each, with suspiciously little to say about what kind of secular or ecclesiastic order will follow. Despite a clear grounding in the Christian end-time narrative, "Wilhelm Friess" seems almost secular and anarchic in comparison to its source. The lack of an impending end of history led Volker Leppin to categorize the prophecy as nonapocalyptic.[11] While Leppin's classification is appropriate for a theological study, the literary and cultural context of "Wilhelm Friess" lies firmly within the tradition of reworking and adapting the apocalyptic narrative. Perhaps "Wilhelm Friess" should be considered an apocalypse of a different kind.

Why Frans Fraet Had to Die

Understanding the source of "Wilhelm Friess" helps make clear what Frans Fraet was doing in Antwerp. While the Dutch astrological prognostications of Willem de Vriese were not used as a textual source for the prophecy of Wilhelm Friess, Frans Fraet may have thought that he recognized an unnamed source for de Vriese's prognostications in a redaction of the *Vademecum.* The closest point of contact between the astrological prognostications and Rupescissa's prophecy is found in their proclamations of woe upon the clergy, where the astrological prognostications are at their most prophetic. The image of clerical humiliation, impoverishment, and flight in the *Vademecum* redaction is similar to that found in de Vriese's practicas, although it is also found in pseudo-Vincent Ferrer and other works.

Reading "Wilhelm Friess" against the *Vademecum* also helps us to understand what may have attracted Fraet to the text and what role he played not only in printing but also in adapting it. Certainly Fraet would have found much in the *Vademecum* with which he could sympathize, including its eschatological material, its predictions of troubles for the clergy, and its promise of relief from persecution for true Christians. According to Hofman, the whole philosophy of Fraet might be summarized as "evil oppresses good, but good will eventually prevail,"[12] a view consistent with the tribulation followed by salvation foreseen in the *Vademecum* and in "Wilhelm Friess." The prophecy culminates in a spiritual utopia without hierarchies, where authority for scriptural interpretation and access to divine inspiration are held in common and where no authority can be maintained by resort to weapons of violence.[13] Scott argues that the utopian vision of a "leveling of worldly fortunes and rank," emphasizing solidarity and equality, is typical of the religious convictions of the dominated.[14] In "Wilhelm Friess," it can be recognized as a protest against what Fraet saw around him in Antwerp.

If there were just one reason that Frans Fraet had to die, it is most likely to be found in the prophesied uprising of small birds against the birds of prey. In prophetic literature from the late Middle Ages and early modern period, the eagle had been a symbol of the Holy Roman Emperor and his dominion. The use of eagles and other birds to represent the nobility and their lands did not require explanation or comment in the numerous fifteenth- and sixteenth-century prophecies where they appear. While the eagle itself is absent among the birds of prey that sparrows, larks, and other small birds would attack and kill in great number in the prophecy of Wilhelm Friess, the threat to the Netherlands' Habsburg regents would have been unmistakable, especially as the uprising of little birds against the birds of prey immediately precedes a prophesied rebellion of the common people against the nobility.[15]

The allegorical prophecy of birds, beasts, and worms in "Wilhelm Friess" exemplifies the prophecy's subversive function. On the surface, "Wilhelm Friess" makes use of well-known elements of traditional imperial prophecies, but it turns those elements into a covert critique of imperial power and a veiled threat of rebellion, by creating ambiguity over the identities of the expected Last Emperor and the heathen false emperor, permitting the Habsburg emperor to be displaced from the starring role to that of the villain. In Antwerp, "Wilhelm Friess" was an example of what Scott terms "critiques within the hegemony," because it turned the empire's own narratives against Habsburg rule. Traditional symbols were manipulated to create messages "accessible to one intended audience and opaque to another." If the censors did understand the concealed message, retaliation was complicated, because "sedition is clothed in terms that also can lay claim to a perfectly innocent construction."[16]

Certainly Fraet had the rhetorical talent and experience to have been both the printer and the redactor of "Wilhelm Friess." One might compare his role in printing the prognostication of Willem de Vriese with his editorial interventions in publishing a collection of religious songs, where Fraet not only selected but also corrected, improved, and extended the song texts.[17] Fraet may have planned to resolve the conflict between state-imposed censorship and public demand for pro-Reformation literature by printing a pamphlet that appeared to reiterate imperial narratives but, beneath the surface and behind the mask of "Wilhelm Friess," subverted imperial discourse. Seeing a hidden message in "Wilhelm Friess" is not reading too much into the text: we can be quite certain it was there, because Fraet was executed for it. Whether Fraet was the redactor or only the printer, suggesting that lower things might violently end their subordination to higher things was why Frans Fraet had to die.

From Antwerp to Nuremberg

At several critical junctures in the transmission of "Wilhelm Friess" from Dutch into German, the identities, locations, and motivations of those who adapted and printed the text are entirely unknown. For several steps in the path of transmission, our only guide is what happened to the text itself, so we will have to consider the textual history of "Wilhelm Friess."

Textual history, source studies, and recension criticism are, at their core, arguments based on probability.[18] The claims that one text is descended from another or that two texts share a common ancestor say, in effect, that the similarities between two texts are so striking and pervasive that it defies all reason to suppose that the two could have arisen independently. The possibilities of human language are so numerous that no two writers, even if they share personal backgrounds and historical contexts and intentions, would write precisely the same thing.

Yet some texts defy the odds. What seem to be improbable coincidences are made possible by the redundancy found in all languages, a common stock of phrases and literary influences, similar contexts and concerns, and shared knowledge of a traditional narrative. Two editions of the same version of "Wilhelm Friess," for example, change the impending downfall of the "Christian cities" to the downfall of the "godless cities" (478). While the two editions are closely related, assuming that the change was inherited from a common source or borrowed from one to the other leads to multiple intractable problems, leaving independent innovations, motivated by a common wariness about seeming to predict Christian decline, as the least unlikely, if still unsatisfying, option. That a single change is not completely reliable evidence of shared ancestry is particularly the case with deletions, as shared anxieties about prophesying disruption and uproar could motivate two redactors to independently omit the same passage. The less significant a textual difference is, the more likely it is that it could arise independently. For binary choices—to break a sentence or not, to include an *and* or not, to treat a noun as a singular or an unmarked plural, and so on—the descendants will probably follow the choice of the ancestor but may choose the opposite, so that apparent similarities with other versions arise without a genetic connection between them. The relationships between the various editions of the most popular version in particular must be determined on the basis of the cumulative probability of a handful of minor distinctions. Our confidence in the reconstructed textual history is necessarily lower, and we must be content with general observations in some places. The least unlikely reconstruction of the history of "Wilhelm Friess" does not account for every similarity or difference, and it is still a history in which a number of improbable things must be assumed to have occurred. The extant editions are only the visible surface of a complex and often subterranean transmission history in both manuscript and print.

Textual history is not always precisely equal to print history, as two different editions might have identical texts, although this does not seem to occur among the editions of "Wilhelm Friess." The opposite can also take place, where a single edition can have textually significant differences between copies because of corrections carried out during the course of printing. There is one example of this among the editions of "Wilhelm Friess," where different states of one edition (identified as N16, as described shortly) are the precursors to two textually distinct editions (N17 and N18; see the list of editions in appendix 3 for fuller bibliographic records).

In classical textual criticism, the controlling assumption is that innovations can only be inherited by texts that descend from the innovator. The textual history of "Wilhelm Friess," however, requires the assumption of multiple contacts between separate branches of the family tree, which complicates the work of identifying and describing the relationships between versions.[19] Because of these contacts—"contaminations" in the terminology of textual criticism—and because of the dialectal differences between the known editions and the original Dutch text, it is impossible to precisely reconstruct the original wording. At most, we can say that shared innovations as compared to the French redaction indicate a shared history among versions of "Wilhelm Friess," either through common descent or by borrowing.

But recovering a lost original is not our aim here. After all, we already have good models of what the original text looked like, in the *Vademecum* of Johannes de Rupescissa and in the French redaction. Instead, we are interested in discovering what a text meant to those who produced or read it, including both Frans Fraet and his executioners, as well as the translators, redactors, and printers who spread the prophecy to new audiences. For this, both the textual ancestors of the lost Antwerp edition and its German textual descendants help us determine what that edition must have contained. Each later edition had its own historical context and target audience, and we are also concerned with describing them. Every edition of "Wilhelm Friess" is potentially significant.[20]

The prophecy of Wilhelm Friess is found in four versions, which we will refer to as D (for Düsseldorf, where the only copy is found), N (for Nuremberg, where several editions were printed), L (for Lübeck, where its two editions were printed), and B (for the Bavarian State Library in Munich, where the sole copy is found). Not all versions were equally popular. The versions recorded in one of the Low German dialects of northern Germany, D and L, are known from just one and two editions, respectively. The High German version B is also known from a single edition, while the other High German version, N, is found in fifteen editions printed in or around 1558 and in all seven of the prophecy's seventeenth-century attestations. All four versions state on their title pages that Wilhelm Friess of Maastricht had recently died and that the prophecies were found after his death. The titles of D and N indicate prophecies for the years 1558–63, B specifies the years 1559–63, and the title pages of the L editions indicate prophecies for 1558–70. That an edition belongs to one redaction or the other is clear in all cases, but the relationships between redactions and between the various editions of the N version are more complicated. Each of the four versions offers unique material, including both distinctive innovations and preservations of wording from the original text.

Figure 1 represents the relationship between versions D, B, N, and L, as well as the sources of the prophecy. In the following pages, I will discuss the relationships between texts that are asserted in the figure, as well as areas of uncertainty that the diagram cannot easily express, and I will examine the historical surprises that lurk behind seemingly inconsequential differences between closely related texts.

Version D

This version and version L both appear to be descendants of a common ancestor, which is designated as y in figure 1. Version D is somewhat shorter than the others. It does not include later additions to the text

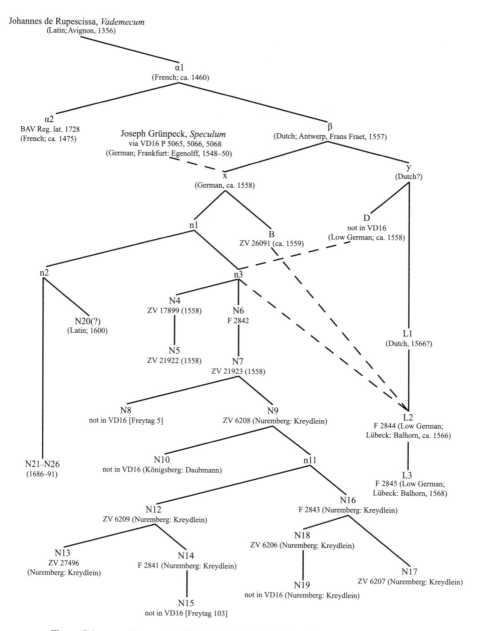

Fig. 1. Diagram of textual relationships between the editions of "Wilhelm Friess" and its sources. Items in lowercase are not attested by extant editions or historical records. Where not specified, the language is German, and most estimated dates are omitted. Borrowings are represented by dashed lines. Some relationships are general rather than exact, and the reconstruction of unattested versions has been minimized.

found in the other three redactions, it omits several passages that were found in the source, and a few passages have been moved to new places in the text (see the edition in appendix 1). The Latin mottoes on the title page and at the conclusion, "Fiat voluntas Dei, sicut in coelo sic et in terra" and "Soli Deo honor, nunc et in secula," which other versions render in German, are curiously similar to the two Dutch mottoes known to be used by Frans Fraet, one for his signed editions and the other for his anonymous ones: "Alst God belieft" and "Gheeft God die eere."[21] As mentioned earlier, several passages that echo the language of the French redaction, preserved only in this version, suggest that it is perhaps only a generation or two removed from the original Dutch edition. To provide an additional example, a passage found only in the D version preserves a rhetorical contrast that has been leveled in the other three versions. All others predict flooding in many cities, with water so high that everyone will be terrified. Two versions, D and B, include an additional emphatic phrase, but only D's phrasing—every man will be terrified of the flooding "no matter how bold [köne] he is"—yields good sense, contrasting fear and courage. In version B, every man will be terrified "no matter how pious he is"; the contrast has been lost (191). The other versions omit this phrase entirely, although it was found in the original source, with the same contrast between courage and fear found in the D version. The one edition of this version, a pamphlet of four leaves, fills the verso of the last leaf with three additional short prophecies. These include excerpts from the *Prognostication for Twenty-Four Years* of Paracelsus (actually combining two of its chapters and omitting some inconvenient lines about *magica*), a passage from the *Extract of Various Prophecies* (a section originally from Lichtenberger, who attributes it to Cyrillus), and a short Latin prophetic verse about the year 1560.[22] The title page of the one D edition uses a decorative element that appears to be identical to one used by the Wittenberg printer Hans Lufft in three editions of 1558–59 (VD16 W 945, L 3452, and L 3345), but the printed text does not match Lufft's typographic material, so the origin of this edition may lie in the region of Wittenberg but the printer is not likely to have been Lufft.

X: Gnesio-Lutherans and the Polemic Use of Prophecy

"Wilhelm Friess" took a different path into the High German dialects of southern Germany. Unlike version D, which omitted several passages, the common ancestor of versions N and B (which we will call x) preserved nearly all of the original text but expanded it by adding a new conclusion and sharpened and redirected its polemics. The x translation not only repeated the prediction that church prelates would be deposed but also added the gratuitous jab that they were currently living "in all forms of blasphemy and abominable filth," a parenthetical aside not found outside the N and B versions (69–70). Compared to its exemplar, the German translation tended to indulge more often in superlatives and to engage more frequently in devotional exhortation.

The distinction between the descendants of x and y are most clearly seen in the shared innovations of the y redactions D and L, but there are also a few passages found only in N and B but not in the y redactions or in the French manuscript. The injunction for all who seek mercy to turn their hearts to God, for example, is an intrusion into the text that separates predictions of woe for France and Italy that is found only in N and B (206–8). The text is not so much extended by this passage as it is interrupted by it. The result is a separation of formerly connected thoughts, almost like the drift of tectonic plates, so that new material pushes apart coastlines that were once locked together.

The common ancestor of the N and B versions added a new conclusion (464–503), most of which it borrowed from a text that had already appeared in many German prophetic pamphlets and compilations of the sixteenth century. The passage first appeared in the *Speculum naturalis coelestis et propheticae visionis* of Joseph Grünpeck (1473–1532), first published in Latin and German in 1508.[23] In Grünpeck's *Speculum*, this passage forms the beginning of a sermon attributed to a prophet who had recently arisen in France, so the original source of the passage may well be older than 1508. Grünpeck was a humanist and scholar who had risen to a prominent position at the imperial court of Maximilian I before a syphilis infection led to Grünpeck's dismissal. Following this, Grünpeck authored a number of works that spanned both astrology and prophecy, with the *Speculum* being his most substantive contribution in that arena.

Grünpeck was a serious student of rhetoric, but the passage as it appears in "Wilhelm Friess" does not give his talents their proper due. In its original form, Grünpeck sets up a striking contrast: "You have begun to be foolish and neglectful in the exercise of virtue, but very wise, cunning, and careful in doing evil."[24] Around 1516, an anonymous redactor compiled sections of Grünpeck's *Speculum* together with passages taken from the *Prognosticatio* of Johannes Lichtenberger (ca. 1440–1503). The *Prognosticatio* was the most successful and influential prophetic compilation from its first printing in 1488 into the sixteenth century, and it was reprinted well into the late seventeenth century. The anonymous compilation, or *Extract of Various Prophecies*, was immensely popular in its own right, with twenty-one editions between 1516 and 1540 and several more appearances in compilation with other works. A Dutch translation of the pamphlet also appeared (although the date it bears, 1509, is certainly too early, perhaps by several decades).[25] The Dutch translation of the *Extract of Various Prophecies* was not the source of the passage that is quoted in the prophecy of Wilhelm Friess, however. The prophecy instead cites the version found in a series of prophetic compilations published between 1532 and 1550 by the Frankfurt printer Christian Egenolff.[26] While Egenolff's compilation was originally a collection of sibylline prophecies, he began adding other texts to the collection in the early 1530s, including the *Extract of Various Prophecies*. The process of accretion culminated in a sizable collection of over one hundred leaves that included the *Prognostication for Twenty-Four Years* of Paracelsus and the complete *Prognosticatio* of Johannes Lichtenberger, as well as several shorter texts. Grünpeck's rhetorical contrast of slothful virtue and crafty evildoing survives in the *Extract of Various Prophecies*, but in the compilations of Christian Egenolff, it was leveled to the simpler form later found in the prophecy of Wilhelm Friess.

The addition of German prophecies is significant because the earliest German editions of "Wilhelm Friess" also preserve an unusual reflex of the *Vademecum*: an enemies list. The original Latin and the French redaction look forward to the time when "Jews, Saracens, Turks, Greeks, and Tatars" would be converted. The earliest prophecy of Wilhelm Friess instead provided a list of sects that would be reconverted, which was omitted in all but a few later editions, as denouncing other Christians was a politically risky act that furthermore alienated potential customers. In the two earliest known editions of the N version, however, the list of sects remains intact and allows us to pinpoint quite precisely the religious setting of the prophecy's entry into Germany, if not the geographical location. In one edition, the list includes "Papists, Calvinists, Adiaphorists, and Interemists," while the other mentions "Papists, Calvinists, Adiaphorists, Majorists, Menianists, and Interemists" (38–40).

The first German readers of "Wilhelm Friess" were therefore not just Lutherans but Lutherans of a particular kind. Following the defeat of the Lutheran Schmalkaldic League in 1547, the Holy Roman Emperor Charles V imposed the Interim, a cessation of Lutheran worship that lasted until 1552. While few Lutherans were satisfied with this development, some sought ways to accommodate the emperor's decree while

maintaining Lutheran beliefs. These moderates included most prominently Philipp Melanchthon, who took part in the negotiations and
held that compromise was possible on matters that were not essential to
faith, called *adiaphora* (from the Greek for "indifferent things"). Those
who held similar views were sometimes referred to as Adiaphorists or
Philippists. Other Lutherans—known as "Gnesio-Lutherans," from the
Greek for "genuine"—demanded unyielding resistance to the Interim,
rejecting any concession as a compromise with the Antichrist. The disagreement between Philippists and Gnesio-Lutherans initiated a series
of arguments within Lutheranism that lasted for several years.[27] The
Lutheran theologian Georg Major (1502–74), who sympathized with
Melanchthon, held that good works were necessary for salvation. Out-
spoken Gnesio-Lutherans, including Andreas Osiander (1498–1552),
Nikolaus von Amsdorf (1483–1565), and Mathias Flacius Illyricus
(1520–75), rejected this view as a weakening of the doctrine of grace. In
1552, another theologian, Justus Menius (1499–1558), responded with
a criticism of Osiander's teachings on grace.

The sects listed in the German translation of "Wilhelm Friess," the
"Papists, Calvinists, Adiaphorists, Majorists, Menianists, and Interemists," thus comprise a list of the theological opponents of the Gnesio-
Lutherans in the 1550s. The German translation of "Wilhelm Friess" was
not the only time that leading Gnesio-Lutherans had appealed to older
prophecies in their polemics. Decades earlier, Andreas Osiander had
published German translations of a prophecy of Hildegard of Bingen
and, together with Hans Sachs, he had published the cycle of prophetic
papal images known as the *Vaticinia de summis pontificibus*.[28]

More recently, Mathias Flacius had enlisted Hildegard of Bingen in
his polemics as early as 1550, when he published a prophecy attributed
to her concerning the papacy's ruin and the reformation of the church.[29]
Flacius was born in 1520 in what is today Croatia. His studies brought
him to Wittenberg by 1541, where he became an associate of Luther and
Melanchthon. Although Flacius's academic talent was initially rewarded
with a professorship in Hebrew, conflict over the Interim with Melanchthon following Luther's death led Flacius to leave Wittenberg in 1549.
His ability and unyielding positions made him a leading voice among the
Gnesio-Lutherans, but constant conflicts with other theologians limited
the toleration for his presence in any place he stayed for the remainder of his life. After leaving Wittenberg, he held academic positions of
short duration in Magdeburg, Jena, and Regensburg before traveling
to Antwerp in October 1566 to lead the Lutheran congregation there.

Protestant setbacks in the Dutch Revolt forced Flacius to leave Antwerp in February 1567 and travel first to Frankfurt and then to Strasbourg. Even Strasbourg was not a permanent refuge for him, as he was forced to leave Strasbourg in 1573 for Frankfurt, where he died two years later.

At the same time that Matthias Flacius was publishing diatribes against Georg Major and Justus Menius (not to mention against Osiander and Nikolaus von Amsdorf), he included several medieval prophecies in his *Catalogus testium veritatis* of 1556, a compendium of witnesses for the truth in all centuries of church history.[30] Flacius cited as witnesses for the decadence of Catholicism such prophetic authorities as Lactantius, the sibyls, Osiander's edition of the papal images, Joachim of Fiore, Hildegard of Bingen, Birgitta of Sweden, (pseudo-)Vincent Ferrer, Savonarola, (pseudo-)Methodius, Wolfgang Aytinger's commentary on Methodius, Johann Hilten, Joseph Grünpeck's *Speculum*, Dietrich von Zengg, and the *Vademecum* of Johannes de Rupecissa.

Flacius's collection attests what Lutheran readers saw in the *Vademecum* less than a decade after Wolfgang Lazius had included excerpts from the *Vademecum* in a pro-Habsburg compilation of prophecies.[31] In the reading of Mathias Flacius, the *Vademecum* was a witness that the pope was a minister of Antichrist, that the cardinals were false prophets, and that the Catholic clergy was facing imminent tribulation that would restore clerical poverty and return clerical wealth to the laity. In Flacius's view, these things were in the process of being fulfilled.[32] We do not know enough about the earliest history of "Wilhelm Friess" in Germany to say that Mathias Flacius was responsible for its translation or publication, but Flacius's published works provided an opportunity for him or for others to take an interest in prophetic texts such as "Wilhelm Friess," and we can be certain that whoever did translate and publish the first German version shared both Flacius's religious perspective and his interest in the polemical use of prophecy.

The early circulation of "Wilhelm Friess" among German Gnesio-Lutherans tells us something about Frans Fraet's activities in Antwerp. Frans Fraet was hardly a Gnesio-Lutheran and was more likely influenced by both Luther and Calvin, at a time when Dutch Protestantism was in a state of transformation.[33] Yet Fraet clearly printed a text with which German Gnesio-Lutherans could sympathize and that they could adapt further for their own uses. Certainly, following the bitter experience of the Interim, a veiled critique of the Holy Roman Emperor would have found a sympathetic reading among German Gnesio-Lutherans. At every stage of its existence, "Wilhelm Friess" continued to be transmitted because it was valuable to those who read and published it. At the time of its first translation into German and its dissemination in Germany, it was a text that spoke to the situation of unyielding Lutheran hard-liners like Mathias Flacius Illyricus.

Version B

While the earliest German translation may have been stridently Gnesio-Lutheran, printing and selling such a work would have been fraught with political and commercial difficulties. Later editions mostly preferred milder rhetoric. The most rigorously moderate of the four versions is version B, a revision of x that omitted several passages and altered others. As a general rule, many prophecies and most astrological prognostications were printed either late in the year prior to or early in the year of the most imminent prediction. This rule of thumb can help establish an approximate timeline for undated editions. Version B foresees an onset of tribulations in the year 1559 and was therefore most likely printed in late 1558 or early 1559, around a year later than the first editions of the D and N redactions and a year after Fraet's edition. Consequently, several passages in N that refer to the year 1558 have been altered or omitted in B.

Other passages that were changed in version B reflect an aversion to anything that seemed too radical. Where the N and L versions describe uproar in both human affairs and the animal kingdom, version B omits the list of small birds and any mention of their attack on the birds of prey, leaving it to the worms to attack the large birds. Where the original text foresaw rebellion among the common people against their lords, the B version more circumspectly predicts that the "common people will call on the LORD in great reverence" (153–54). (Even the original prophecy of "Wilhelm Friess" was far less radical than the *Vademecum*, which foresaw the nobility falling to the sword of popular justice; in "Wilhelm Friess," it is the rebels who will face the nobility's merciless retribution.)[34] Predicting invasion and catastrophe is one thing, but the anonymous publisher of the lone B edition appears to have taken pains to remove suggestions that smaller things, whether people or birds, might rebel against their place in society. Pamphlets that prophesied small things rising against larger ones could easily have been understood as a threat against the hierarchical order of early modern society and may have attracted unwanted attention from civic authorities, and we can imagine the printer of B hesitating to print a text that dwelt too long on that point. In addition, the pamphlet removed the steps that one might take to prepare for the foreseen disasters, whether practical or spiritual, and reduces the ministries of the false prophets, the Angelic Pope, and the Last Emperor, but it adds that the Last Emperor will leave good governors to rule in his place upon his abdication (423). On the whole, version B takes care to avoid anything that might be taken as seditious or that would suggest practical responses to the text, rather than contemplative responses.

What may have been a politically prudent editorial intervention was not, however, a path to commercial success. The B version, which eliminated much of the prophecy's sectarian polemic, is known only from a single edition. The earliest editions of the N version instead retained and at times even sharpened the rhetoric—for example, by attributing clerical wealth not to the clergy's benefices, as do other versions, but to their lies and murdering (80–81). It was not the B version but this other descendant of x that became a best-selling pamphlet in Nuremberg and enabled "Wilhelm Friess" to go from Nuremberg out into the world.

CHAPTER 4

From Protest to Propaganda

Establishing the relationship of one edition of "William Friess" to another is a slow and wearisome process in which slight and seemingly inconsequential variations are identified, compared, and categorized. I have reserved most of the details for the appendixes. Even for the brief summary presented here, it can be helpful to keep one eye on the schematic diagram of textual history in figure 1 (in chapter 3). The result of this effort is a view of how the text changed on a fine scale as it was transformed from political agitation, to sectarian polemic, to a commercial ware that could be openly printed and sold—and how it became, almost twenty years after its first printing, a prophecy that demanded a response.

The Tangled History of N

The most frequently reprinted version of "Wilhelm Friess," the N redaction, split early on into two subfamilies. One of them, the "left branch," is known only from the latest appearances of "Wilhelm Friess" in print at the end of the seventeenth century, which will be considered at somewhat greater length in chapter 7. Although these late editions altered the text substantially, they are similar in several places to the B version, which suggests that the exemplar for these editions of the 1680s and 1690s was a very early member of the N redaction. For example, where the conclusion of "Wilhelm Friess" warns that tribulation will quickly appear if people do not repent of their sins, both the latest editions and the B version add that the tribulation will quickly appear "upon you" ("über euch," 483).

Johannes Wolf's excerpt from the prophecy of Wilhelm Friess in his *Lectionum memorabililium,* his monumental, two-volume collection of histories, prophecies, and curiosities published in 1600, appears to provide another witness of the same branch of the N version.[1] Apart from a short excerpt concerning clerical poverty from the end of "Wilhelm Friess," Wolf included only the prophecy of woe upon the clergy, rendering what is clearly the N version of the prophecy into Latin and one word of Greek (115). Curiously, Wolf gives the year of Friess's prophecy not as 1560 but as 1360, and one wonders if Wolf might have been aware of the connection between "Wilhelm Friess" and Johannes de Rupescissa. Wolf's translation of the prophecy into Latin obscured the features that would make it possible to place Wolf's excerpt any more specifically within the N tradition—with one exception. According to the French redaction of the *Vademecum,* the chastised clergy will no longer wear "purple, scarlet, or any other rich apparel." Wolf's Latin extract follows this closely ("*Praelati Ecclesiarum non serico, non purpura, coccino, bysso, aut aliis preciosis vestibus induentu*"), as do the B and L versions of "Wilhelm Friess," while the editions of the 1680s and 1690s unfortunately omit this passage. The other branch of the N version, however, changes the purple clothing or rich apparel to "velvet, scarlet, or colorful cloaks" (61–63). Wolf's Latin rendition appears to reflect an older version of the N redaction and, one is tempted to conclude, the same left branch as the late editions, although conclusive proof is elusive.

Curiously, a similar description of the clergy's new clothes as colorful rather than purple appears in the genealogically distant D version. This and several other shared passages suggest that what distinguishes the two branches of the N family is not the age of the editions but, rather, contact between the "right branch" and the D redaction (or some precursor from the y side of the family; see figure 1) that resulted in the borrowing of several passages into the right branch but not the left. When "Wilhelm Friess" predicts that people will be troubled and frightened, versions D and L, from the y branch, add that the people's sorrow will be due to "torments and deprivation" ("*van der qualinge unde ungenochte*" or "*van wegen der groten quale unnd ungenöchte*"), a phrase that is lacking in the French redaction, the B version, and the left-branch N editions of the late seventeenth century. The phrase has an equivalent, however, in the right branch of the N redaction, where it appears as "trials [literally, "crucifix"] and suffering" ("*des Creutzes und leidens halben,*" 152). The similar wording of the D and L versions would be difficult to explain if the borrowing had proceeded from N to D, rather than in the other direction. A similar innovation in D that was then borrowed by the right branch of the N version is the remark that the highest bishop would live such a holy life that he would be a "mirror of all virtue" (355–56). Another sign that the right N branch was influenced by the D version can be found in the doubled passages that include the readings found in both versions. The D version predicts that many people will be terrified by famine, while the left branch of the N version predicts that many people will die of famine. The right branch makes both predictions, using awkwardly redundant phrasing: "There will be such awful distress and deficiency because of famine and hunger in all lands that many people will likely die because of hunger and famine, and all people will be frightened because of the famine's severity" (267–73). Similar doublings can be found in other passages.

If we have reconstructed the genealogy of "Wilhelm Friess" correctly, at least ten generations separate the earliest translation of x into German from the latest editions of the N redaction, all of which most likely appeared during 1558. While the N version was being so frequently reprinted, the text was also changing. Along the way, "Wilhelm Friess" lost some of the sharper polemical barbs. Where both branches of the N version had assailed the wicked emperor of the west for his "tyranny," an edition on the right side that would become the ancestor to all others (N6) accused him instead of "cruelty," avoiding the political overtones of an accusation of tyranny (231). On the basis of the typographic material, this edition might cautiously be attributed to the workshop of Urban Gaubisch in Eisleben.[2] The next edition in the chain of transmission (N7) reduced the chance of offending possible customers by omitting the list of the Gnesio-Lutherans' opponents as sects that would eventually be reconverted or destroyed. In addition, where the original conclusion had assailed Christians for casting the word of God into the puddle of filth ("Unreinigkeit"), this edition berated them for casting God's word into the puddle of disunity ("Uneinigkeit"), which again blunted the prophecy's political message (470). Some of the latest editions of the N version even avoid referring to Catholic rites similar to absolution and masses for the dead as "other kinds of devil's filth," instead preferring the more circumspect formulation "other things of that nature" (368). For "Wilhelm Friess," becoming printable entailed a long process of adaptation that preserved enough polemical heat to attract readers while removing passages that would strike too many readers or too powerful of observers as subversive. Eventually, the text printed anonymously by Frans Fraet in Antwerp became something that a printer in Nuremberg could openly print under his own name.

The changes that affected the right branch of the N redaction, by far the most popular version of "Wilhelm Friess," are closer to those treated by classical textual criticism. The alterations in one generation were passed on to the next, which, in turn, introduced new changes that were inherited by later generations. It is possible to construct a chart of textual variants with the original text at the top and the innovations below and with the oldest editions on the left and following generations arranged in order to the right, so that the chart resembles one side of a step pyramid, as each generation is separated from the previous one by a half-dozen, mostly minor variants.

The development of the N version of Wilhelm Friess is unusually well documented compared to most prophecies and other pamphlets of the fifteenth and sixteenth centuries, although some stages of the process remain obscure. The examination of relationships between redactions and the changes between editions enable us to consider it as a model for the development of prophecies in print. The earliest stages of transmission are characterized by rapid and significant revision by a limited but highly motivated audience that had access to multiple versions of the text. Consequently, the earliest texts are the most variable, as readers intensely studied, compared, and combined different redactions, thereby creating new versions of the text. Translation provided the opportunity for significant changes as the text crossed linguistic boundaries. In later stages of transmission, the pace of change slowed from edition to edition (though the editions may have appeared quite rapidly) as the text stabilized into a form that expanded its popular appeal while avoiding official sanction and that could therefore be printed and profitably distributed to a wide audience.

This type of textual history is reminiscent of "mouvance," Paul Zumthor's term for the mutability and instability of medieval texts that became a central concept in the New Philology of the late twentieth century. One might also compare this textual variability to what Joachim Bumke observed concerning medieval German epics, where the most variable texts and most uncertain relationships are found in the oldest manuscripts, while the more recent manuscripts can be much more neatly classified, in contrast to the assumptions of traditional textual criticism. According to Bumke, the greater variability of the older manuscripts is due to pronounced changes in literacy and the use of the written word between the twelfth and the fifteenth/sixteenth centuries, when the youngest manuscripts were copied.[3] For scholars influenced by New Philology as well, the variability of medieval texts was a consequence of pre-modern oral and scribal culture. In the case of "Wilhelm Friess," however, we find much the same kind of textual mutation occurring in print and within the space of a few years during the second half of the sixteenth century. As Bumke notes, textual transmission follows rules that are particular to a given time, place, and context. The complicated family tree of the prophecy of "Wilhelm Friess" is the consequence of a prophetic text that was being intensively read and revised at a dramatic pace before it reached Nuremberg, where it began to achieve a stable form as it was issued from the press of Georg Kreydlein and his imitators.

"Wilhelm Friess" in Nuremberg

One remaining puzzle is why the reception of "Wilhelm Friess" in southern Germany was so different from the bloody trail it left in Antwerp. While Frans Fraet was executed for printing a seditious prognostication, Georg Kreydlein of Nuremberg published at least eight editions of a similar text, usually with his own name on the title page. Kreydlein appears as a printer as early as 1554, but the single edition of that year was not followed by any others until 1558, when he published his editions of "Wilhelm Friess" and seven other pamphlets. The workshop address Kreydlein gave in 1554 and again in 1558—"auffm newen baw," or "at the new building," in Nuremberg—is the same as that used by another printer, Georg Merkel, from 1552 to 1557.[4] Merkel was briefly imprisoned in 1557 because of conflicts with his wife, Barbara. Barbara Merkel appears as the press's sole proprietor in 1560, until Georg Merkel briefly resumed business in 1561–62 before his death. To what degree Kreydlein cooperated with Georg or Barbara Merkel and how the turbulence in the Merkels' press operation affected Georg Kreydlein are unknown, but it is clear that Kreydlein was attempting to establish his own workshop in 1558.

At this critical juncture in his printing career, Kreydlein published multiple editions of only three different works: two editions of a description of the entry of the Holy Roman Emperor Charles V into Prague, five editions of a prophetically tinged astrological prognostication for the years 1559–65 by Nikolaus Caesareus, and eight editions of "Wilhelm Friess." Kreydlein's editions used three different title woodcuts, all of which show Christ standing with the apostles beneath astronomical signs of the times and against an urban background (see figure 2). In VD16, one of these editions (N14; VD16 F 2841), which combined the prophecy of "Wilhelm Friess" with the astrological prognostication of Nikolaus Caesareus, is dated to 1557, but the dating is certainly wrong. Caesareus's prognostications for years beginning in 1559 would hardly be printed in 1557, and none of the other nine editions of Caesareus's work are earlier than 1558. Caesareus furthermore foresaw that the common people would rebel against their rulers but would be violently defeated, "like the peasants in the Peasants' War [of 1525] thirty-three years ago." This edition likely appeared in late 1558.[5] The catalog of the Herzog August Bibliothek in Wolfenbüttel considers this edition to be a possible Erfurt reprint of a Nuremberg edition and dates it to 1558. Kreydlein continued publishing reports of tyranny, persecution, visions, prodigies, funerals, and other standard forms of pamphlet literature until his death in 1561. All forty-five of Kreydlein's editions, nearly all of them booklets of four to eight leaves, are in German rather than Latin.

In the textual history of "Wilhelm Friess," the Kreydlein editions form, except for one gap, a compact and continuous chain of transmission from one edition to the next. The editions N16–N19 are particularly similar to each other, sharing a title woodcut, text and decorative types, and much of their page layout. The type was changed significantly during the printing of N16, so that existing copies represent two different states of the type. The differences between later editions indicate only a partial resetting of type, affecting between 10 and 80 percent of the text for N17–N19.

At least two other printers found Kreydlein's product promising enough to reprint. Johann Daubmann printed an edition under his own name in Königsberg (where the prophecy would also have been able to reach a Polish-speaking audience). Kreydlein's multiple editions and the rapid reprinting of "Wilhelm Friess" by others are sure indications of a popular and successful pamphlet. Moreover, that there are twelve editions known from a single copy, two editions known from two copies, three known from three copies, and two known from five or more copies suggests that there may be several more editions that have not yet been discovered or that have disappeared entirely.

At the time that Georg Kreydlein was printing his pamphlets, Nuremberg was near the height of its political, commercial, and cultural ascendancy. The city had long been one of the free cities of the Holy Roman Empire, so it was subject to no other sovereign besides an emperor who

PROGNOSTICATIO.

Etliche seltzame Pro-
pheceyung/geweyssaget von dem Alten M. Wilhelmo Friesen/von Mastrich/
welcher newlich gestorbē/die bey jme gefunden nach seinem Tode/von 1558. biß
ins 63. Jar sich erstreckende/Inn
denen sehr seltzame vñ gräwliche veränderung geweys-
saget werden.

Marthæi vi. Lucæ xi. Actor. xxi.

Dein will geschehe wie im Hymel/
also auch auff Erden.

Gedruckt zu Nürnberg/durch
Georg Kreydlein.

Fig. 2. Title page of the first prophecy of Wilhelm Friess, showing Christ in dialogue with his disciples. VD16 F 2843 (N16). Nuremberg: Georg Kreydlein, [1558]. Herzog August Bibliothek Wolfenbüttel: A: 151.27 Theol. (11).

was usually occupied with matters elsewhere. Territorial acquisitions in the preceding decades had brought neighboring lands under Nuremberg's control, resulting in the largest geographic extent of any imperial city at midcentury. In addition to its economic significance, Nuremberg was also one of the most important printing centers of southern Germany, with several large and capable workshops operating within its walls. The Protestant Reformation, following the principles of Martin Luther, had been introduced in Nuremberg beginning in 1525, with Andreas Osiander providing substantial impetus. But while an uncompromising Gnesio-Lutheran text such as the earliest editions of the N version of Wilhelm Friess may have found many buyers in Nuremberg, it would not have been tolerated by the city authorities. In 1547, Charles V had soundly defeated the Lutheran nobility in the Schmalkaldic War, forcing their territories to accept the widely despised Interim, which brought Protestant worship to a halt and threatened to end the Reformation altogether. Nuremberg's civic leaders accepted the Interim just enough to stave off invasion by the forces of the Holy Roman Emperor but attempted to avoid the most contentious compromises with Catholic forms of worship, in order to avoid popular revolt.[6] The city's printers were subject to censorship, and even after the Interim was lifted, the city maintained its position in support of Melanchthon and against the unyielding Gnesio-Lutheran orthodoxy exemplified by Mathias Flacius.

How could a pamphlet that meant a death sentence for Frans Fraet in Antwerp become a best seller for Georg Kreydlein in Nuremberg? The answer is a matter of geography: the meaning of "Wilhelm Friess" changed as it traveled from Antwerp to Nuremberg. If one overlooks the half-concealed sedition of "Wilhelm Friess"—and in Nuremberg, unlike Antwerp, there were few reasons to look for it—the prophecy appears little different from many other narrations of the end-time drama with an anticlerical sentiment that were published in the fifteenth and sixteenth centuries. The actors in "Wilhelm Friess" are the stock characters of the Christian end-time narrative, and the future disasters that "Wilhelm Friess" warns of are entirely stereotypical. It lacks only the specific mention of the Antichrist, who had become a controversial figure that some Protestants rejected as a Catholic legend.[7] "Wilhelm Friess" instead contrasts the Last Emperor with a "false heathen emperor from the west" who will "join with those in the east and come down upon the entire land," where he will "persecute and torment the Christians with utmost cruelty and spare nothing, but rather devastate and destroy everything over which he gains power" (225–33). Unlike the nominal allegiance owed the emperor by the free imperial city of Nuremberg, Habsburg rule over Antwerp was stern and direct, and the geography of the false emperor was profoundly different. In Antwerp, the tyrant from the west with eastern allies who cruelly oppressed Christians could easily be read as a reference to Habsburg dominion emanating from Spain and Austria. It was certainly all too clear to Dutch Protestants that these lands were the source of their persecution. From the perspective of Nuremberg, however, the political geography of the Netherlands was much different. In the "Wilhelm Friess" pamphlets, the only time the Netherlands are mentioned is when the title pages refer to Wilhelm Friess's citizenship in Maastricht. This city lay not far to the west of Aachen, which was the traditional site of the Holy Roman Emperor's coronation as King of the Romans following his election and was also where Charlemagne was buried. For the customers of Georg Kreydlein in Nuremberg, Maastricht, once at the core of the Carolingian realm and then, in the sixteenth century, a part of the Habsburg hereditary lands, could serve together with Nuremberg as a point on the central axis of empire.

In southern Germany, imperial propaganda had long sought to connect the emperors of prophecy with whoever happened to hold the imperial scepter at the moment. Frederick III, great-grandfather of Charles V, had been compared to the Last Emperor in the mid-fifteenth century (to cite but one example).[8] In Nuremberg, 650 kilometers to the southeast of Antwerp, there was little question that the Last Emperor was a Habsburg (and, hopefully, the current emperor or at least the next one). At the same time, the false emperor from the west and his eastern allies fit the geography of national rivalry with France and anxieties over Turkish incursions. One anonymous edition of "Wilhelm Friess" (N8) encouraged this identification by illustrating the title page with a woodcut of two turbaned soldiers putting children to the sword while a reclining figure looks on passively from his bed. King Francis I of France had been among the contenders in the election that made Charles V the Holy Roman Emperor in 1519, and war with France was nearly perpetual during Charles's reign. Another constant of his reign was strife with the Ottoman Turks in Hungary, in North Africa, and at the gates of Vienna in 1529. From 1536 onward, France and the Ottoman Turks maintained a strategic alliance that included joint action against the forces of Charles V. In contrast to the printing by Frans Fraet, Georg Kreydlein's printing of pamphlets lauding the emperor and his victories did not conceal any secret agenda. If it required no explanation in Antwerp that the false emperor with eastern allies could only refer to the Habsburg tyrant, it was equally clear in Nuremberg that only the Holy Roman Emperor could be the righteous Last Emperor of prophecy.

The status of the Last Emperor and other figures of the traditional end-time narrative was not at all clear in 1558, however. Like the Angelic Pope, the Last Emperor was a central figure in what was ultimately a pre-Reformation drama that was, in many ways, out of place in Lutheran Nuremberg. Charles V had begun his reign auspiciously with the 1527 sack of Rome, the very seat of the papal Antichrist in Protestant propaganda, and he had ended his reign as the Last Emperor was supposed to, with a formal renunciation of lands and offices. Charles had announced his abdication in 1556, and it was formally accepted in February 1558. According to the traditional narrative, however, the true Last Emperor was supposed to put off his crown on the Mount of Olives after defeating all heretics and enemies of Christendom. The Holy Land had not been reconquered, Christianity was divided against itself, the Ottoman Turks and other enemies remained a threat, and Ferdinand I had been crowned the new emperor. Clearly, the world was not yet ending. How did the new political reality fit the traditional narrative?

The accomplishments of Charles V in the realm of religion during his reign were even more troubling for Lutherans. While Charles had tolerated the Protestant Reformation in those cities and principalities where he had been powerless to stop it, he had strictly opposed it elsewhere and imposed the Interim on Protestant territories following the Schmalkaldic War. For apocalyptically minded Lutherans, the clash of the true faith with the diabolical enemy had ended not in ultimate fulfillment of evangelical hopes but, rather, in a negotiated settlement. In 1555, the Peace of Augsburg had regulated German religious affairs by establishing that individual territories would follow the religious dictates of their sovereigns.

What made "Wilhelm Friess" such a compelling product for German readers and printers was its insistence on the continued validity of the traditional end-time script at a time of political and religious change. As a new emperor began his reign and a new religious regime was implemented, the unusual specificity of the eschatological timeline in "Wilhelm Friess" forcefully reinscribed the present moment and the realigned political and religious foundations of German and European society into the traditional end-time narrative. As is often the case with printed prophecies, "Wilhelm Friess" was, in a German context, essentially conservative, placative, and optimistic. The prophecy insisted that future political and religious leaders would be wise and righteous men who would rule in harmony with each other, defeat all enemies, and fulfill the collective hopes of German society. For Georg Kreydlein, the hopes and fears of the Protestant citizens of the imperial city of Nuremberg represented a market opportunity that all but demanded something like "Wilhelm Friess." Frans Fraet had concealed the subversive message of "Wilhelm Friess" so well that the surface message could be taken at face value. The imperial prophecies that had been appropriated to subversive ends in Antwerp were reappropriated to sell imperial hegemony in Nuremberg.

The Restless Ghost of Wilhelm Friess

The success of "Wilhelm Friess" in Nuremberg was a product of how it fit the ideological needs of a specific time and place, but that moment had come and gone by 1560. Almost certainly, all editions of the D and N versions were printed in 1558 and the one edition of the B version by 1559. Although "Wilhelm Friess" continued to find at least some readers into the 1570s, its prophecies for specific years had begun to diverge too noticeably from actual events for it to continue functioning as an interpreter of the present moment.[9] In the following years, the prophecy of Paul Severus and the astrological prognostications of Nikolaus Weise for the years up to 1588 took the place of "Wilhelm Friess" in the market for popular prophetic pamphlets.[10]

The prophecy of the pseudonymous Paul Severus appeared in fifteen editions by 1563, most of which reproduce only the last section of what had been a longer astrological prognostication.[11] In several passages, the prophecy of Paul Severus seems to echo "Wilhelm Friess," including a prediction of tribulation for the Catholic clergy: "The pope and his people will abandon the seat in Rome and flee into the wilderness out of great fear in order to live safely there, and there will be no more pope. Churches and cloisters will also be destroyed everywhere in Germany, and the clergy will be chased out and driven away, and they will have no more benefices, and there will be great lamentation among the clergy everywhere in Germany."[12] A tyrant from the west will oppress Christians in the Netherlands, but God will cast him down. In another scene reminiscent of the conclusion of "Wilhelm Friess," the prophecy attributed to Severus (hereinafter referred to as "Paul Severus") foresees misfortune lasting from 1564 until 1570, when a new Reformation will bring about order and good laws and when a righteous emperor in the north will establish peace and reclaim Hungary, Constantinople, and Switzerland for Christendom and the empire.[13] "Paul Severus" orients its prognostication with reference to the four cardinal directions more strongly than in "Wilhelm Friess," and it includes a version of the prophecy that the Ottoman Turks would invade Germany and devastate the land but eventually be defeated. In the traditional version, the climactic battle takes place near Cologne on the Rhine, but "Paul Severus," perhaps due to local patriotism, foresees that all Germans will gather for battle in Saxony.[14] The context and influence of "Paul Severus" remain largely unknown, but it found its way to readers both in the 1560s and later; the astrologer and Lutheran dissenter Paul Nagel borrowed passages from "Paul Severus" for a prophetic work published in 1605.[15]

It would not be surprising if "Wilhelm Friess" had dissolved into nothing more than an influence on later prophetic texts such as "Paul Severus," but odd things began happening that attest a prolonged effect of "Wilhelm Friess" on prophetic writing in Germany and the Netherlands. In 1562, when the printer Christian Müller of Strasbourg published an extract of Theodore Simitz's astrological prognostications for 1563–66, he supplemented Simitz's work, according to the title page, with "the prophecy that was made by the old Wilhelm Friess of Maastricht about the years 1563 and 1564."[16] The text attributed to Friess begins with a section about eclipses: "Now the evil and shocking years 1563, 1564, and 1565 are coming, for in these years great changes in the empire will occur whose equal has not happened in a hundred years."[16] Several observations concerning upcoming eclipses and planetary conjunctions follow, as well as citations of various astrological authorities on what these astronomic events portend. This text, printed together with Simitz's prognostication under the name of Wilhelm Friess, was not "Wilhelm Friess" at all. It is not entirely unfamiliar, however. The text was an extract from the astrological prognostication by Nikolaus Caesareus that Georg Kreydlein had printed so frequently and, at least once, together with "Wilhelm Friess." Other printers had reprinted Kreydlein's editions of "Wilhelm Friess," and now a printer was appropriating Friess's authorship for the prognostication of Nikolaus Caesareus, just as Frans Fraet had once borrowed the authorial name of Willem de Vriese from pamphlets printed by Hans van Liesvelt. One might be inclined to regard Christian Müller's attribution of Nikolaus Caesareus's astrological prognostication to Wilhelm Friess in 1562 as a simple oversight on the part of the printer, were it not for the pattern of applying the name of Wilhelm Friess to new texts, which began with Hans van Liesvelt and Frans Fraet and would continue well beyond 1562.

The prognostication of Nikolaus Caesareus that was attributed to

Wilhelm Friess has few parallels with the prophecies that Kreydlein had printed in Nuremberg. One does find a passage, however, that is similar to what Willem de Vriese had once written in Antwerp: the frequent conjunctions of Saturn, Jupiter, and Mars will cause the rise of new sects, "great changes in the empire and in matters of religion, devastation of many lands and cities, and the clergy will in truth be sorely attacked." The upper planets will further "instigate the common people to war and rebellion against their rulers and against the clergy so that they will persecute them with great enmity and rob them of their honors and possessions and harm them." The end, as already seen above, is foreordained: the rebellion will end as badly as the Peasants' War had done in 1525.[17] Just as the name of Willem de Vriese had once been attached to a variety of texts in Antwerp, the same had now happened to Wilhelm Friess in Germany. Rather than identifying a specific text, the name of Wilhelm Friess was on its way to identifying a type of prognostication at the intersection of prophecy, astrology, and reform.

Wilhelm Friess in Antwerp and Lübeck, 1566–68

VERSION L

The L version of "Wilhelm Friess" is known from two Low German editions printed by Johann Balhorn the Elder in Lübeck. The title pages of the two editions claim to contain prophecies for 1558–70, of which the last four years would be particularly turbulent. Not only do they identify the prophecy as something found under the pillow of the elderly "Wilhelm de Frese," doctor and astronomer of Maastricht, after his death, but they also state for the first time that Friess was the author of the prognostication as well. The texts of the two editions differ little from each other, but the title woodcuts used very different strategies to attract customers. Balhorn's first edition used a crude image of a scholar in robes and a cap as its title woodcut, but the next edition opted for a more dramatic scene: amid prostrate bodies, men and women raise clasped hands in pleading toward Christ, who is seated on a rainbow in the sky amid sun, moon, stars, comets, and fiery stars falling to the earth.

The L version has the most complicated textual history of any of the four redactions. It is the version with the most substantial additions and omissions, while still preserving some original passages found nowhere else. Because one of the editions has been misdated, the historical context of these editions has gone unrecognized.

Johann Balhorn also printed his two editions with a disconcerting lack of care. One of the lengthier additions found in the L version concerns the Whore of Babylon from Revelation 17:3. In Balhorn's editions, she sits not on a red beast but on a "terrible Finnish beast," a "growsamen fennischen derte" (85). This formulation may be a deformation of the Dutch *rozijnverwich* as found in the Biestkens Bible printed several times after 1558, which was based partly on the Bible of Jacob van Liesvelt.[18] The curious phrase suggests that the sources of the L version include Dutch texts, and it also indicates the modest editorial care and comprehension to be found in Balhorn's Lübeck workshop. One notes that the German verb *verballhornen*, meaning "to corrupt or mutilate a text, especially through well-intended attempts at improvement," arose from a disastrously edited book printed by Johann Balhorn's son.[19]

All versions of "Wilhelm Friess" retain traces of its original geography. Even in translation, the false emperor of the west and his eastern allies come down upon the land (*niderwartz*), that is, toward the Low Countries (228). One of the lengthy passages added in the L version contains the prediction of pestilence in *averland* (37), the higher elevations found in Germany, again reflecting a Dutch geographical perspective and suggesting that the substantial additions to "Wilhelm Friess" found in L were added to the text while it circulated in the Netherlands.

Several features shared with the D version place L firmly in the y branch, including the reordering of a lengthy exhortation to repentance that both versions move from its original location to the position immediately following the advice to store food for five years (47–52). As a representative of the y branch, the L version preserves some material omitted in D. Its prediction that monasteries would be destroyed uses a verb, *vordestrueret*, that echoes the phrasing of the French redaction, "les abbayes destruira" (56). In the other versions, the tormented clergy confess that their punishment is just. Only in the L version do they say that their punishment is also good, echoing the French "a bon droit" (98). When the small birds assault the large birds, only version L includes not just particular species but also a rendering of the collective term *les grans oiseaulx de proie*, or "birds of prey" (147), found in the French *Vademecum* manuscript. The phrase used in Balhorn's first edition, however, is the nonsensical *groff Vögel*, which Balhorn perhaps misread from Dutch *roofvogel* ("bird of prey"; one might be tempted to see *groff Vögel* instead as a misreading of High German *große Vögel*, "large birds," but that phrase does not appear in any of the High German editions). Balhorn's second edition mistakenly corrected the passage to *graue Vögel*, or "gray birds."

The L version leaves us with some unsolvable mysteries. All other versions cite Job—according to the B version, the seventh chapter (21)—that life is a war with the devil. That chapter says nothing about life as a war but emphatically states that life is vanity. Balhorn's editions assert that life, according to Job, is the devil's organ works ("ein Orgelwerck des Düvels," 23). This is nonsensical, but might it reflect an early deformation of French *orgueil*, or "vainglory," which the other versions turned into "warfare" (Low German *orlog*, High German *urlog*) in order to make sense of the passage? Or is it a late deformation of Dutch *oorlog*, or "war"? Where the N and B versions affirm that the worms who will attack the larger animals will appear as if one could easily ("leichtlich") conquer them, as does the French redaction, Balhorn's editions state that the worms will shine brightly ("licht") over the earth (139–40). The use of the same root for descriptions that are entirely different in meaning points toward an inheritance from the original source, but the paths by which Balhorn's worms achieved their luminescence are inscrutable.

In addition to its inheritance from the y branch of "Wilhelm Friess," the L version borrowed from both the B and the N versions of the x branch. Only the B version omits mention of the little birds and instead states that the worms will attack birds of all kinds (145). The L version borrowed the B version's innovation, even though it was redundant in the L version. Another passage expresses hope that God would turn aside his punishment if people repent, just as he spared the people of Nineveh, or as the B version puts it, "if we turned ourselves [*uns kerten*] to virtue." The L version borrows and distorts the same phrase: "if we convert our hearts [*unse herten*] to virtue" (31). A telling case of borrowing from B involves the timeline of tribulation. The original text, as seen in versions D and B and the French redaction, had foreseen five years of catastrophe. Version B, printed a year after the D and N editions in 1559, changes the prediction to four years of disaster, which the L version borrowed despite a stated expectation of twelve years of tribulation (165). The borrowing from High German editions probably occurred in Lübeck, as Balhorn's second edition corrected one innovation in his first so that it read more like the original text of the B version, changing *unordentlike teiken*, "disorderly signs," back to the B version's *unerhörde teiken*, "unheard of signs" (136). This correction and a few others that make Balhorn's second edition more like the N version (18, 56) illustrate the complex textual history of printed booklets. A printer like Balhorn who printed a second edition would often have two or more exemplars on hand in the form of the original exemplar and the first edition, making every later edition potentially the result of "contamination" between a prior edition and an older exemplar. Because of this, the fact that one edition has a text more faithful to the original in a few places may be the result not of textual precedence but of reverting to the exemplar through correction.

Version L also borrowed numerous passages otherwise found only in N but not in the D or B versions or in the French redaction, such as the passage foreseeing not just a pestilence, as in the other versions, but one worse than anyone could imagine (184–85). The N and the L versions are likewise the only ones to add that there will be many of the foreseen false prophets (348). Where the D version follows the French redaction quite closely in stating that unrepentant sinners who were not killed in war would die in other tribulations, the N version states that they would be taken from the world in other ways, a formulation that the L version adopted (310). Where the French redaction and the D and B versions describe the Last Emperor's conquest of the "Holy Land," the N version refers to it as "das gelobte Landt," the "promised land," which the L version borrows as "dat landt van geloffden" (414).

A borrowing from either N or, perhaps more likely, the B version occurred early enough that the L version even preserves more faithfully than any other known edition a few words of the conclusion largely borrowed from Grünpeck by way of Egenolff. The conclusion calls on readers to put on the clothes of repentance and regret ("busse unnd rewe" in the N version), but the clothes of penitence and sorrow in the original ("penitentzen unnd leyd"). Only the L version has a combination of the older wording and the newer, "tehet an dat kleid der penetentien / unde draget ruw und leidt" (479). Those who fail to do so will flee to the shore and call on the water to gently accept them, or, in the original and in the L version, to gently receive their lives (485; "ewer leben" or "iw levent").

The editions of "Wilhelm Friess" do not offer any single version that is a reliable guide to the original text in all cases. While the N version may be the most complete and overall the least altered, the complicated history of transmission and borrowing between versions means that unique fragments of the original can be found almost anywhere. The L version appears to have translated into Low German a Dutch text that had been expanded since 1558 and then to have extended it with borrowings from two different High German versions of "Wilhelm Friess," but even

Johann Balhorn's handiwork did not erase all its unique fragments of the original text.

According to auction records now over two centuries old, a Dutch edition of "Wilhelm Friess" was printed in 1566, coincidentally the same year that Mathias Flacius traveled to Antwerp to oversee the Lutheran congregation there. Although no copy is currently known, the Dutch edition was very likely similar to the Lübeck editions: its title page also promised its readers prophecies for the years 1558–70, and it specified that the prophecy had been found under the head of Willem de Vriese ("onder zihn hooft"), just as only the Lübeck editions state that the prophecy had been found under Friess's pillow ("under synem Höuet küssen").[20] This lost Dutch edition could have been Johann Balhorn's source, as Balhorn's first edition was almost certainly printed not in 1558 (as it is dated in VD16) but, instead, no earlier than 1566. Balhorn's second edition bears the year 1568, while the first has no date. The dating of the first edition to 1558 in VD16 would make sense based on a title page that mentions prophecies for the years 1558–70, but the existence of editions printed in 1566 and 1568 should raise some suspicion about the dating of the first edition, and a look beyond the title page shows that these suspicions are justified. Despite the claim of prophecies beginning in 1558, all references to the years 1558–64 have been removed or shifted seven years into the future. Version L adds a new prophecy that the years 1566–70 will be marked by pestilence, signs, and wonders. The only reference to the years before 1566 in the L version is a prediction that there would be a severe famine from 1561 to 1566 (37). By 1566, this prediction no longer required any special insight: one history of the year 1566 in the Netherlands is entitled simply *Het Hongerjaar* (the year of hunger).[21] In Johann Balhorn's editions, the terrible reign of the false emperor is much reduced, as are the troubles predicted for France. Following the conclusion of France's Italian Wars in 1559 with the Peace of Cateau-Cambrésis, the prediction of impending war between France and Italy no longer had a place in "Wilhelm Friess," especially since the growing influence of Protestantism among the French nobility let some Dutch Protestants hope for support from France in the struggle against Habsburg domination.[22] Johann Balhorn's first edition should certainly be dated no earlier than 1566, which makes a source in a Dutch version of "Wilhelm Friess," perhaps the lost Dutch edition printed in 1566, a distinct possibility. Valkema Blouw surmised that the missing Dutch edition of 1566 was a reprint of Fraet's edition, but if similar dates of tribulation can be taken as a reliable indicator, the lost Dutch edition belonged to the L redaction and was some generations removed from the text printed by Fraet.[23]

Beyond the reappearance of the prophecy a decade after its first appearance in print, something even more extraordinary happened with the L editions. Between 1566 and 1568, the prophecy of Wilhelm Friess—or at least part of it—came true.

CHAPTER 5

A Horrible and Shocking Prophecy

---⚘---

The Appalling Accuracy of "Wilhelm Friess"

With a better understanding of when the L version of "Wilhelm Friess" was printed and how the text took shape, we have come full circle, returning once again to Antwerp and the Low Countries. In Dutch history, 1566 is the *wonderjaar*, the "year of miracles," which saw the outbreak of open hostilities and the initial successes of the Dutch Revolt against Habsburg rule.[1] The events were so remarkable that Godevaert van Haecht, a Dutch Lutheran observer of events in Antwerp at the time, thought that a prophecy made seven years earlier that had foreseen a miraculous year was then being fulfilled.[2] Although the prophecy van Haecht referred to was probably not "Wilhelm Friess," the context in which the lost Dutch edition of "Wilhelm Friess" was circulating included the sense that long-awaited events were coming to pass.

Like the earliest editions of the N version, the two editions of the L version provide a list of sects that makes clear its Lutheran perspective. The sects—which, in the L version, will be not just converted but destroyed—include "Papists, Calvinists, Jovists, Anabaptists, Sacramentarians, etc." (38–42). "Sacramentarians" was another name for Calvinists, while "Jovists" (*Jovisten*) is perhaps a misreading of "Joristen," followers of the Anabaptist leader David Joris. These are not the religious enemies of German Gnesio-Lutherans in the 1550s found in the N version. They are, instead, the religious opponents faced specifically by Lutherans in the Netherlands during the age of confessionalization, as the mainstream Protestant churches were taking separate paths and drawing harder boundaries between Lutheran and Reformed doctrine and worship, a process that gained particular force in the Netherlands in the decade following the abdication of Charles V.[3]

The Dutch Revolt began with a wave of vandalism directed at religious images and church altars. The L version updated the prophecy accordingly. Where all other versions of "Wilhelm Friess" predicted only the destruction of cloisters, the L version foresaw the destruction and also the plundering of both cloisters and churches (56). In the wake of the rioting, the Habsburg central government lost the ability to impose its will in much of the Netherlands, and even reputable printers began openly publishing seditious pamphlets and Protestant religious works.[4] Just as "Wilhelm Friess" had predicted, the common people had risen up against their rulers.

The rebellion emphasized the contrast between Calvinism and Lutheranism with respect to one of the sorest points of contention between the two strands of Protestantism. Where Calvinist preachers had justified underground worship, Luther had counseled cooperation with the government in religious matters, even if it meant delaying the Reformation in an area until the local sovereign could be converted. Consequently, Calvinists were more likely to approve violent resistance to unrighteous secular rule, while Lutherans were more likely to oppose revolution and to accept the feudal political hierarchy led by the Holy Roman Emperor.[5] The emperor from the west who persecutes Christians may be wicked in "Wilhelm Friess," but the L version adds that he has been sent by God for just that purpose (230). Although Frans Fraet was executed for printing a seditious prophecy, "Wilhelm Friess" had always regarded popular revolt with ambivalence at best. Unlike the sword of popular justice in store for the nobility in the *Vademecum*, the earliest versions of "Wilhelm Friess" foresaw that the nobility would violently suppress the revolt of the common people. Where other versions of "Wilhelm Friess" foretell the death of those who refuse to repent, the L version adds rebellious people to the list of the doomed (42) and includes a new prediction that no more sects will arise. Opposing views on the sacrament of the Lord's Supper were another source of contention. When both the sacramental host and wine were offered to Protestants in Antwerp in the fall of 1566, the Calvinists mocked the Lutherans—whose religious views did not contrast as sharply as theirs with Catholicism—as idol worshippers, flesh eaters, and blood drinkers.[6]

Lutherans who distanced themselves from the revolt saw their loyalist position vindicated in 1567, when the Calvinists of Antwerp experienced a series of traumatic defeats. On 13 March 1567, residents of Antwerp standing on the city walls were spectators to the Battle of Oosterweel, in which Calvinist rebels led by Jan van Marnix, elder brother of Philips van Marnix, faced an army of experienced soldiers led by Filips van Lannoy, captain of the Habsburg governor's bodyguard. As the Calvinists of Antwerp watched the annihilation and massacre of the rebels, they began arming themselves in order to come to the aid of the defeated soldiers outside the walls. William of Orange, as duly appointed *burgraaf* of Antwerp, prevented this action by sealing the city gates and told the Calvinists that any attempt to interfere would only lead to their deaths. Within a few months, William would abandon his position and become a leader of the revolt, but in March 1567, he still recognized his obligation to the Habsburg monarch who had appointed him.

Despite William's orders, the Calvinists of Antwerp did not stand down. They began to assemble and arm themselves with their own weapons and with weapons plundered from city merchants. Calvinist leaders demanded the surrender of city authority, threatened to expel all Catholic clergy and believers from the city, and rejected the accord of religious peace that had been in force in Antwerp since September 1566.[7] William of Orange agreed to let Calvinists keep watch jointly with the city guard over Antwerp's Great Market, the town hall, and the city walls and gates. Despite this concession, a group of Calvinists broke into the Cloister of St. Michael and set about ransacking it.

The next day, William of Orange continued his frantic riding between the city's civic and religious leaders in order to negotiate a peaceful settlement, but his initial attempts were rejected, and Reformed preachers began to threaten that the Lutherans, derided as "new papists," would meet the same fate as Catholics if they did not lend their support to the uprising.[8] In reaction to this, William signaled that all those who were loyal to the king, the city of Antwerp, and the Lutheran Augsburg Confession should form an army, with arms and artillery provided by the city's armory. The Lutherans and three companies of the city guard assembled on the Oever, a market near the banks of the river Scheldt. The Calvinists who had held watch at the Great Market and city hall retreated to join the main Calvinist force on the Meir, a market to the southeast, while the vandals who had broken into the Cloister of St. Michael found themselves cut off from the main Calvinist force and agreed to disperse peacefully. William of Orange gathered additional aid in the form of two hundred horse and riders from the German residents of Antwerp and the "Easterlings," or merchants of the Hanseatic League, who rode in from Antwerp's new district and, upon finding the Great Market well defended, continued on to the Oever. The Lutherans and city guard were soon joined by many Catholics, who recognized that a Calvinist victory would result in their expulsion or worse. Upon seeing the Lutheran army assembled and recognizing the particular enmity that many of the common people held against them, the Italian, Spanish, and Portuguese merchants assembled a force of a thousand armed men and took up position between St. Jacob's Church and the Kipdorp Gate, just a few streets from the Calvinists assembled on the Meir. Van Haecht estimated the Calvinist army as ten thousand men at arms, while the army gathered by William of Orange had eight thousand soldiers and so many additional supporters in surrounding streets that their numbers seemed countless to him.[9] Observers expected violence between the two immense armies within the city to break out at any moment, with a fearful vengeance to be wrought afterward against the homes and families of the losing side.[10]

The Calvinist leaders finally recognized that they were surrounded and outnumbered. The Lutherans and their supporters lined the whole length of the Oever and the streets on either side in ranks nine deep almost as far as the town hall and Great Market, which were well defended by cannon and companies of the city guard, cutting off access to the Scheldt. The Spaniards, Portuguese, and Italians blocked movement toward the new city and merchant shops to the north and the closest city gate to the east.

The tactically hopeless situation of Antwerp's Calvinists made their figurative isolation all too clear. They could see with their own eyes how the Lutherans had made common cause with the Catholics and how representatives from the nations of Europe on all sides had united against them. On 15 March, the Calvinists lay down their arms and dispersed according to the terms of what seemed to them a humiliating defeat, which remained a source of resentment against the Lutherans into the seventeenth century. Some Calvinists accused the Lutherans of having become Catholics, as there were so many Catholics in their army.[11] It must have been all the more galling that the Lutheran prophecy of Wilhelm Friess, which foresaw the uprising of the common people ending ignominiously, had been proved correct. Back in Germany, Mathias Flacius defended himself against the accusation that he was to blame for the recent unrest in the Netherlands in similar terms, treating ruthless suppression as the consequence of revolt against legitimate rulers: "And what else did [the Calvinists] accomplish in the end by their rebellion against the civil government except for falling into even greater calamity, burdening the gospel of Christ and all those churches with the foul name of sedition, and finally giving their persecutors a worthier cause for such anger against them?" Following the Battle of Oosterweel and other defeats at the hands of the multinational Habsburg armies, many Dutch Protestants began fleeing in April 1567 to refuges abroad. News of the dramatic events in Antwerp spread quickly. At least one pamphlet about them appeared in Augsburg in 1567, and it is known from other cases that news of Dutch events could appear in German-language pamphlets as little as three weeks after the fact.[12]

The new editions and revised text of "Wilhelm Friess" in 1566–68 were reactions to recent events in the Netherlands, and they offer an additional example of how the text changed form and took on new meanings in new places and different times. The L version provides the link to and the impetus for yet another text attributed to Wilhelm Friess, which again claimed to have been found with him after his recent death in Maastricht and which became a new best-selling prophetic pamphlet beginning in 1577, this time not in Antwerp or Nuremberg but in Basel. The origins of this new prognostication do not lie in Basel, however. Its genesis traces to a decade earlier instead, to 1567 and the trauma inflicted on Dutch Calvinists in Antwerp.

The Horrible and Shocking Prophecy of Wilhelm Friess

In 1577, Wilhelm Friess had his second posthumous best seller when the printer Samuel Apiarius of Basel published a "horrible and shocking prophecy or prediction concerning Poland, Germany, Brabant, and France," which had been "found in Maastricht with a God-fearing man, Wilhelm de Friess, after his death in 1577" (1–4; parenthetical references in this discussion indicate lines from the edition of the second prophecy in appendix 2).[13] Friess's name had appeared as "de Friess" only in the Lübeck and lost Dutch editions, which suggests that the L version was the specific catalyst for this new prophecy. While the pamphlets that Apiarius printed in Basel claimed to contain prophecies found in the same way and from the same author, the text of "Wilhelm Friess II," or "Friess II" (as I will here designate this second prophecy), has little in common with "Wilhelm Friess I." Its attitude toward the future and the contemporary political situation is fundamentally different. Instead of optimistically foreseeing the speedy fulfillment of traditional end-time expectations, the second prophecy of Wilhelm Friess is a nightmare vision of utter devastation from which only a few can hope to escape.

While "Wilhelm Friess I" describes future events and offers advice on how to prepare for them, the authorial voice of "Friess II" reports the narrator's own visionary experience. Although the title page places the narrator's residence in Maastricht in the Netherlands, the geographic site of "Friess II" clearly comprises the German-speaking lands. The text of the earliest edition printed by Apiarius (designated as F7 in appendix 3 and in figure 4, which appears later in this chapter) begins,

> On 24 April 1577, as I lay on my bed awake at midnight, a beautiful young man came to me and said: "See what will happen and diligently take note of it." Then I stood up, and immediately it seemed to me that I was on a high mountain in the middle of Germany. (cf. 15–18)

One of the few points of similarly between "Friess I" and "Friess II" is that both foresee invasion at hand. In "Friess I," the false emperor and his allies attack from the west and east, while the narrator of "Friess II" sees an invasion approaching from four directions. Invasion was just one among many catastrophes predicted by the first prophecy, but the second prophecy makes invasion a singular and all-encompassing disaster.

> Then the young man said to me, "Turn to the north. I will show you how terribly God will punish the world." I did so, and I saw a great horde approaching Germany. They had many banners, riders, and foot soldiers. Their flags were black with white crosses, and they came to a great water. Then a large strong man rode to the front on a black horse. His clothing was covered in blood and he held a large horn in his hand. He said to his people, "You should halt and wait until we call our allies to join us." And he blew the horn, and one heard it far and wide.
>
> Then the young man said to me, "Turn and look toward the west," and I did so and saw a large and terrible multitude drawing toward the north. They were fearsome and had many banners like the others, but their flags and clothing were white and red, with a red cross on them. One who looked like an evil spirit rode at their fore on a red horse. Lions and bears followed them and drove them forward ferociously and instantly attacked any who delayed. A clear voice went out among them saying, "Make haste to eat flesh."
>
> I was filled with such terrible fear that I became dizzy and was

about to faint. Then the young man strengthened me and said, "Be
comforted and do not despair, for I want to show you more." He said
to me, "Turn toward the east," and I did so. There I saw again a horrible host journeying toward the north with riders and banners like
the previous ones. Their banners were red with a fiery sword on them,
and their clothes were also red and spattered with blood. A mighty armored man went to the front who was so large that I have never seen
his equal, and his armor gleamed beyond all measure and had many
golden letters on it. He called out ferociously to his folk, "Make haste,
for we want to ruin their plans." Then I asked the young man who
that man was. He answered, "He is the Destroyer." And I asked him
again, "What are those letters written on him?" He answered, "All the
plagues and punishments that he will carry out." (cf. 19–46)

The title "Destroyer," or *Verderber*, is otherwise used primarily for the
Destroying Angel of the Passover account in sixteenth-century Bibles
and devotional literature. This figure is both diabolic and divinely sanc-
tioned.

And they made haste and quickly drew near. When they had come
together, they made a plan and were all of one mind to punish and
plague all lands. There was such a countless mass of people there that
I was amazed there could be so many. I said to the young man, "Who
can count this multitude or how many flags there are?" Then he said
to me, "There is a great number of people, while the number of banners is one hundred sixty-four thousand." And they armed themselves
powerfully while they were on the water's shore. (cf. 46–52)

Even the Destroyer is not the supreme leader of the horrors unleashed
on Germany, however. After the three armies have arrived from the
north, west, and east, a fourth host arrives from the northeast.

When they had gathered, a horrible and dreadful man came to them
from the northeast. He had a dreadful host with him who did just
as the bears had done, and they killed whomever they came upon
except the people mentioned above who were without number. The
army divided itself and let that horrible man proceed through their
midst and take his place at their front. He held a golden cup full of
blood in his right hand, and in his left hand he held a young child.
(cf. 52–59)

The cup of blood and the child are then consumed in a cannibalistic desecration of the Eucharist.

> He drank from the cup, and after that he ate for a time from the child. He did that so long until he had drained the cup and had eaten all but the child's head. After that he took the cup and the child's head and threw them down among the armies, and they trampled it with their feet. At that moment a bloody sword descended slowly from heaven, and he received it into his fist and cried with a loud voice, "Woe to you, Germany! Woe to you, Brabant and France! Woe to you, all lands! Woe to the Earth! O how happy is that person who has not given birth upon you, for I, your Destroyer, am coming and will not depart. Woe to the young men and young daughters! Woe to the proud lads and great lords, for the land will be filled with my hand." And when he had said this, he departed and the entire host with him, and he killed and horribly mistreated all those he found. He did that so far and wide until it seemed to me that he was very close to me. (cf. 59–71)

The narrator faints and then awakens to an earth covered in blood.

> Then I fell down and departed from myself, and I do not know how long I lay in that place. Then the young man came and took me by the hand and said, "Stand up, for it is finished." I did so and looked far around me, but I saw no one alive. It seemed to me that the entire Earth was full of blood from the killing and murder that they had done.
>
> Then I said to the young man, "Is there no one left alive on the Earth?" He said, "Turn to the south," and I did so. There I saw a little gathering of people wearing black clothes drawing toward me. They carried white banners, and a fine honorable man with a gray beard led them. He had a golden book in his left hand and a golden trumpet in his right hand, and he blew it and let forth a mighty blast. Then a few survivors emerged from the dense bushes and from over the high mountains. They also put on black clothes and they sat together at a great water like the Rhine. The man who had the book taught them the fear of God from it, and he directed those who had been deceived onto the path of God. When he had finished teaching, they kneeled and prayed to God. Then the man stood up with all the people and said, "Let us depart from here and mourn the earth." (cf. 71–88)

The final part of the vision warns the Romance-speaking nations and German nobility of a great tribulation that approaches.

> O you Latin world, now begin to cry and wail, for great pain is approaching you because of your great sins. For the wind has whipped up a fire that cannot be quenched. Many people think that it does not concern them because they cling to both sides, but their backs will be bent in the same game. They take no heed that the time is coming and the fire begins to burn them. Perhaps they need a cook to prepare their food for them. Many Germans will gather when the fire begins to reach them and the smoke is upon them. No count or lord will be safe. They will feel the wind of the great storm. O how much blood will they shed among those who seek domination and want to rule unjustly. O Brabant, O France, O Germany! Cry and wail, you shepherds and rulers, and put off the clothes of joy. Clothe yourself with ashes and put on a hair shirt as if you were born with it and say, "I have raised and nurtured my people, but they have despised me. To me it has become like a lion that lies in wait for someone." O you poor folk, what kind of strangers have risen up among you? They are not rulers but destroyers, not protectors but oppressors of orphans and widows throughout all Germany. It will seem to the Germans that it does not concern them, so that the common folk will say, "One is so and the other so."
>
> When these speeches were finished, the young man led me again to my room, and when I awoke the clock had struck four.[14] (cf. 88–113)

While the horror of this vision is palpable, its precise meaning is not immediately clear, due partly to its use of opaque symbolism and partly to its original context being unknown. The sheer number of editions indicates that "Friess II" was a popular pamphlet, but the passage of time, the shift to Basel as the center of printing activity, and, above all, the entirely different text mean that the reasons for its popularity were much different than those for "Friess I." Precisely what led customers to buy the two dozen editions over more than a decade is not immediately apparent. Barnes describes the second prophecy of Wilhelm Friess as a "complex and obscure vision about the nations of Christendom."[15]

For the publication of "Friess II," Samuel Apiarius of Basel played an even more dominant role than Georg Kreydlein did in publishing "Friess I." Apiarius printed thirteen editions, half of all editions known, or at least one edition nearly every year between 1577 and 1588, almost always giving his name and the place of publication, while three further editions identify themselves as reprints of pamphlets first published in Basel (F13, F25, and F26). With twelve editions of "Friess II" known from a single copy, seven from two copies, and six editions known from three copies, we must again assume a significant number of missing editions.

While the title page of the earliest Basel edition (F7) lacks illustrations, Samuel Apiarius used woodcuts of several different kinds on the title pages of following editions. For another edition of 1577 (F8), Apiarius used two small woodcuts that show a dining monarch on the left and a man pouring out two decanters onto the ground on the right, above which he quoted 1 Thessalonians 5:19–21 (in the New Revised Standard Version, "Do not quench the Spirit. Do not despise the words of prophets, but test everything; hold fast to what is good"). Perhaps the two woodcuts contrast wise acceptance and foolish rejection, or they may illustrate the consumption of wisdom and rejection of vanity, but their function as a sober visual metaphor and encouragement of prudent reading practices is clear. For an edition of the following year (F10), however, Apiarius selected a woodcut that directly invoked the disaster predicted by "Friess II" (see figure 3). Retaining the same title formulation and motto, the woodcut shows a personified Germania raising her right hand to her head in distress while a group of armed women, identified as the Turkish menace by the cardinal direction *oriens* (east) and a banner with a crescent moon and star, approaches from the left. To the right, or west, a second group of women, identified by a banner with an imperial eagle, appears to be departing and casting back glances in derision. Below and to the north, another banner with a crescent moon and two stars marks a second front of Islamic threat. Above, or from the south, a comet, armed cavalry, and a papal crown dominate a sky filled with storm and stars. Later editions also depicted disaster on their title pages, such as two editions of 1579 (F13 and F14)—one from Apiarius and one a reprint from another press—that selected a scene of a city in flames and a fortress under siege beneath a zodiacal ram.

But these title woodcuts do not provide more than a surface interpretation of the text. To puzzle out what "Friess II" was trying to say and why it was so popular, we will have to start by disentangling its textual history. For all the effort of Samuel Apiarius, we will have to look beyond Basel and before 1577 to uncover the origins of the second prophecy of "Wilhelm Friess."

Ein Grawsame vnnd

Erschröckliche Propheceihung / oder weissa=
gung vber Teutschland / Braband vnnd
Franckreich.

(v. p. 6459. 2.)

Dise Propheceyhung ist gefunden worden / in Ma=
strich / bey einem Gottsfürchtigen Mann / Wilhelm
de Frieß / nach seinem Todt / 1577.

1. Thessalon. am 5. Capitel.

Den Geist leschet nicht auß / die Prophecey verachtet nicht /
Prüffet es alles / vnd behaltet das gute.

¶ Gedruckt zu Basel / bey Samuel Apiario / Anno 1578.

36.

Fig. 3. Title page of the second prophecy of Wilhelm Friess, showing
besieged Germania. VD16 ZV 6212 (F10). Basel: Samuel Apiarius, 1578.
Herzog August Bibliothek Wolfenbüttel: A: 218.11 Quod. (36).

The Textual History of Wilhelm Friess's Second Prophecy

Unlike "Friess I," the second prophecy of Wilhelm Friess exists in only a single version, so the relationships between editions can be depicted as a relatively uncomplicated family tree, and the textual differences are mostly less substantial than those of "Friess I." Comparing the various editions of "Friess II" reveals only small discrepancies in the text until the end of the vision, where the differences are quite apparent. The larger discrepancies make it possible to reconstruct the textual history of "Friess II," which, in turn, makes some of the prior, seemingly minor changes take on new significance.

At the conclusion of the vision in the 1577 editions of Samuel Apiarius, the honorable man from the south teaches the few survivors on the banks of the Rhine, leads them in prayer, enjoins them to depart and mourn the earth, and then pauses for a lengthy speech directed not at the survivors but, first of all, at the Romance-speaking lands. "O you Latin world, now begin to cry and wail," the honorable man begins, apparently ignoring the band of survivors who had gathered around him. Then he harangues Brabant, France, and, above all, the German nobility, seemingly unaware that all these lands had just been utterly destroyed by demonic armies. This section of the honorable man's speech seems incongruous for good reason: it was entirely lifted from two other works.

The first unmarked citation (88–98) consists of two unconnected passages from "Dietrich von Zengg," a brief and highly obscure prophecy with scant scholarly literature.[16] First attested in manuscript as early as 1465, the tract was relatively popular in print, with sixteen editions between 1503 and 1563.[17] Most title pages attribute the prophecy to a Brother Dietrich, a Franciscan monk residing in what is now the Croatian town of Senj. The quotation in "Friess II" does not come from an edition attributed to any Brother Dietrich, however. Instead, the quotation closely follows a version of what is clearly the same text as "Dietrich von Zengg," though it claims to be a prophecy written by a nameless Carmelite monk of Prague in the year 462 (perhaps 1462?) and allegedly found in Altenburg Castle in Austria. Two editions of this version were printed in 1522 and 1523 in Freiburg and Speyer, with two more, including the probable source of the citation, following in 1562 and 1563.

The citations from "Dietrich von Zengg" stop, but the honorable man's speech continues. "O Brabant, O France, O Germany! Cry and wail, you shepherds and rulers," he says. After calling on the nobility to clothe themselves in hair shirts and ashes, he refers to the rulers as foreigners and oppressors. The second half of the speech (98–106) seems like a tissue woven of biblical citations (see Jeremiah 25:34, 6:26; Isaiah 1:2; Jeremiah 12:8; Isaiah 1:23), but "Friess II" was not the first to weave them together. The second citation in the honorable man's speech is a reworking of a passage from Lichtenberger's *Prognosticatio.* The passage is not taken from the German version of the *Prognosticatio* first printed ca. 1490 but instead follows the text as it appeared in a new translation first published in 1527, an edition for which Martin Luther had provided a preface. This passage, like most else that appears in the *Prognosticatio,* is not original to Lichtenberger. It appeared at least as early as 1422 in an accusation, probably written by a Bohemian Catholic, against Holy Roman Emperor Sigismund's manner of waging war against the Hussites. One hesitates to call even this the original source, as the author was explicitly collecting reports then in circulation.[18]

Recognizing the citations from "Dietrich von Zengg" and Lichtenberger in "Friess II" is the essential insight that allows us to reconstruct the history of the text. As the citations come as jarring intrusions into the honorable man's speech, one suspects that they were added after the prophecy's original composition. In the 1577 editions of Samuel Apiarius, however, the vision concludes immediately after the citation from Lichtenberger: the vision guide leads the narrator back to his room, where he awakes. If the citations of Lichtenberger and "Dietrich von Zengg" are indeed additions that displaced the end of the honorable man's speech, one can surmise that there must have been an earlier state of the text that did not include the expansion.

1639: The Earliest and Latest Wilhelm Friess

There is, in fact, one edition (F1) that ends with the honorable man's speech, uninterrupted by quotations from other prophecies. It concludes the speech with a passage that fits the preceding lines much better than the citations from "Dietrich von Zengg" and Lichtenberger: "For injustice has been taken from them. Let us also bury all those of ours who have died, for their souls rest in peace. Praised be the Lord our God, for his judgment is just" (109–11). The edition that concludes the speech in this way is also the one printed last, in 1639. Despite its late date, its updating of language that had become archaic, and its additional changes to the text, the 1639 edition is a witness of the earliest text of "Friess II." The title page of the 1639 edition does not mention Friess or Maastricht but instead calls "Friess II" a "horrible and shocking old prophecy or vision about Germany" that a devout man living in Emden—a notable center of Dutch Reformed publishing in exile—had extracted on 23 February 1623 from an old manuscript written by a deceased notary. According to the title page, the prophecy had been printed in Dutch in 1638, but an edition in German was warranted because the significance of the prophecy and its fulfillment could be observed daily.[19] In a foreword to the reader, the editor, who refers to himself only as "J. Schr." and claims to have been trained in theology at Wittenberg, notes that an unnamed informant had read the same prophecy in German ten years earlier and that the close agreement of both versions was a sign of the vision's reliability, as it had not suffered from corruption at the hands of uncomprehending copyists.[20]

The Second Generation

Two additional editions (F3 and F4) include both the citations from other prophecies and, following the passage from Lichtenberger, the rest of the honorable man's speech as found in the 1639 edition. The two parts of the speech have been driven apart in these editions by the insertion of citations from other prophecies, much like the matching coastlines of distant continents that have been separated by tectonic expansion. Both of these editions were published anonymously, but F4 bears the date of 1577, while F3 is dated variously to 1580 in VD16 and to "ca. 1574" by the catalog of the Herzog August Bibliothek. The close agreement between the two editions suggests that ca. 1577 would be a better date for F3 as well. The same combination of texts, with the end of the honorable man's speech following the two citations, is found in the one manuscript copy of "Friess II" (F2). This manuscript, dated to the seventeenth century and traceable to Augsburg, collects printed and manuscript curiosities, prophecies, and devotional works, along with printed broadsides and copperplate etchings.[21] It seems to represent the same textual generation as F3 and F4 while not being a descendant of either one.

While reconstructing the textual history of "Friess I" was greatly aided by knowing its source text in the French redaction of the *Vademecum*, we lack that advantage with "Friess II," apart from the two citations from other prophecies. For those passages, we can compare the editions of "Friess II" to the source texts, and we find not only that the F3 and F4 editions are more extensive than those of Samuel Apiarius but that they preserve the quotations from "Dietrich von Zengg" and Lichtenberger (88–106) more completely and accurately. Both editions also include an additional sentence following the citation from Lichtenberger and before the conclusion of the honorable man's speech. This added passage places "Friess II" squarely in the context of Calvinist confessional rivalry with Lutheranism: "Also the Lutheran priests of the north will become so puffed up in haughtiness and greed and cause so much contention in matters of faith, but eventually it will go badly for them" (106–8). The author of at least this passage was determined to draw boundaries between his or her own branch of the Reformation and Lutheranism, whose clergy are referred to as the *Leutersche Pfaffschap*, little better than Catholic priests.[22]

Because of a few passages where F3 follows the 1639 edition while the text of F4 differs in ways also found in later editions, we will assign priority to F3. The anonymous printer of F4, "Printer A," printed two more editions in 1577. (Based on the similarity of types used, it is not impossible that "Printer A" printed F3 as well, although the title woodcut of F3 differs from that used by "Printer A" for F4–F6.) The text of F5 and F6 differs in important ways from their predecessors, but it anticipates, in many ways, the text of "Friess II" as printed by Samuel Apiarius. One of the most notable changes occurred when a redactor removed the pointed remark about the Lutheran clergy but, wielding a dull scalpel, removed the end of the honorable man's speech as well. The types and decorative material of "Printer A" may be those used after 1582 by Gerhard von Kempen in Cologne, but the source of von Kempen's types is unknown, and "Printer A" remains stubbornly anonymous.[23]

Samuel Apiarius

Samuel Apiarius had established a printing workshop in Bern in 1554 and relocated to Solothurn in 1565, but he spent the majority of his printing career, from 1566 until his death in 1590, in Basel. The city had belonged to the Swiss Confederation since 1501 and had followed the Reformed branch of the Protestant Reformation for nearly a half century by the time Apiarius printed his first edition of "Friess II" in 1577. He took as his exemplar one of the later editions by "Printer A" (F6). What is likely Apiarius's first edition (F7) introduced several changes found in all his later editions, but it otherwise followed the text of F6 closely. It was the only one of Apiarius's editions to include two short prophecies—

attributed to a sibyl and to Birgitta of Sweden—that are otherwise found only in the editions of "Printer A." There are also a number of unique variants found in F7, however, so the textual history of "Friess II" in the vicinity of F7 may be somewhat more complicated than figure 4 indicates, or we might see here another case where a printer corrected later editions against the exemplar, as Johann Balhorn seems to have done with his second edition of "Friess I." Just as with the Kreydlein editions of "Friess I," the Apiarius editions of "Friess II" form a stable core of orderly succession from one edition to the next and a successful commercial product that other printers copied, but they represent the third stage in the edition history of "Friess II" (see figure 4). Like Georg Kreydlein, Samuel Apiarius reprinted and popularized as a commercial product a text that had already undergone several changes and that had previously only been printed anonymously.

With a better understanding of the textual history of "Friess II," details that might, at first glance, be ascribed to a printer's whim or a typesetter's mistake turn out, instead, to be crucial for identifying the time and place of the prophecy's origin. Material shared by the 1639 edition, the manuscript copy, or the anonymous editions previously mentioned (F1–F4) should be acknowledged as belonging to the original version of Wilhelm Friess's second prophecy, even if omitted in all other editions, and several details of precisely this kind take on critical significance.

These editions all date the vision of "Friess II" not to 1577 but to 24 April 1574, so we will search for a historical context in that year. These editions also include a geographic point missing in all later editions: when the honorable man gathers the survivors to teach them on the shore of a great water like the Rhine, it seems to the narrator to be in the vicinity of Strasbourg ("und dauchte mich es ware umb Straßburg," 84–85). The search for context will therefore center on that city. While the remark against the Lutheran clergy may not have been part of the original text, it was an early addition that indicates the religious convictions of the elements of German society among which the prophecy first circulated. The appearance of so many editions in the Reformed city of Basel is a further indication that we are dealing with a redactor—and likely an author as well—whose allegiance was more to Calvin than to Luther. Where the L version of "Friess I" had specifically rejected Calvinism, "Friess II" sided with Calvin against Luther. Just as we saw with the textual history of "Friess I," the antipathy of the early redactor toward Catholicism did not stop him or her from reading and citing pre-Reformation German prophecies.

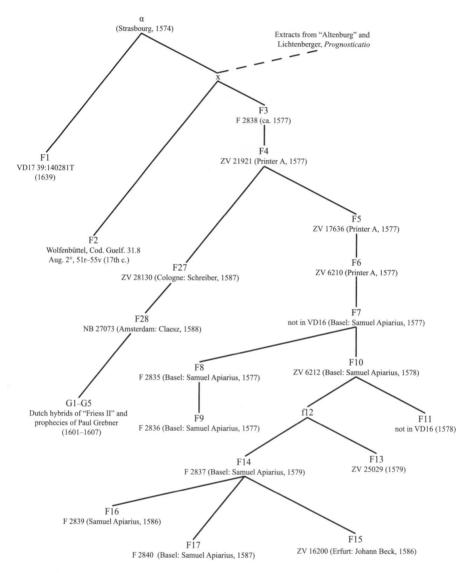

Fig. 4. Diagram of textual relationships between the editions of "Wilhelm Friess II" and its sources. Items in lowercase are not attested by extant editions or historical records. Borrowings are represented by dashed lines. Some relationships are general rather than exact, and the reconstruction of unattested versions has been minimized. Most editions of 1580 and later are not shown.

Although the F3 edition is undated, there is one more reason to give it precedence over other editions: it is the only one whose title page recognizes the astronomical symbolism on which the second prophecy of Wilhelm Friess is based.

The Stars over Strasbourg

By devouring a child, the demonic commander of the combined armies in "Friess II" reenacted the depiction of Saturn devouring his children, a well-known image that was the standard anthropomorphic icon for Saturn in early modern astrological pamphlets.[24] The sword descending from heaven into his hand may be an allusion to the appearance of a comet. Astrologers were not reluctant to predict the appearance of comets as harbingers of doom, and contemporary sources record the appearance of comets in 1572, 1573, and 1574 (although mentions of a "comet" could refer to a variety of atmospheric and astronomical phenomena).[25] In the same way, the mighty armored man from the east whose army carried red banners with fiery swords is an unambiguous reference to the iconography for Mars. The monstrous captain from the north who blows a horn is identifiable as Mercury, in this case bearing not his usual caduceus but the panpipes with which he lulled Argus to sleep. While most depictions of Mercury in the sixteenth century show him with his caduceus, the prognostication of Ambrosius Magirus for 1568 is one example that showed Mercury with both implements.[26] The leader of the fourth army, who was followed by lions and bears, does not fit any planetary iconography, but the lions and bears may have been inspired by the rotund faces and fiery manes used to depict lunar or solar eclipses.

That, at least, is the configuration of heavenly bodies that the F3 edition selects for its title page (see figure 5): a conjunction featuring armored Mars and child-devouring Saturn to the left; Mercury, with his caduceus, in opposition to the right; and the figure of Justitia, a winged woman holding a scourge and scales, in the center. Below the gods, the title woodcut depicts an almost entirely eclipsed lunar disc and a partially eclipsed solar disc.

There is enough information in this title woodcut to firmly establish that it was meant to describe the configuration of the heavens in the year 1574. Mars and Saturn were in conjunction, near to each other in the night sky from the perspective of an earthly observer in August

XXXVI·

Ein Grausame vnd Er-

schreckeliche Prophezeygung oder Weissagung

vber Teufchlandt/ Brabandt vnd Franckreich.

Diese Prophezeygung ist gefunden worden in Ma-
stricht/ bey einem Gottforchtigen Mann Wilhelm
de Frieß nach seinem todt.

j. Thessalon. am v. Capit.

Den Geyst löschend nicht auß/die Prophecey verachtend nichts
Bewärend es alles/vnd behaltend das gut.

Fig. 5. Title page of second prophecy of Wilhelm Friess showing Mercury in opposition to Saturn and Mars, as well as solar and lunar eclipses. VD16 F 2838 (F3). [N.p.: n.p., ca. 1577]. Zentralbibliothek Zürich: Ms F 34, 96v.

1574. Conjunctions of these planets happen approximately every two years, so the woodcut would not fit the configuration of the heavens in 1577. According to the planetary tables of Cyprian Leowitz published in 1557, Mercury was expected to be in opposition to Mars and Saturn on 20 and 26 April 1574, respectively, just before and after the date of the narrator's vision in "Friess II."[27] Contemporary astrologers saw the opposition as an ominous sign. Georg Winckler's prognostication for 1574 states that the opposition of Saturn and Mercury will poison Mercury's otherwise friendly influence, so that in matters of war and peace, the coming year will see "many vexing, miserable, and amazing things." Winckler states that for the teachers of God's Word, an eclipse portends things more ominous than he was willing to write. The movements of the planets in combination with the solar eclipse seemed so threatening, according to Winckler, that many learned people thought that the Last Judgment might be approaching or even that the end of the world had arrived.[28] The title page of the F3 edition of the second Friess prophecy depicts eclipses of both the sun and the moon, and there was a partial solar eclipse visible in Germany on 13 November of that year, the only solar eclipse visible in Germany between 1567 and 1582. Like the eclipse of 1574, over half the sun's disc is obscured in the title woodcut, while the eclipses of 1567 and 1582 were expected to darken the sun to a much greater (1567) or much lesser (1582) degree.[29] There was no lunar eclipse in 1574, but contemporary astrologers emphasized that the lunar eclipse of 8 December 1573 would not exert its influence until the next year. While 1573 would be a fruitful and peaceful year, 1574 would be full of hate and enmity "because of the lunar eclipse that will occur on 8 December, which will show its effect in the following year."[30] Cyprian Leowitz noted in 1564 that Mars, Jupiter, and Saturn would be in opposition in the years 1573 and 1574, which, in combination with a solar eclipse, would have a dire effect on the weather and on human society. He predicted "unusual heat and dryness of the air, from which violent dissension between brothers, relatives, and neighbors will arise." This is much the same scene as the lower plane of the title woodcut, where winds emanating from a face and a skull fall on a city in the background as two men draw swords against each other. In addition, Leowitz foresaw conspiracies and sedition, "savage military actions, conflagrations, and plundering and pillaging of fields, towns, castles, and cities," as well as the deaths of princes, changes in policy and religion, and a particular threat to Spain.[31]

Almost no year went by without ominous astrological predictions of some kind, and every year offered a few dozen conjunctions and oppositions from which astrologers selected the most significant ones, yet the astronomical events depicted on the title page of F3 match both the actual configuration of the heavens in 1574 and contemporary astrological discussion of astral influences, so that it seems most likely that the title woodcut was made specifically for that year. It is possible that the woodcut was created first for an astrological prognostication and then used later for the edition of "Friess II."[32] It appears certain that this edition was printed by someone who had access to an early version of the text and who understood the connection of "Friess II" to the year 1574. The second prophecy of Wilhelm Friess is much more than a transformation into prose of that year's planetary motions, and the translation of astrology into prophecy is, in any case, approximate rather than exact, but the title page of this edition is the only one to recognize the astronomical inspiration for the monstrous generals of "Friess II."

The three editions of "Printer A" (F4–F6), including the edition that Apiarius took as his model, were all printed in 1577 but used a copy of the title woodcut from Victorin Schönfeld's astrological prognostication for 1575 on their title pages.[33] The scenes are mirror images of each other and show four armored men standing in groups of two. A reclining skeleton in the foreground holds up a skull and an hourglass as a reminder of death's inevitability. In the background, an army marches on a distant town, upon which a face in the sky blows down destruction. The title woodcut for the three "Friess II" editions is arranged as a horizontal rectangle, rather than a vertical one, and it carefully erases the astrological iconography, including Mercury's caduceus and winged shoes, the scepters held by the Sun and Moon, and the scorpion in the heavens and on the army's banner. The title woodcut of the three "Printer A" editions therefore represents a transition from the F3 edition, whose astrological iconography corresponds to the text, to a generalized visual depiction of four armed men without identifying characteristics. The earliest editions of Samuel Apiarius, as we have seen, use title woodcuts that omit any reference to the four demonic leaders of the invading armies. Samuel Apiarius did not start decorating the title page with woodcuts of anthropomorphic planets (following the conventions of annual prognostications) until 1586, and he chose from a variety of planets: Saturn, the Sun, and Jupiter in 1586 (F16), followed by Mercury and Mars in the next year (F17).

Not only is the F3 edition closer to the source than Apiarius's editions, but its choice of illustrations exhibits a better understanding of the text. Because of the significance of the year 1574 and the city of Strasbourg in the one manuscript copy, in the early F3 and F4 editions, and in the 1639 edition—and thus in the original text—the key to solving the riddle of the second prophecy of Wilhelm Friess lies in investigating what was going on in that time and place. There was, in fact, a man in Strasbourg who had a specific reason for considering the course of the planets, among his many other concerns, in late spring 1574.

CHAPTER 6

"Wilhelm Friess" in Strasbourg

———— ❧ ————

Despair at the sight of enemies on all sides and from all nations, which is so vividly depicted in "Friess II," had also been the experience of the embattled Calvinists of Antwerp in March 1567, whose defeat would have been made more humiliating by the stridently Lutheran prophecy of "Friess I" circulating in the Netherlands at that time. Seven years later, a rejoinder appeared in the form of the second prophecy of Wilhelm Friess. Although the earliest known editions of the second prophecy appeared in 1577 and were primarily printed in Basel, we have been able to establish Strasbourg as the place, 1574 as the year, and Reformed Protestantism as the religious environment of the origin of "Friess II." The connection between "Friess I" and "Friess II" that links Antwerp and Basel remains to be explained.

The second prophecy of Wilhelm Friess not only offers a number of parallels with other sixteenth-century texts but also appears to be part of a literary tradition of prophetic writing in southwestern Germany. As this chapter will argue, the second prophecy of Wilhelm Friess, one of the most intricately constructed prophecies of the sixteenth century, employs multiple symbolic systems to address the interrelated theological and geopolitical concerns of Strasbourg's Calvinist sympathizers at a specific time. The prophecy united geographic, astrological, and religious symbolism with a skill that rivaled those who, in 1574, were completing a new astronomical clock for Strasbourg's cathedral. While evidence for the authorship of "Friess II" is largely circumstantial, it suggests an unusual combination of religious sympathies, international orientation, intellectual ability, and rhetorical talent. There was just such a person with these characteristics among the clock builders' associates in Strasbourg, which offers intriguing evidence that the author of "Friess II" was Johann Fischart, the most skilled satirist of sixteenth-century German literature.

The Home of Wilhelm Friess's
Second Prophecy: Sources and Templates

Apart from the quotations drawn from Lichtenberger and "Dietrich von Zengg" noted in the previous chapter, "Friess II" does not borrow passages from other works. Instead, it makes use of elements and structures found in earlier prophecies, what we might call their "prophetic vocabulary" and "prophetic grammar." The allegory of worms, beasts, and birds in the first prophecy of Wilhelm Friess encoded its political significance using living creatures, a prophetic vocabulary that was common since at least the Middle Ages and that Rupert Taylor considered as one of the two basic symbolic systems of prophecy.[1] The second prophecy of Wilhelm Friess took a different approach, and several elements of its symbolic inventory are consistent with a geographic origin in the region around Strasbourg.

As Barnes has noted, "Friess II" has elements in common with a late fourteenth-century text known as the "Gamaleon" prophecy.[2] The text of that prophecy has a complex manuscript transmission history in various Latin and German versions, and it is usually regarded as a German reaction against the pro-French prophetic compilation of Telesphorus of Cosenza that appeared in 1386.[3] The "Gamaleon" prophecy enjoyed a resurgence of interest beginning in the mid-sixteenth century. It was printed as a separate pamphlet only once, by Johann Prüß of Strasbourg in 1538, but it also appeared in the collections of primarily Latin prophetic material published by Wolfgang Lazius in 1547, by Matthias Flacius in 1556, and by Johannes Wolf in 1600. The similarity in some motifs is so specific that it is likely that the author of "Friess II" knew "Gamaleon." Like "Friess II," it opens with a young male vision guide waking the narrator and directing him to view the four cardinal compass points. In "Gamaleon" as in "Friess II," letters are interpreted, objects are cast down, and terrible armies approach.

While "Friess II" appropriates prophetic vocabulary and grammar from "Gamaleon," they are used to express a very different message, as the two prophecies are nearly opposite in outlook. The casting down of a golden chalice and a child's head in "Friess II" are the gruesome conclusion of a perversion of the sacrament of the Lord's Supper, while the young vision guide himself dashes his own crown against the ground in "Gamaleon." The letters engraved on a demonic general's armor in "Friess II" represent the plagues he will inflict, while the images engraved on each piece of the vision guide's crown in "Gamaleon" represent seven ages of the world. Similar to the hellish *Völkerwanderung* of "Friess II," a cruel and terrible host comes from the north in the "Gamaleon" prophecy, while a false emperor wearing red armor and holding a bloody sword and a royal orb arrives from the south and is crowned by the pope. In "Gamaleon," however, the terrible people from the north, whose reign will last until the end of the earth, apparently represent the German nation against whom none can prevail. The conclusion of the "Gamaleon" prophecy invokes an emperor, selected in infancy, who will regain the Holy Land, subdue his neighbors, overthrow the papacy and clerical power, and establish Germany as the seat of secular and spiritual dominion. The anticlerical sentiment, regard for an all-powerful German emperor, and hopeful outlook found in the "Gamaleon" prophecy are much closer to the optimism of "Friess I" than to the hopeless desolation of "Friess II." Despite the differences in intention between these prophecies, we can recognize in "Gamaleon" a template for prophetic expression that influenced the writing of "Friess II." Just as the citations borrowed from "Dietrich von Zengg" derive from a version whose two earliest editions were printed in the southwestern cities of Freiburg and Speyer, the only pamphlet edition of "Gamaleon," printed in Strasbourg in 1538, also suggests an origin in the German southwest.

Those who composed, read, and revised "Friess II" in the 1570s were clearly interested in Strasbourg and in prophecies from decades earlier. Over forty years before the honorable man of "Friess II" knelt with his surviving followers on the banks of the Rhine near Strasbourg, the radical reformer Melchior Hoffman (ca. 1495–1543) had declared that Strasbourg was the prophesied New Jerusalem.[4] One of the most esteemed members of Hoffman's circle of Strasbourg prophets was Ursula Jost, whose visions Hoffman regarded as equal to those of the Old Testament.[5] The Strasbourg printer Balthasar Beck printed Jost's visions together with a preface and conclusion by Hoffman in 1530. Jost made use of a visionary vocabulary reminiscent of that found in "Friess II," with armies, riders, banners, blasts delivered on horns or trumpets, and helpful vision guides contrasted with the approach of threatening figures. In the twenty-third vision, Jost sees the wounded Christ, as well as armies and a man with a horn: "After the previous crowd of people, a great swarm of riders came riding who had peacock feathers hanging from their hats down their backs. I saw further that a large man came after these armies who let forth a strong and mighty blast of wind and water."[6] In the seventy-second vision, Jost sees the approach of a man in black armor riding a white horse, as well as "two standing next to him who smeared the armor dark and black so that he might travel safely through all lands."[7] The menacing figure in the sixty-fifth vision is another horribly large man who becomes embodied as a darkness that is accompanied by black tears full of the Eucharist wafer.[8] Melchior Hoffman died in prison in Strasbourg in 1543, but those who were influenced by him and his prophets, such as the "Lichtseher" movement of Martin Steinbach, continued to be active in and around Strasbourg into the late 1560s.[9]

One of the most recent prophecies of the German southwest prior to "Friess II" was a pamphlet that claimed to have been written in a Franciscan cloister in the year 1300 and whose one edition was printed by a pseudonymous "Christian Mundanus" of Freiburg in 1573. This prophecy of "Brother C." describes the death of Martin Luther and the Interim quite exactly and then predicts three invasions by a false emperor from the north and south.[10] The French king would be deposed for persecuting the faithful but would then be returned to the throne as a true Christian, and a certain Friedrich of the Rhine would come to power (probably Friedrich III, Count Palatinate of the Rhine in 1559–76). All of this would be accomplished by 1578 or 1579, after which a time of peace and harmony would follow.

In addition to a particular prophetic vocabulary that appears to have been popular in southwestern Germany, "Friess II" has an internal structure that might be summarized as a guided prophetic vision according to the four cardinal directions. Not only is this structure found in "Gamaleon," but it occurs already in Ezekiel's temple vision (Ezek. 40–48) and, to a lesser extent, in Zechariah's vision of chariots drawn by horses of various colors (Zech. 6). The advent of ominous riders on various types of horses was a motif of the Apocalypse (best known from the woodcuts of Albrecht Dürer) and had also stirred the interpretive faculties of Martin Luther and Melchior Hoffman.[11]

The compilations of Martin Luther's writings as prophetic oracles that were published by Johannes Timann and others following Luther's death in 1546 emphasized a pessimistic view of German geography. As a consequence of greed and ingratitude, Luther foresaw that the "Turk,

Pope, and uncountable other devils from Italy, Spain, and all corners of the world" would come and plague the German people.[12] Already in a commentary on Psalm 124 written in the early 1530s, Luther had compared the situation of the evangelicals to that of Israel under siege: "We Jews are like the lowest dregs of the globe and the least part of humanity. Men rise against us, that is to say: Kings, princes, rich men, wise men, and whatever is powerful and great in this age, all of them neither oppose nor hate us in the usual way, but rather they rise up against us in the attempt to overwhelm and annihilate us completely. If you turn to the east, to the northeast, to the north and south and consider how many and how powerful are the kingdoms that surround us, and with what deadly hatred they are angered against us, clearly we can be considered to be little sheep encircled by a hundred wolves, and every moment they try to attack and devour it."[13] Although "Friess II" takes sides with Calvinism against Lutheranism, it shared the pessimistically prophetic view of German geography found both in Luther's writings and in compilations of his teachings published after his death.

Strasbourg and Sacraments: The Religious Home of "Friess II"

Strasbourg, like Nuremberg, enjoyed the status of a free imperial city. It was the leading economic force of its region, and its significance as a printing center extended throughout southwestern Germany. After the Reformation took hold in Strasbourg in the early 1520s, the city became known for its religious tolerance, and several radical leaders and various Anabaptist groups found a home there for a time. Beginning in the 1530s, however, the city became harsher in its treatment of nonconformists, and most Anabaptists eventually left the city or were reconciled with mainstream Protestantism. Under the city's guiding reformer, Martin Bucer, Strasbourg charted a middle course between Martin Luther and Jean Calvin from the 1520s into the 1540s. From 1538 to 1541, Calvin lived in Strasbourg and attempted to win Anabaptists for the Reformed cause. In later decades, Calvinism in Strasbourg continued to receive strength from Huguenot refugees, as French Calvinists were frequently forced to seek refuge abroad.

In the decades after 1550, however, any Strasbourg resident who chose to follow the tenets of Jean Calvin found himself or herself in an increasingly untenable position. The years following Bucer's death in 1551 were marked by confessional conflicts between Lutheranism and

Calvinism in which orthodox Lutheranism gained firm control over the city's institutions. Reformed teaching and worship were threatened with official sanction and eventually forbidden. Calvinist worship had been increasingly forced underground after 1563, and in February 1577, the city authorities closed the French Calvinist congregation that had served Huguenot refugees. Johann Sturm, the first rector of Strasbourg's humanistic school (which he had led since the 1530s) and a proponent of Reformed views, was forced from his office in 1581, after years of conflict with the second generation of the city's Lutherans leaders.[14] By the end of the century, Strasbourg had committed itself to orthodox Lutheranism and prohibited its citizens from participating in Reformed services.[15]

The confessional conflicts that set Lutherans against Calvinists in Strasbourg included a fierce controversy in the 1570s over the sacrament of the Lord's Supper. In the New Testament accounts of Christ's last meal with the apostles on the evening before Christ's arrest and crucifixion, Christ "took a loaf of bread, and after blessing it he broke it, gave it to them, and said, 'Take; this is my body.' Then he took a cup, and after giving thanks he gave it to them, and all of them drank from it. He said to them, 'This is my blood of the covenant, which is poured out for many'" (Mark 14:22–24 NRSV). What exactly Christ meant when he said, "This is my body," has been subject to vigorous discussion up to the current day. All strains of Protestantism rejected the Catholic doctrine of transubstantiation, which held that the Eucharistic wafer and wine were transformed into the substance of the body and blood of Christ, but common ground among Protestants in the matter of sacramental theology nevertheless remained elusive. In 1529, Luther and Zwingli had debated the merits of two alternative interpretations that would eventually become one of the key points of separation between the Lutheran and Reformed churches. Zwingli and the Reformed churches after him held that the bread and wine of the sacrament of the Lord's Supper were only symbols of Christ's body and blood. Luther, however, insisted on a literal understanding of "This is my body," which he interpreted as implying Christ's real presence in the sacramental emblems. Luther's position was eventually formulated as the doctrine of ubiquity, which many Reformed regarded as little better than transubstantiation and a return to Catholic heresies. Attempts to negotiate a sacramental theology agreeable to both sides over the following decades ended in failure, and the differences became increasingly bitter. Already in 1532, Martin Luther recorded that followers of Zwingli had mocked the Lutherans as flesh eaters and blood drinkers.[16] This was precisely how the Calvinists of Antwerp insulted their Lutheran fellow citizens in the fall of 1566, as Godevaert van Haecht recorded ("gy syt vleescheters en bloetdrinckers").[17] The L version of "Friess I" is the only version to include a reference to the Whore of Babylon and her bitter cup, a frequent image in contemporary polemics concerning sacramental theology, providing another point of contact between "Friess II" and the L version of "Friess I."[18] In the environment of acrimonious contention over sacramental theology, the Lutherans enshrined the doctrine of ubiquity in the 1577 Formula of Concord, which struck many Calvinists as all but establishing an alliance between Catholics and Lutherans.[19]

It was perhaps inevitable that "Friess II," a prophetic expression of a society's hopes and fears, written in the religious environment in or near Strasbourg in the 1570s, would take the sacrament, the central symbolic ritual of Christianity, as its central concern. In the final scene before the narrator's collapse, the narrator witnesses the monstrous leader of the combined armies holding a golden cup full of blood in one hand and a young child in the other. The demonic general drinks the blood and consumes the child, then casts the remnants down to be trampled. This perversion of the sacrament is not only Saturnine and diabolical but also a rather uncharitable Reformed reading of Catholic and Lutheran sacramental theology. If the blood of Christ were truly present in the sacramental wine, participation in the sacrament would involve a ghoulish drinking of blood. If Christ had a deified human nature from the moment of his birth and if his body were truly present in the sacramental wafer, the Eucharist must involve the ghastly act of consuming a child. Such were the doctrinal stakes for Calvinists while Lutheran theologians were constructing the Formula of Concord, and its ratification in 1577 helped make the second prophecy of Wilhelm Friess newly relevant and a steady seller for Samuel Apiarius in Reformed Basel for the following decade.

"Friess II" arose in a religious environment that was shaped by hardening confessional boundaries between competing Protestant denominations and, as Lutheranism gained the upper hand, a growing sense of besiegement. Particularly in terms of civic power, the Calvinists of Strasbourg were a weak and embattled flock, and "Friess II" refers to the few survivors of the envisioned catastrophe as a "klein haufflein Folcks," a "little gathering of people" (78). One finds a similar outlook among Dutch Protestants under Habsburg oppression, who used the same and similar terms, referring to themselves as "the 'little gathering of the elect,' the 'congregation covered in blood'" that had been driven out of the land to live in exile.[20] Another image common among Calvinists in the Netherlands compared the Reformed to the Hebrew slaves in Egypt or to the exiled Israelites wandering in the desert.[21] The "hidden transcript" of "Friess II" is its veiled critique of Lutheran sacramental theology at a time when Lutheran orthodoxy was decisively establishing its hold over Strasbourg's civic and religious institutions. For the Calvinists of Strasbourg in 1574, doctrinal concerns had an additional political dimension. If we follow the interpretation of Aby Warburg, the planets in astrological prognostications can also refer to particular social classes.[22] In this reading, the author of "Friess II" saw not just enemies on all sides but also attacks emanating from particular occupations and social classes: Saturn would represent church prelates, Mars would lead the armored might of secular power, and Mercury would direct the scholars and other learned figures in their oppression of the embattled Reformed congregation.

The Geopolitics of "Friess II"

Beyond local struggles, Calvinists in Strasbourg in 1574 faced threats on a larger geographic scale. In France to the west, the struggle between the Reformed Huguenots and the Catholic king Charles IX was, on the whole, going quite badly. The Duke of Anjou, who was the king's younger brother and a commander of the Catholic armies, had led the royal forces to victories at Jarnac and Moncontour in 1569. The truce signed in 1570 had been shattered in August 1572 by the St. Bartholomew's Day Massacre, in which thousands of Huguenots had been killed in Paris. Following the outbreak of renewed hostilities, the Duke of Anjou led a months-long siege of La Rochelle, the Huguenots' most important center of power in France. The siege ended with a negotiated settlement only because the Duke of Anjou, as Henry of Valois, had been elected king of Poland. Henry began his reign in February 1574, but it would not last long: Charles IX died in May, and Henry left Poland in June 1574. He was crowned King Henry III of France in February 1575.

The religious and political events threatening the Reformed cause in the early 1570s were reported widely in pamphlets printed throughout Germany.[23] Pamphlets published in 1573, which reproduced a letter allegedly written from Poland by Cardinal Charles de Lorraine to French legates, further incited fears of invasive religious persecution. According to these pamphlets, the cardinal proposed an alliance—between

Spain, France, and the pope—that would eradicate the Huguenots of France and the Calvinists of the Netherlands, assist the Spanish invasion of England, and prepare a worse fate for the German Lutherans than the French Huguenots had experienced on St. Bartholomew's Day in 1572.[24]

However credible such pamphlets may have been, actual developments were ominous enough to justify a bleak outlook among Calvinists in 1574, particularly in Strasbourg. In addition to their losing struggle against Lutheranism at home, their antagonism toward Lutheranism and enmity toward Catholics left the Reformed seemingly surrounded by enemies: German and Scandinavian Lutherans to the north; French Catholics to the west; and Habsburg Catholics and, beyond them, Ottoman Turks to the east. The impending arrival in France of Henry III, former leader of the victorious Catholic armies, from Poland to the northeast, would have been an omen of even worse persecution to come.

The geography of religious oppression faced by the Calvinists of Strasbourg in the 1570s is not only reminiscent of what the Calvinists of Antwerp had experienced in 1567, when they had found themselves surrounded on every side by enemies from every nation, but is also precisely the geography of horror in the second prophecy of Wilhelm Friess. In "Friess II," with its demonic invaders from the west, north, east, and northeast, the monstrous leader approaching from the northeast was meant to be understood as Henry III arriving from Poland, a figure with whom Calvinists were already familiar. While the orientalist Francis Balodis considered "Friess II" to be based on the Russian czar Ivan IV's violent waging of the Livonian War (1558–83), an understandable interpretation for a Latvian scholar writing in 1941, the second prophecy of Wilhelm Friess dealt with more immediate concerns of Calvinists in southwestern Germany.[25] While later editions of "Friess II" omitted any reference to Strasbourg, at least one contemporary reader suggested a similar geopolitical interpretation in marginal notes that identified the approaching armies as the Poles, a coalition of the pope with Spain and Austria, the Turks, and the Tatars.[26]

Two of Samuel Apiarius's 1577 editions of "Friess II" preserved the significance of Poland, calling the work a prophecy upon "Poland and Germany, Brabant and France," but the later editions of Apiarius omitted Poland from their titles, until one of the last Basel editions of 1587 added it again. After Henry had ascended the throne of France, the reference to Poland lacked political significance and it was dropped from later title pages. Fortunately for French and German Protestants, the fears expressed in "Friess II" proved unfounded, as Henry III took a moderate approach to religious affairs during his reign as king of France. After a Dominican monk assassinated Henry III in 1589, pamphlets announcing the news in Germany commemorated the king with a few lines of verse, allegedly a century old, that had prophesied his death.[27]

It is conceivable that part of the motivation for composing "Friess II" in 1574 was to oppose Henry's election to the French throne or to hinder his return to France through German territory. There were precedents for enlisting prophecies in the cause of dynastic politics: for example, the "Alofresant" prophecy, which foretold glorious things for a certain Habsburg heir, may have arisen in the contested election of 1519 that ultimately brought Charles V to the imperial throne.[28] If "Friess II" was meant to oppose Henry III, it would not be the only prophetic comment on his coronation. The oration of Jan Dymitr Solikowski to the French and Poles in support of Henry III's election and greater cooperation between the two nations, published in Basel in 1575, closed with an excerpt from Lichtenberger's *Prognosticatio* that foresaw the conjunction of the lily and the eagle of the north, to which Solikowski added a point-by-point explication to prove that the prophecy referred to Henry III.[29] The prophecies of Paul Grebner, known only from later sources but dated to 1574, also addressed Henry's reign in Poland and France.[30]

If the leader of the combined armies in "Friess II" represented Henry III of France, then the "honorable fine man" from the south with a gray beard, a "golden book in his left hand and a golden trumpet in his right hand" is likely a reference to Jean Calvin. Calvin had been headquartered south of the Alps in Geneva, and for many German Calvinists, Switzerland was an unspoiled island amid the corruption of imperial Europe.[31] In "Friess II," the honorable man's followers come from over the mountains and emerge from the forests, and they are identified by their black clothing. Not only is Calvin the eponymous originator of black clerical garb, but sixteenth-century Lutheran sources report seeing the devil wearing black robes like Calvin's.[32] Calvin had died in 1564, so his followers a decade later had to rely on his doctrine and writings. Fittingly, the implements of teaching borne by the "honorable fine man," his trumpet and his book, stand in stark contrast to the diabolical ritual objects held by the leader of the combined armies.

The second prophecy of Wilhelm Friess was not the only German-language work of 1574 that connected the persecution of Protestants and the election of Henry III. That year also saw, for example, publication of a "thorough and true description of how the reformed religion has been persecuted in France by Henry II and his sons Francis II and Charles IX up to the present day," to which was attached a report on how "Henry, Duke of Anjou, was elected and crowned king in Poland and then departed to Venice."[33] In Strasbourg, Bernhard Jobin printed a report in 1574 on Henry's election in Poland and, in the next year, published one French and two German editions of the *Reveille matin* attributed to the French Protestant Nicolas Barnaud. The *Reveille matin* had been intended to convince the Polish nobility not to elect Henry to the Polish crown.[34] Referring to the St. Bartholomew's Day Massacre, the author of the *Reveille matin* wrote, "No house or family in the entire world is so besmirched by such shameful disloyalty and betrayal as this House of Valois," and the author encouraged the Polish nobility to elect a "cow herder or an ass driver" rather than "one of these murderers or bloodhounds."[35] These works share not only a pro-Calvinist, anti-Valois outlook but also the identity of their compiler or translator: Bernhard Jobin's brother-in-law Johann Fischart (1545/46–91).

Johann Fischart, Author of the Second Prophecy of Wilhelm Friess?

Johann Fischart is today acknowledged as the most talented satirist and one of the most important German writers of the sixteenth century. Born in Strasbourg, Fischart likely began his schooling at Johannes Sturm's academy. Fischart's student travels took him to the Netherlands, Paris, Italy, and perhaps England as well, in the late 1560s. On his return to Strasbourg in the early 1570s, Fischart began working with his brother-in-law and publishing his early works, primarily religious polemics. Fischart remained in Strasbourg until the summer of 1574, when he traveled to Basel to complete his legal education.[36]

The wanton attribution of anonymous sixteenth-century works to Johann Fischart has a long history that is rightly met with more skepticism now than it was in the nineteenth century.[37] One hesitates to add to the tradition, especially on the basis of circumstantial evidence. "Friess II" lacks any of the features that might provide positive evidence for Fischart's authorship, such as using his motto ("Alors comme alors") or one of his known pseudonyms, and it largely lacks Fischart's characteristic inventive use of language and playful word creation. Despite this, the accumulation of evidence brings Johann Fischart into question as the author of "Friess II." What we know about the composition and outlook of "Friess II" corresponds to Fischart's biography, views on religion and politics, and authorial method, and there are connections between the prophecy and Fischart's works of the 1570s.

Fischart was in the right places at the right times to acquire the knowledge and form the views that are expressed in the second prophecy of Wilhelm Friess. Fischart was born in Strasbourg and spent much of his life there. The texts that served as sources and templates for "Friess II" circulated within his vicinity, and he shared the prophecy's high estimation of his native city. After secondary schooling in Worms and university study in Tübingen from October 1564 to July 1566, Fischart traveled to Paris to study there in 1567, but he most likely left Paris later in 1567, after the expulsion of Protestants by royal decree.[38] From Fischart's report, in his 1571 *Life of St. Dominic,* that he had heard a Dominican preach in Flanders, a region that includes Antwerp, it is clear that Fischart's travels had taken him to the Netherlands by then, most likely either just prior to his studies in Paris or on his return from there in 1567.[39] Fischart was thus in the vicinity of Antwerp around the time of or shortly after the dramatic conflict between the Calvinists and the city's other residents, when the L version of "Friess I" was in circulation in the Netherlands. Following additional study in Siena, Fischart returned to Strasbourg and worked there in the workshop of his brother-in-law Bernhard Jobin from 1570 until 1574, which was also Fischart's most productive literary period.[40] In the early summer of 1574, Fischart left Strasbourg to complete his academic qualification in Basel, where he was named a doctor of law in August 1574.[41] The stations of Fischart's biography, including Antwerp, Strasbourg, and Basel, are also those of the second prophecy of Wilhelm Friess.

Fischart's path from Antwerp to Strasbourg runs curiously parallel to that of Mathias Flacius, who has appeared already as a possible link between Gnesio-Lutheran polemic prophecies and Antwerp at the time of the Dutch Revolt. Flacius had come to Antwerp in the autumn of 1566 to tend the Lutheran congregation in Antwerp, but he was forced to flee by the outbreak of violence in 1567.[42] Flacius sought refuge first in Frankfurt and then in Strasbourg, where he remained until 1573, two years prior to his death in 1575. In 1571, Tobias Stimmer created a portrait of Flacius that was printed on the press of Bernhard Jobin along with laudatory verse written by Johann Fischart.[43] Fischart's verse praises Flacius's continuing willingness to face the enmity of the world in the fight for truth, although Fischart did not share Flacius's unyielding commitment to Lutheran orthodoxy. Another broadside with Flacius's image printed by Jobin in 1577 contains a somewhat more extensive biography in Latin that notes all the stations of Flacius's life, including his time in Antwerp.[44]

Johann Fischart's religious allegiance was as complicated as the religious affairs of Strasbourg itself. In 1541, his father had been a witness at the wedding of the prominent author and spiritualist nonconformist Sebastian Franck. Fischart purchased Franck's collection of proverbs in 1584, and Fischart's *Die Geleherten die Verkehrten* of the same year was based on writings by Franck, which had earlier been read and owned by Fischart's family.[45] During the 1570s, as Lutheran orthodoxy was being enforced in the civic institutions of Strasbourg, Fischart was becoming increasingly aligned with Calvinism.[46] Bruno Weber refers to Fischart as a "devout Calvinist," and Wilhelm Kühlmann calls him a "resolute partisan for the Calvinists," although Kühlmann sees Fischart as avoiding internal Protestant disputes until 1579.[47] One notes, however, that Fischart appears to have dissented on the point of sacramental theology with a particular vehemence. He opposed the Lutheran Formula of Concord, and in his 1576 verse interpretation of the Strasbourg cathedral's animal figures, he wrote that Catholic usage turned the sacramental chalice into the "Whore of Babylon's cup, fitting for the Antichrist." Adolf Hauffen, the leading scholar on Fischart in the early twentieth century, surmised that Fischart's criticism of the doctrine of transubstantiation was so excessive that it also injured Lutheran belief in Christ's real presence in the sacrament and offended the civic leaders of Strasbourg.[48] While Fischart's personal religious convictions during the 1570s are not entirely unambiguous, his growing allegiance to Calvinism and understanding of sacramental theology are in accordance with the perspective of "Friess II."

In addition to his religious views, Johann Fischart's international interests and sympathies are quite clear from early on in his literary career. He lent his support to the French Huguenots in their struggle against the Catholic monarchy and to the Dutch Protestants in their struggle against Spain.[49] Fischart aided their causes by his own propagandistic writing and by translating anti-Catholic and pro-Protestant works from French and Dutch, such as the *Bienenkorb des heiligen römischen Immenschwarms* (Hive of the Holy Roman bee swarm) of Philips van Marnix. Fischart also held Switzerland in particular regard.[50] In his 1576 verse tract *Das Glückhafft Schiff von Zürich* (The fortunate ship from Zurich), Fischart recalled and encouraged the renewal of the alliance between Strasbourg and the Swiss cities of Zurich, Basel, and Bern. Fischart also took note of the reign of Henry III, and Weber cautiously suggests Fischart as the author of texts on Henry III published in two broadsides from the press of Bernhard Jobin.[51]

One might object that Johann Fischart, author of *Aller Practick Groß-mutter* (Grandmother of all practicas), a parody of astrological prognostications, could hardly have created a work like "Friess II," which has astrological symbolism at its core. However, Fischart's *Aller Practick Großmutter* does not offer a rational critique of astrology but, rather, satirizes popular gullibility, printers' avarice, and the methodological incompetence of the astrologers.[52] Fischart could not have written *Aller Practick Großmutter*, first published in 1572 and expanded in 1574, without first acquiring considerable knowledge of popular astrology. While the iconography of Mercury as pipe player that was seen in the astrological symbolism of "Friess II" was relatively uncommon, Fischart was familiar with it: his *Geschichtsklitterung*, his reworking of Rabelais's *Gargantua and Pantegruel* first published in 1575, refers to the "Mercurial pipe player who lulls hundred-eyed Argus asleep."[53] Other passages in the *Geschichtsklitterung* refer to Saturn as the devourer of children or orphans. Fischart's monogram, *JFGM*, standing for *Johann Fischart genannt Menzer*, also appears in a mythologically coded resolution as *Jove Fovente Gignitur Minerva*, "Minerva is born with Jupiter's favor." Fischart knew the Lutheran antiastrological contraprognostication of (probably pseudonymous) Urban Luginsland, published in Strasbourg in 1569 and 1574 following earlier editions in the 1550s. From references in his *Catalogus catalogarum*, a satirical list of real and fictional books, it is clear that Fischart also knew contemporary "planet books," popular compilations of astrological knowledge, as well as the authoritative ephemerides of Cyprian Leowitz.[54]

Fischart was not reluctant to engage with astrological symbolism and prognostication in his own writing. In 1573, Bernhard Jobin printed a broadside addressing the supernova of 1572 from a devotional perspective. The verse text treats the appearance of this "comet" as an omen of the world's end and calls on Christ to save his *Völklein*, his "little band of people" from the Beast and from tyranny. The preceding prose introduction, which Hauffen also attributes to Fischart, notes that the "comet" portends drought, war, plague, and fever, among other kinds of misfortune, and states that astrological prognostications are not worthless when they are in accordance with God's will and scripture.[55] In 1578, in response to recent appearances in the heavens, Bernhard Jobin printed a broadside that combined a woodcut presumably by Tobias Stimmer and a text attributed to Johann Fischart. The text calls two recent lunar eclipses and a recent comet God's miraculous preachers (not *Wander-*

prediger but *Wunderprediger*), whose responsibility for earthquakes, pestilence, and war goes without saying.[56] The broadside devotes most of its attention to a discoloration of the sun among the clouds that was recently observed near Tübingen. Echoing the prophetic vocabulary of "Friess II," the broadside describes how soldiers and cavalry in black armor had seemed to emerge from a cloud and travel to the east, followed by a gigantic man and then another army splattered in blood. Such appearances in the heavens, the broadside concludes, are God's warning to the world and should be met with a willingness to repent.[57]

Johann Fischart also had a specific cause for contemplating the stars over Strasbourg in 1574: the completion in late June of that year of the cathedral's astronomical clock. It was built by the mathematician Konrad Dasypodius and decorated by Tobias Stimmer, an artist whose woodcuts had frequently appeared in print together with texts from Fischart. The publication of laudatory broadsides and pamphlets marked the clock's completion.[58] For a broadside published by Bernhard Jobin in 1574, Fischart himself composed a poem to accompany an illustration of the astronomical clock.[59] Strasbourg's clock was a technological marvel. In addition to marking the passage of the hours, each day of the week was represented by one of the seven planets in human form drawn by wagons, a form often seen in the "planet books." The clock included both a celestial globe and an astrolabe that displayed the positions of the planets, which were flanked on each side by tables of solar and lunar eclipses visible from Strasbourg for the upcoming decades.[60] The first lunar and solar eclipses displayed on each table are those for December 1573 and November 1574, the same two depicted on the title page of the earliest edition of "Friess II."[61]

Between the tables of lunar and solar eclipses stood a circular calendar whose outer disc rotated once each year while the inner disc rotated once in a hundred years. The calendar displayed the day, year, number of years since the Creation, and information that was necessary for determining feast days. The corners behind the circular calendar each bore a representation of one of the four historical world empires: Assyria, Persia, Greece, and Rome.[62] The iconography of these four figures is, in most cases, threatening: Assyria is represented as a turbaned man whose shield bears a winged lion; Persia is represented as a crowned man whose shield displays a bear; the Greek representative has a laurel crown and a shield with a winged, four-headed leopard; and Rome is represented as a helmeted warrior whose shield displays a beast with ten horns—one notes the allusions to the beasts seen in the visions of

Daniel and the Apocalypse (Dan. 7:1–7, Rev. 13:1–2). At the center of the calendar, unmoving, was a circular map of Germany on a rectangular field, most prominently displaying the Rhineland.[63] Each side of the map was labeled with a cardinal direction, while Strasbourg's cityscape occupied the center. As Fischart composed verses praising the clock and its capabilities, it is clear not only that he knew the configuration of the heavens for 1574 and the anthropomorphic symbolism through which the planets were represented but also that he had a particular cause to contemplate Strasbourg's place in the world in that year. The geography of "Friess II," with four armies approaching Germany, corresponds to this representation of Strasbourg and Germany surrounded by four world empires, which suggests that "Friess II" can be seen as an apocalyptic ekphrasis inspired by the astronomical clock in Strasbourg.

In addition to astronomical and astrological works, Fischart also knew the prophetic pamphlet literature of which "Friess II" is an example. The "Parat oder Beraitschlag," an introductory chapter in the *Geschichtsklitterung*, mentions Lichtenberger and refers to an episode in the *Sibyl's Prophecy*.[64] Fischart owned a copy of Savonarola's *Oracolo della renovatione della chiesa* (Prophecy concerning a renewal of the church), as well as a prophetic explication of mysterious characters discovered in fish (VD16 J 217). Fischart left numerous marginal notes and underlinings in his copy of this work, most prominently at a passage predicting that God would bring all the peoples of the world together.[65] In the mid-1570s, Fischart worked on a translation of Wolfgang Lazius's work *De gentium migrationibus*, including chapters on the ancient Germanic tribes and the relationship of their languages to Greek and Latin. (Another of Lazius's works, the *Fragmentum vaticinii*, contains excerpts of many prophecies, including Lichtenberger's *Prognosticatio*, "Dietrich von Zengg," and "Gamaleon," but it is unknown whether Fischart knew this work, and the excerpts found in Lazius's compilation are not from the same versions or same passages as those found in "Friess II.") Fischart's reference to Lazius's *De gentium migrationibus* in his *Catalogus catalogorum* places the migration of peoples in the context of cardinal directions and eschatology, calling it a "prophecy that the Japhetic language of the north will decree laws and measures to the whole earth shortly before the end of the world, and also that monarchies have always moved from south to north." The prophecy is attributed to "D. Wickart of Mainz," which is possibly a reference to Fischart himself.[66]

One might be reluctant to regard Johann Fischart as the author of "Friess II" because the prophecy lacks the typical linguistic features and spelling conventions used by Fischart in Jobin's workshop and shows no sign of the inventive word creation that is the signature of Fischart's style. Language and orthography may be less of a concern, as the early F3 edition, probably printed around 1577, was likely not printed in Bernhard Jobin's workshop, where Fischart was employed only until 1574. A later typesetter or one working at another press need not have followed Fischart's patterns of language and orthography. Fischart's linguistic artistry characterizes much of his work, but not all of it. For example, Fischart's prologue to the *Emblematum tyrocina* of Mathias Holzwart lacks the playful word invention typical of Fischart, as does *Das Glückhafft Schiff von Zürich.*[67]

In its original version, the second prophecy of Wilhelm Friess was perhaps not entirely lacking in wordplay. The monstrous leader of the demonic armies and the fine honorable man with a gray beard are implicitly compared by their emblems and what they do with them. The demonic general holds a child and a golden cup, which he empties, while the righteous leader has a trumpet and a golden book, from which he teaches the people until his preaching is completed. "Friess II" notes his completion with the phrase "Und als er nun außgeleret hat" (and when he completely taught them), using the unusual construction *außgeleret* (86). That word is a homophone of *ausgeleeret*, a more common word meaning "drained, emptied" that could easily describe the monstrous general's draining of the chalice full of blood. The printed text in the earliest editions uses not this word but forms of *austrinken* (60), however.

While the second prophecy of Wilhelm Friess may not display Fischart's typical wordplay, it does have several other features of his writing. As others have noted, Fischart's works often addressed current affairs in Strasbourg and responded quickly to the literary marketplace. Fischart enjoyed creating complex puzzles in which to conceal the meaning of a text from his audience, and his works combined popular elements with learned ones, such as the mythological encoding extensively used by Fischart. Vulgarity and grotesque excess were other characteristic features of Fischart's work.[68] All of these traits can be found in "Friess II," a work that hides its meaning behind a combination of learned mythological symbols and the form of popular prophecy and whose central message is found in a scene of demonic cannibalism—surely a grotesquely excessive way to critique sacramental theology. Wilhelm Kühlmann notes Fischart's "vigorous emphasis on the narrator," which can perhaps be seen in the contrast between the impersonal reporting of future events in "Friess I" and the creation of a narrative voice who reports on a vision in "Friess II."[69]

Fischart's contemporaries were already aware that he published many works anonymously or under pseudonyms. Johann Jacob Frisius's 1583 revision of Conrad Gessner's catalog of literary works included a brief biography of Fischart that notes that Fischart "also wrote many other things that were published with his name either changed or omitted."[70] As Jan-Dirk Müller notes, Fischart created his works in dialogue with other texts more than did any other sixteenth-century German author, through "translation, paraphrase, amplification, parody, allusion, citation and other methods, usually—but not always—in comical distortion."[71] To the extent that we understand the composition and publication of "Friess II," its development matches the methods of Johann Fischart. As Fischart was accustomed to revise his own work and publish it in expanded versions, he may also be the redactor of "Friess II" who added excerpts from Lichtenberger and "Dietrich von Zengg," along with the pointed remark against the Lutheran clergy.

If the interpretation of "Friess II" and the attribution to Fischart are correct, the second prophecy of Wilhelm Friess may not have been the first time that Fischart addressed the threat he saw in Henry III in the guise of a geopolitical prophecy. Fischart is regarded as the author of an anonymous tract that Jobin printed in 1574 (using the pseudonymous imprint "Valetin Gutman von Wildtberg"), entitled *Von erwölung des Königs in Poln / samt kleiner weissagung ihres nachgestelten erholten dancks* (On the election of the king in Poland, together with a small prophecy of their subsequent gratitude).[72] The author of this verse tract, who castigated the Poles as fools, grievous sinners, and dishonorable oath breakers for allying with France rather than Austria so soon after the St. Bartholomew's Day massacre, foresaw the same kind of ignominious end for Henry III that Elias had foretold for Jehu and Jezebel.[73] If the French and the Polish, bordering Germany on the east and west, should think to make a joint attack, their lands would be visited by "armies and whatever belongs to and is necessary for such things: armor, weapons, shield and spear," not to mention artillery and cavalry.[74] The pamphlet compares the future fate of the Poles to the fates of the Anabaptists of Münster and the peasants who rebelled during the Peasants' War, and it foresees a fearful invasion from Russia, "burning your whole land, murdering both wife and man."[75] Any promise of aid from the Turks is unreliable, because as soon as an impoverished Poland no longer offers tribute, the Turks will join in the invasion.[76] The Poles' only recourse lay in repentance, faith in Christ, and leading a life of good works, including the correct use of the Eucharist instead of the heresies taught by Caspar Schwenckfeld and the pope.[77] The pamphlet warns that Germany, which is beset no less than Poland by sin, could also expect punishment, but it adds that the Germans had never in their history broken their oaths.[78] Although the predicted invasions are of similar severity, *Von erwölung des Königs in Poln* sees Henry of Valois as the trigger of attacks on Poland from Germany and other nations, while "Friess II" treats the same king's ascension in France as the final step in Germany's utter devastation.

As a citizen of Strasbourg who had contact with Antwerp and Basel, was engaged with astrological symbolism in 1574, sympathized with Calvinism and rejected the Lutheran view of the sacrament, and had the habit of expressing himself anonymously through a combination of the learned, the popular, and the grotesque, Johann Fischart was in the right place at the right time and had the right rhetorical talent, perspectives, and sympathies to come into consideration as the author of "Friess II." Moreover, several points of similarity exist between "Friess II" and other works attributed to Fischart. While the case for Fischart's authorship is circumstantial, the similarities are so numerous and so striking that the author of the second prophecy, if it was not Johann Fischart, must have been something like Bernhard Jobin's other brother-in-law.

If we accept the attribution of the second prophecy of Wilhelm Friess to Fischart—and there are grounds for caution; one noted expert on Fischart, Ulrich Seelbach, finds it entirely implausible—we gain a somewhat different understanding of the most accomplished satirist of sixteenth-century German literature.[79] We discover an earnest, rather than playful, Fischart, vehemently rejecting the Lutheran doctrine of ubiquity and engaging in confessional debates some years earlier than previously thought, and Fischart's travels to Paris and Flanders in 1567 gain additional significance for his later work. Above all, if we read the prophecy of Wilhelm Friess as an apocalyptic ekphrasis on Strasbourg's astronomical clock, we discover a Johann Fischart whose usual biting sarcasm gave way to an earnest pessimism in view of the ominous portents he observed in the late spring of 1574.

CHAPTER 7

The Last Emperor and the Beginning of Prophecy

―――― ⌇ ――――

"Friess I" versus "Friess II"

The previous chapters have allowed us to connect the numerous editions of "Friess I" printed in Nuremberg in 1558 with the appearance of "Friess II" in Basel beginning in 1577 by establishing a chain of textual and historical connections through Antwerp in the 1560s and Strasbourg in the 1570s. Rather than two isolated events twenty years apart that share only a name and a genre, "Friess I" led to the publication of "Friess II" through a sequence of cause and effect and a network of personal relationships. The first prognostication of Wilhelm Friess, printed by Frans Fraet in Antwerp, had mounted a critique from within the hegemony of Habsburg power, using the narrative elements of imperial prophecies to attack Habsburg rule over the Netherlands. In Nuremberg, however, "Friess I" appeared as a text that reiterated and stabilized narratives of the existing order of society at a time when their foundations had become uncertain. The L version of "Friess I" continued working out a specifically Lutheran loyalist position with respect to secular authority. Following the humiliating Calvinist surrender of 1567 in Antwerp, the second prophecy of Wilhelm Friess reacted to the galling accuracy of the Lutheran prophecy by turning the logic of "Friess I" on its head, much as Fischart did with Catholic saints' lives in his Protestant polemics and with astrological argumentation in *Aller Practick Großmutter*. Some parts of the web of connections between the two prophecies are clear and robust, while others are fainter or only partially visible. If one strand proves untenable—for example, if it could be definitively shown that Johann Fischart was never in Flanders during 1567—that connection could be replaced by a less visible alternative, such as the quite likely possibility that Fischart read about the tense standoff between Calvinists and Lutherans that had taken place in Antwerp.

While "Friess I" and "Friess II" both claim to be prophecies found with Wilhelm Friess of Maastricht after his death, they had different religious contexts and therefore distinctive views of the future. Lutheran apocalypticism, as Barnes has shown, foresaw gloom and decay for Germany that would be repaired only by Christ's Second Coming.[1] Rather than undermining medieval fears of the world's imminent end, the Reformation heightened them, leaving Lutherans looking in increasing anticipation for the fulfillment of biblical prophecies.[2] Following this tradition of Lutheran apocalypticism, "Friess I" presented the traditional end-time drama as still valid in the religious and political context of the late 1550s, with a bishop and emperor playing their customary roles in the fulfillment of eschatological hopes. The L redaction, printed in 1566–68 in a time of hardening confessional boundaries, explicitly condemned Calvinism along with Catholics and Anabaptists. "Friess II," in contrast, represented Reformed Protestantism of the late sixteenth century. Although Samuel Apiarius's editions omitted the prophecy's warning to the Lutheran clergy (the one overt reference to confessional strife in "Friess II"), the second prophecy was printed predominately in Basel, a center of Swiss Reformed Protestantism, and by a printer whose voluminous output included many works of Reformed theology and devotion. Where "Friess I" had recalled the Angelic Pope of pre-Reformation prophecies in the form of a highest bishop, the Reformed churches had eschewed the office of bishop, and the fine honorable man in "Friess II" holds no ecclesiastic office. After the Calvinists' interests had been entirely ignored by the Peace of Augsburg in 1555, emperors and bishops were figures not of hope but of oppression.

Reformed apocalypticism in the later sixteenth century usually lacked the Lutheran sense of pessimism and expectation of decline, instead displaying, in most cases, a characteristic militant optimism and expectation of gradual improvement. There were notably few Calvinist counterparts to the many Lutheran apocalyptic pamphlets published at the time.[3] One exception is found in the work of Wilhelm Misocacus, a Dutch Calvinist refugee living in Danzig, who disguised anti-Habsburg agitation as astrological prognostications from 1579 to 1591.[4] Perhaps due to the unique circumstances of Strasbourg in 1574, the bleak outlook of "Friess II" represents a departure from the Calvinist apocalypticism found in other sources of the same period.

As a consequence of their allegiance to opposite sides of the widening confessional divide, the understanding of imperial geography in each prophecy is fundamentally different. For Georg Kreydlein and his customers in 1558, the imperial city of Nuremberg, lying halfway between Vienna and Maastricht, easily took its place along the central axis of empire. Basel, however, where Apiarius maintained his workshop, had not been part of the Holy Roman Empire since 1501. From the point of view of Switzerland's Reformed Protestants, Vienna and Madrid were aligned with Rome in the Antichrist's own triple alliance.[5] For customers of Samuel Apiarius in Basel, Wilhelm Friess's home of Maastricht, newly engaged in the struggle to leave the Habsburg political sphere, was a potential fellow member of an independence-minded bloc at the margins of the empire.

"Friess I" viewed the Holy Roman Empire hopefully and from within. For all the radical intentions of Frans Fraet in Antwerp, the prophecy that was popularized in Nuremberg was one that saw the culmination of history in the continued validity of traditional medieval narratives about church and empire. "Friess I" consequently saw the prophesied disasters as the occasion for introspection, unity, and repentance. In contrast, "Friess II" surveyed the geography of imperial Europe at a distance and foresaw only blood-drenched catastrophe in its future. In "Friess II," the nobility do not fulfill national destiny. They are instead alien tyrants. "O you miserable people," the prophecy concludes in Apiarius's editions, "what kind of foreign people has risen up among you? They are not rulers but destroyers, not protectors but oppressors of orphans and widows throughout Germany" (appendix 2, 112–14). The only hope foreseen in "Friess II" lay in escaping from imperial narratives, as the Swiss had done decades earlier and the Dutch had just recently started to do. As viewed from the Netherlands, the Holy Roman Empire would become a foreign country by the early seventeenth century.[6] For "Friess II," salvation is not the culmination of empire but exit from it.

The Long Afterlife of "Wilhelm Friess"

The later receptions of the first and second prophecies of Wilhelm Friess are as different as their origins and outlooks. Fortunately for the inhabitants of Germany, the years 1558–63 did not turn out to be as dire as the first prophecy of Wilhelm Friess had predicted, although a severe famine and the outbreak of the Dutch Revolt did make "Friess I" a printable commodity again in 1566–68, at least after some revision. The days of the Last Emperor as a figure in the Lutheran apocalyptic narrative were limited, however. In a book published in 1596 and again in 1597, the Lutheran clergyman Andreas Schoppe (1538–1614) condemned false prophets who claimed to know the time of the Second Coming. He specifically attacked the invocation of the Last Emperor by "Wilhelm Friess from Nose-Wipe," as clear evidence that the prophecy was the devil's handiwork. Responding to the Last Emperor's abdication, Schoppe asked in indignation, "How could such a pious, God-fearing, and peaceable secular ruler and a loyal caretaker, nurturer, and protector of the true church and religion lead a holier life than by remaining in office and serving God and man according to his calling?"[7] For mainstream Lutheranism, the swan song of the Last Emperor appears to come not long after 1568. Johannes Wolf did include a Latinized version of "Friess I" in his *Lectionum memorabilium*, but Wolf's excerpt of the prophecy included only the sections on clerical poverty. Except for Schoppe's mocking rejection and Wolf's antiquarian collection, the record of popular interest in "Friess I" falls silent after 1568.

Active engagement with the second prophecy of Wilhelm Friess continued rather longer. Where the text and title pages of Georg Kreydlein's editions of "Friess I" remained much the same, Samuel Apiarius and other printers of the second prophecy continually altered the title woodcuts and title formulations, combined the prophecy with other texts, and moved the year of Wilhelm Friess's death into the more recent past. An anonymous edition printed in 1579 dates Friess's vision to that year, while the 1586 edition of Samuel Apiarius specifies that Friess had his vision on 28 December 1585 and died in 1586. Johann Beck's Erfurt edition of the same year omits the date of Friess's vision and the fact of his death altogether (appendix 2, 15). In similar fashion, later editions preserved the details of the "horrible and shocking prophecy" but altered the context in which it was presented. For editions of "Friess II" in the later 1580s, Apiarius adopted the title page configuration from practicas, annual astrological prognostications with title illustrations composed from small woodcuts of the year's governing planets. Apiarius's 1587 edition (F17) illustrated the title page with Mars and Mercury and changed the title to *Ein Grausame unnd Erschröckliche Pratica oder Propheceyung* (A terrible and shocking practica or prophecy). Some of the latest editions (F24–F26) took the generic migration one step further by titling the pamphlet "Recent Events" (using the protojournalistic formula of *Newe Zeittung*) and combining the second vision of Wilhelm Friess with signs of the Last Days and a report of notable events in France. Where the earliest title pages of "Friess II" had invoked sober reflection, later illustrations turned to alarming scenes of greater emotional force. But by the late 1580s, the support of another author or genre was needed to make the prophecies of "Wilhelm Friess" marketable.

"Friess II," unlike "Friess I," did not begin as a Dutch text, but it was translated into Dutch at least once. In 1587 and 1588, one German and one Dutch edition (F27 and F28) combined "Friess II" with the "Short Prophecy for 1587–88 of the Pilgrim Ruth Hidden in the Forest," a prophecy that elsewhere is attributed to "Johannes Doleta." The Dutch edition from the press of Cornelius Claesz in Amsterdam identified itself as a translation from German.[8] This translation was later combined with a prophecy of Paul Grebner in five Dutch editions published between 1601 and 1607 (G1–G5) and attributed variously to Grebner or to "Jerrassemus van Eydenborch" or "Johannes Ulpus." The "Pilgrim Ruth" was an authorial pseudonym used by Johannes Lichtenberger in the first editions of his *Prognosticatio* a century earlier, while "Johannes Doleta" is the same as "John of Toledo," the authorial name sometimes attached to the twelfth-century "Toledo Letter." The "Short Prophecy" printed together with "Friess II" in these editions is a combination of the "Toledo Letter" and a few extracts from Lichtenberger's *Prognosticatio.*[9] Following a comprehensive study of the centuries-long transmission of the "Toledo Letter," Dirk Mentgen concluded that the prophecy was absorbed into the controversy over the second deluge predicted for 1524 and that it did not reappear after that.[10] The "Toledo Letter" was only lying dormant, however. The "Johannes Doleta" version of the "Toledo Letter" was printed in at least five pamphlet and four broadside editions in 1586–88, and another version was printed in 1629.[11] Prophecies, it seems, are not forgotten once unfulfilled. Instead, they hibernate for a time and then return.

Andreas Schoppe regarded "Friess I" as a prophecy that had failed in most points, and he rejected its hope for a Last Emperor, but the prophecies of doom offered by "Friess II" fared better in later decades. Wilhelm Eon Neuheuser, author of numerous prophetic works between 1594 and 1626, gave "Friess II" an optimistic reading in 1618 as a prophecy that true Christians would escape from papal oppression and "finally gain the advantage under a large white flag in which perhaps stands the sign of Tau, as has already begun to be done in the Netherlands."[12] Neuheuser was referring to Ezekiel 9:4, where the inhabitants of Jerusalem who lament the sins committed there are marked on the forehead with a sign, which some traditions and translations identified as the Greek letter tau. Those who do not receive the sign are slaughtered. In a scene reminiscent of "Friess II," the prophet Ezekiel falls on his face at the sight of this vision, but the explicit reference to this chapter is found in "Friess I."

"Friess II" enjoyed a longer continuous reception than "Friess I," partly because the Germany of the following decades more often resembled a desolate battlefield than the site of a golden age of peace and harmony. The latest known edition of "Friess II," published in 1639, reflects international involvement in the ongoing Thirty Years' War: the first demonic general in the 1639 edition commands his army to wait specifically for its "Danish allies" (appendix 2, 25). Considering the devastation wrought by foreign armies on many German regions during the Thirty Years' War, it is not surprising that "Friess II" would strike observers as an all-too-accurate vision of the times in which they lived.

The influence of the second vision of Wilhelm Friess can be seen not only in the number of editions but also in how it provided a template for later prophecies. Just as "Friess II" made use of elements of earlier prophecies, the prophetic grammar and vocabulary of "Friess II" reappeared several times in the seventeenth and eighteenth centuries. While the precise degree and path of influence is uncertain, the use of a similar model in which a vision guide shows scenes to a narrator according to the cardinal directions is strongly reminiscent of "Friess II." The visions of Johannes Kose published in 1601, for example, offer precisely dated visions (the first on a Sunday morning in 1591, the second from 16 to 22 February 1599) in which a vision guide shows the narrator evil spirits and their human followers who assail a small band of pious Christians from the west, followed by the Christians' later salvation approaching from the east, before the vision guide disappears and the narrator regains consciousness.[13] In the Dutch vision of Intje Jansz of Oosterzee, frequently reprinted after the earliest known edition of 1623, the narrator encounters three figures at night on 8 December 1622: one figure gleaming like the Sun and holding a fiery rod that dripped blood, a second figure resembling Death, and a third figure appearing as a warrior with a bloody sword in his right hand. The three figures proclaim woe on Brabant, Flanders, Friesland, and Germany and tell the narrator to look to the southwest, north, and east. The narrator sees the land first full of riders and soldiers and then full of corpses, and he witnesses, among other things, the arrival of a man wearing foreign clothing and a four-cornered hat, who delivers letters from his basket.[14] The precisely dated night vision, the proclamation of woe, the guides who direct the narrator's view to various directions, the armed conflict and bloody desolation, and the arrival of a man with written messages all reflect a pattern previously seen in the second prophecy of Wilhelm Fries.

Gottfried Arnold's *Impartial History of the Church and Heretics*, first published in 1699, records other visions that follow the same template, including Stephan Melisch's prophecy of woe upon Poland, Sweden, and France. In this vision of 19 April 1656, Melisch encounters an unfamiliar man who asks Melisch about his origin (Polish) and religion (Reformed) and also asks if he sang Psalms (enthusiastically). The man then sets Melisch on the south side of a square table, where he sees the king of Sweden sitting to the north; the prince-electors of Heidelberg, Saxony, and Brandenburg to the east; and a cardinal in between the king and the princes. On the west, Melisch sees one like "Ragozi" (perhaps György II Rákóczi, prince of Transylvania in 1648–57) next to several ambassadors and three mighty potentates. The cardinal dashes a papal crown to pieces, a queen arrives, and the guests at the table praise the Swedish king, who then places a new crown on the cardinal's head.[15]

Arnold also records a series of visions following a pattern similar to "Friess II" and seen by Joachim Greulich beginning on 21 May 1653. On midnight of the fifth day, for example, Greulich sees an angel wearing armor and holding in his right hand a bloody sword, with which God will punish the world for its sins. In a vision of 15 July, the armored angel shows Greulich how a king from the Netherlands will lay waste to all of Germany for the sake of God's word, while a Swedish king will resist the Dutch king. Then Greulich sees two armies battling within his bedroom, as a precursor of the devastation that awaits Germany. The angel lifts two crowns (one to the east and the other to the west), states that the kingdom will be entirely exterminated, and names himself as the Destroying Angel who has annihilated thousands for their sins. On 23 July, the angel brings Greulich to Poland, where he sees "two mighty armies like Tatars and Cossacks." After the armies join together, they fight against and defeat the Poles, and then the angel says, "Poland, you are cursed by God, and through this land the Turk will come to Germany."[16] On 12 August, the angel commands Greulich to look into heaven, where he sees nine hundred thousand men approaching from the east, leading sixty wagons and calling out, "Where are the Christian dogs, where are the bloodhounds?" Greulich asks the angel about the wagons, and the angel informs him that they are meant to carry the decapitated heads of the Christians in Germany.[17] Numerous additional visions address the fates of European nations and German cities. Although Greulich's complete vision is much longer than "Friess II," it makes use of a symbolic inventory very similar to that found in the second prophecy of Wilhelm Friess.

Even as late as World War I, a circulating "birch tree prophecy," first recorded in 1701, foresaw terrible battles in the middle of Germany between peoples of the north and south, which would lay waste to towns and cities and force their inhabitants to flee into the forests and mountains. In the final, three-day battle, accompanied by a threefold cry of woe upon Germany, the army of the north would be victorious, while their enemies would flee to the shore of a river, where their last remnants would be destroyed.[18] Given the similarity in motifs, one is inclined to see the second prophecy of Wilhelm Friess as one of the precursors of the "birch tree prophecy," although one must assume that a long and complicated path lies between them.

Even the first prophecy of Wilhelm Friess enjoyed one more burst of popularity over a century after the last edition of the L version had been printed in 1568. In 1686, four editions appeared (N21–N24) of a "wonderful prophecy reaching from 1686 to 1691 in which great changes are revealed by a highly learned man well known to the world," attributed in one edition (N21) to a "Christian Engelmann."[19] The attribution to Engelmann and the author's alleged fame are, of course, pure fiction, as the text is the N version of the first prophecy of Wilhelm Friess, a pseudonym that had last appeared in print over a century earlier. The prophecy as printed in 1686 is primarily interested in the tribulations expected in the coming five years (especially the false emperor of the west and his eastern allies), which were updated by the expedient of adding around 130 years to the original dates in most cases. The prophecy of woe to the clergy is deleted, and the careers of the final emperor and highest bishop are reduced to bare mentions of their existence and to the promise of a time of peace and prosperity to come under their leadership.

The new relevance of "Friess I" in the late 1680s is not difficult to understand. France was near the height of its power during the long reign of Louis XIV and had annexed Strasbourg in 1681, while an Ottoman Turkish army again besieged Vienna in 1686. The false emperor of the west and his eastern allies were again an acute threat, which gave the first prophecy of Wilhelm Friess a new relevance and likely led the former owner of a copy of N21 now in Weimar to include it in a volume otherwise composed of pamphlets on the military affairs of the French and Turks.[20] Making predictions, especially about the future, is very easy: one need only have enough patience and sufficient imagination to recognize their fulfillment.

The late version of "Friess I" was printed again in 1689 (N25), in a short compilation of prophetic works. By then, the Turkish threat had passed. But the French king received special mention on the title page, which lodges a "melancholy complaint and appeal to the highest and eternal Majesty on behalf of all the lands and cities of the Palatinate and the Rhineland against the most cruel acts of Louis XIV of France." The compilation was reprinted in the next year (N26), ostensibly because of popular demand.[21] The compilation opens with "Friess I," claiming that the prophecy had first been printed in 1686. The next work is an extract from the "Postilla" attributed to Johannes Lichtenberger and allegedly printed in 1512, although Lichtenberger was not the author and the "Postilla" was likely a recent composition.[22] Luther's 1527 preface to Lichtenberger's *Prognosticatio* comes next, followed by the pseudo-Paracelsian prophecy of a "Lion of the North."[23] The final section is the lament to God against Louis XIV, and then a short conclusion ends the work. The text of the conclusion is familiar: "Wake up, you Christians, from the sleep of sin! Open your ears, sharpen your senses, and hear my words" (appendix 1, 465–68). The compilation's conclusion is, in fact, the conclusion of "Friess I," itself a citation of prophetic compilations going back at least to Grünpeck's *Speculum* of 1508, so that the first prophecy of Wilhelm Friess forms both the beginning and the ending of the entire work.

The Textuality of Prophecy

The literary merit of the prophecies of Wilhelm Friess may not be immediately apparent. They are short pamphlets of a few leaves, and one will not find in them surprising plot turns or characters with rich interior lives. Both prophecies reflect the influence of earlier works, and they were meant to be accessible to a broad audience that included those of modest economic means and limited educational attainment.

Yet each prophecy is, in its own way, a sophisticated work of verbal art. The first prophecy of Wilhelm Friess attempted to subvert traditional imperial prophecies in order to deliver a covert revolutionary message. It failed as a pseudonymous work of anti-Habsburg agitation, but it was a resounding success as a recapitulation and updating of traditional narratives. It concisely expressed one aspect of public perception of the religious and geopolitical situation of Germany in the mid-sixteenth century, and it succeeded so well in this that it was used again for the same purpose at the end of the seventeenth century. Having geopolitical relevance for 130 years is quite an accomplishment for a little pamphlet. The second prophecy, with its ominous armies led by demonic generals, used overlapping systems of geographic, religious, and astrological imagery to express the fears of Reformed believers at a critical moment. In its complex and interlocking symbolism, "Friess II" may be one of the most original and sophisticated prophecies of the early modern period.

Apart from any literary qualities that the prophecies may hold, the visions of Wilhelm Friess are significant for how they changed. Between the annual prognostications of Willem de Vriese in Antwerp, the imperial narratives of "Friess I" printed in Nuremberg, the prognostications of Nikolaus Caesareus that appeared under the name of Wilhelm Friess, and the nightmare vision of "Friess II," four entirely separate texts were attached to Friess's name in the space of two decades. Both prophecies have textual histories that branched into different traditions within the space of a few years, including the four different versions of "Friess I." The variety and frequency of available editions have allowed us to undertake a fine-grained examination of the prophecies' textual history, which brings into new perspective a question raised by Robert Lerner and others: where do prophecies come from? If we have properly understood the history of Wilhelm Friess's visions, we might say that there are four basic moves that typify their development, including how the texts changed over time and how they responded to their historical context.

1. Selective reception of an earlier prophecy

The first prophecy of Wilhelm Friess appears to have responded to the general pro-Reformation tenor of Willem de Vriese's practicas, while establishing a textual continuity, even in the vaguest sense, with only a single passage, the proclamation of calamities upon the clergy. The second prophecy treats "Friess I" in the same way, by adopting, at most, a few details, including the author's name and the prediction of invasion by various enemies. In other cases, such as those of Joachim Greulich and Intje Jansz, prophecies borrowed not a passage of text but a visionary template or prophetic grammar. For these prophecies, faithfulness to the exemplar was not of any concern. What mattered was not the accurate transmittal of a complete text but the recognition of perhaps just a single passage as being of special significance.

2. Expansion into a complete prophecy

Expansion of the borrowed element often took the form of creating astrological scaffolding for prophetic statements or adopting a prophetic framework for an astrological prognostication. The prognostications of Willem de Vriese published in Antwerp appear to have given astrological cover to a prediction of woe for the clergy that ultimately derived from prophecies such as Rupescissa's *Vademecum* or pseudo-Vincent Ferrer. The opposite process is also common. The *Prognosticatio* of Johannes Lichtenberger consists of a few sections from a 1484 astrological prognostication by Paulus de Middelburgo supplemented by extensive borrowings from several prophecies of the late Middle Ages.[24] A dramatic example of prophetic expansion of astrological prognostication is the 1499 compendium of planetary ephemerides of Johannes Stöffler and Jakob Pflaum, which consists of hundreds of pages of astronomical details and one brief note couched in apocalyptic language concerning the planetary conjunctions of 1524. The consequences included popular fears of a second deluge and the publication of hundreds of pamphlets that addressed the ensuing controversy; the citation of Stöffler and Pflaum's apocalyptic passage in prophetic compilations; and the publication, in 1520 and later, of the disorganized compilation of prophetic tropes ascribed to Jakob Pflaum.[25] In similar fashion, layers of meaning built from prophetic tropes were added to the astrological symbolism of "Friess II." Astrological prognostication made it possible for the stars to portend something that could not be desired openly, and then the astrologer's interpretation of the heavens could be extracted and given prophetic coloring.

According to the rules of the textual game of prophecy, it was permissible to supplement a prophetic extract or a complete prophecy by drawing on the stock of prophetic truth wherever it could be found. This might take the form of adding biblical citations and allusions, as the L version of "Friess I" does, or it might entail supplementing the text with something else from the prophecy's conceptual world. In this manner, the translation of "Friess I" from Dutch into German added a citation from the *Extract of Various Prophecies*, itself derived from Grünpeck's *Speculum*. In similar fashion, a redactor of "Friess II" added citations from "Dietrich von Zengg" as preserved in the "Prophecy Found in Altenburg," as well as from Lichtenberger's *Prognosticatio*. Despite occasional protests from some theologians and astrologers, many readers saw prophecy and astrology as belonging to the same conceptual world. As complementary methods of placing the present moment into a narrative that extended from the Creation to the Last Judgment, astrological prognostications and end-time prophecies could be combined without most contemporaries sensing any contradiction.

3. A need to veil the message

Both the first and second prophecies of Wilhelm Friess gave expression to ideas beyond what was permissible to say at the time. The limits on expression were particularly acute in the case of "Friess I" in the context of the Habsburg Netherlands, where sympathizing with the Reformation or resisting imperial domination could end in execution. While Strasbourg in the 1570s was a more tolerant place, criticizing orthodox Lutheran sacramental theology, the primary point of contention with Calvinism, was a precarious undertaking. The recourse to a prophetic mode of communication made it possible to write and publish what was otherwise unprintable. The turn to prophecy and other forms of veiled language was a consequence of a message that exceeded what was permitted to be spoken aloud in the face of censorship and oppression, let alone printed in inexpensive pamphlets and distributed to a wide audience.[26]

4. Adaptation to a new context

Veiling the message has the added and important effect of priming readers to be alert for hidden meaning while at the same time broadening the range of meanings that readers can find in the text. This allows prophecies to be transmitted and thus to survive the passage of time and to gain popularity in new places, even if the meaning that most readers find in the prophecy is fundamentally different from what the author intended. Because so many prophecies from the late Middle Ages and early modern period claimed to have been discovered in old books or found hidden in a trunk or within the walls of a church or similar places, contemporaries mocked the trope as a worn-out stereotype that undermined, rather than added to, a prophecy's authority.[27] Yet the claim of discovery, like the claim of foreign authorship for a prophecy like "Alofresant," may have been a sober acknowledgment that a new significance had been discovered in an older text and that meanings change as geographical borders are crossed. The first prophecy of Wilhelm Friess had to develop in Antwerp, where the context of censorship and religious oppression required the resort to prophecy, but it could only become successful in print in Germany, where it took on an entirely different meaning. "Friess I" would be entirely unknown today if it had not found its way to German Gnesio-Lutherans and then to Nuremberg, where its veiled anti-Habsburg message was lost behind a surface meaning that reaffirmed imperial narratives. "Friess II" arose in the specific context of Strasbourg in 1574 as the former king of Poland was on his way to France to be crowned as Henry III, but the prophecy experienced its success in print beginning in 1577 in Basel. Transmission across language boundaries opened up new gaps in meaning that translators then filled with various levels of artistry and accuracy. Ottavia Niccoli has observed that many readers misunderstood much or all of a prophecy's significance for its prior or original context.[28] But this is not only inevitable: it is necessary. Finding new significance in a text written long ago or in another place is not a regrettable misreading of an author's original intent; rather, it is constitutive of how prophecies are created and preserved as living texts. Because prophecy as a genre depends on crossing boundaries and finding new contexts, prophecies are able to move from marginal or border regions, against the prevailing tides of cultural dissemination, toward the cultural center. While the Reformation may have emanated from Wittenberg to the Netherlands, the mode of prophetic writing made it possible for—or perhaps even required—the first prophecy of Wilhelm Friess to move in the opposite direction.

The four moves of prophetic textuality mentioned above do not necessarily proceed sequentially, and none of them should be considered the logical first step. The generation of prophecies was less a matter of creation followed by dispersal and corruption than a continual and cyclical process of extraction, accretion, and adaptation. This was already true of medieval prophecies, as Lesley Coote and Robert Lerner have separately noted. The thirteenth-century "Cedar of Lebanon" prophecy was "built from extensive plagiarism and provided material from which others plagiarized in their turn," according to Lerner, while Coote notes that "writers, copyists and audience all participated in the creation" of a prophecy "and might go on re-creating it as circumstances changed."[29]

The prophecies of Wilhelm Friess are typical of the early modern period, as virtually all prophecies of any degree of popularity in Germany at that time underwent the same kinds of borrowing and adaptation during the course of their transmission. Where the German translation of "Friess I" expanded by incorporating citations from Grünpeck's *Speculum* into the text, the one edition of the D version filled the last page with prophecies borrowed from Paracelsus and Lichtenberger. These two types of compilation, what we might call "expansion" and "accretion," differ only in degree, and they eventually may not differ at all. Over time, a series of what were once clearly identified extracts can be forged together into a single organic prophecy, as happened in the case of Martin Luther. When extensive compilations of Luther's statements with an apocalyptic tone appeared following his death, the compilers were careful to identify the sources of each quotation. Producers of later pamphlets for broader audiences selected the most noteworthy material, omitted the textual references, and combined the diverse statements into integral prophecies ascribed as a whole to Luther. In a similar way, texts can be combined with their own commentaries, as Robert Moynihan argues for the Joachite *Super Hieremiam.* In his view, an original and authentic short commentary by Joachim of Fiore on the book of Jeremiah was annotated by Joachim's later disciples, and the marginal commentary was subsequently incorporated into the text.[30] What was then printed in the sixteenth century as a prophetic book of Joachim of Fiore was, in fact, a commentary on a commentary.

To trace the relationship from the end back to the beginning, we could say that the second prophecy of Wilhelm Friess was a Calvinist reaction to a Lutheran reworking of a covert anti-Habsburg rendering of a fifteenth-century French redaction of a fourteenth-century Latin prophetic summary, itself a compendium of many contemporary and older prophecies whose author seems, furthermore, to have created two different redactions of the work.[31] In tracing the prophecies of Wilhelm Friess back to the *Vademecum* of Johannes de Rupescissa, we find not the original source but only the earliest point before the chain of transmission is lost in a patchwork of citation, allusion, and commentary. Given the textual cycling and recycling we have observed with the visions of Wilhelm Friess and others, we cannot avoid the possibility that most prophecies are commentaries on commentaries or compilations of extracts from compilations of extracts all the way back, with their moment of origin entirely lost to view. Coote even claims, "It is not possible to create *stemmata* for prophetic texts. There is not, in most cases, an 'original' from which other versions deviate."[32] What we can still hope for—and what justifies the stemmata included in this book—is what we have in the two prophecies of Wilhelm Friess: not the beginning of a text where an author creates something entirely original, but a particular place and time where a writer finds meaning in and gives particular form to an arrangement of preexistent textual building blocks. Because so much of the premodern textual tradition took place outside of our view, we cannot ever be certain that we have found the moment where inspiration first took written form, rather than one more occasion where an existing prophecy was adapted to a new context. Perhaps the right question to ask is not where prophecies come from but, instead, what the discourse of prophecy allows one to do.

While the transmission of prophetic texts permits radical innovation, the textual rules of the genre also constrain what can be done, so that prophecy is both innovative and antiquarian. Frans Fraet was a skilled and experienced rhetorician, but when he printed a critique of Habsburg religious oppression in the form of prophecy, he did not invent a new vision. He instead adapted an existing text, expanding some sections and removing others. A later Gnesio-Lutheran found Fraet's text worth translating into German and, at the same time, supplemented it with additional prophetic elements, including a citation that ultimately derived from Grünpeck's *Speculum.* Even as Frans Fraet violated the emperor's decrees against heresy, he was obeying the discursive conventions of prophecy. As a consequence, later authors recognized Fraet's redaction as something that could speak to their own moment in history, even when they extracted just one passage from the whole, as Johann Wolf did in 1600, or when they supplemented "Friess I" with additional prophetic texts, as the *Wonderful Prophecy Reaching from 1686 to 1691* did a century later. The majority of prophecies in print during the fifteenth and sixteenth centuries were not texts that had been invented; instead, like the prophecies of Wilhelm Friess, they were reworkings of texts that had been found. The imperative for redactors of prophecies was not maintaining textual integrity, as it was with biblical copyists, but following a set of rules that allowed expansion, deletion, and rearrangement in order to make the text a truer and more powerful pronouncement on the present moment. One might say that prophecy is the genre with the greatest discrepancy between its claims of originality and the reality of textual transmission. Both claiming to offer an unmediated divine vision and actually providing a text shaped by numerous borrowings and multiple adaptations are typical elements of the genre.

While "Friess I" and "Friess II" have all the characteristics of medieval prophecy identified by Robert Lerner, including the "assumption of false identity, prediction of events that had already happened, the introduction of meaninglessness, and the resort to plagiarism," these should be seen as more than evidence of fraud, pious or otherwise.[33] While the sixteenth century and earlier times certainly had their share of cynics and deceivers, we have not seen evidence of bad faith in the history of Wilhelm Friess. It is hard to fault Frans Fraet for assuming a false identity when the alternatives were submission to tyranny or a shortened path to martyrdom. It is likewise difficult to accuse Johann Fischart of meaninglessness—if we have correctly identified him as the author of "Friess II"—for using symbolism that was sometimes opaque to express covertly what could not be spoken aloud. Later redactors of the prophecies took pains to create sensible readings when they perceived that meaning had been lost, as might easily happen in the process of translation.

While the L version of "Friess I" printed from 1566 to 1568 indulged in prophecies *ex eventu*, the charge of fraudulently predicting events that had already happened is less grave if one does not conceive of prophecy's primary function as providing knowledge of things to come. The prophecies of Wilhelm Friess were instead comments on how the present moment should be understood with respect to a narrative that included both past and future. In that context, a prophecy *ex eventu* is less a fraudulent claim of accurate prognostication than it is a way for readers to recognize the present moment in the grand scheme of history. Helping readers to orient themselves in society and the cosmos was a function of both apocalyptic prophecies and astrological prognostications.[34] In the same way, the disconcerting regularity with which the year of Wilhelm Friess's death was updated becomes more understandable if we consider that its function was to anchor the narrative to the then-present moment. *Plagiarism*, which implies the illegitimate appropriation of another's text, is the wrong word to use for the extracting and compilation of texts according to the implicit rules of the genre. Prophecies were rhetorical constructions that might be assigned to children as translation exercises in their Latin education, as Andreas Engel recalled in 1597 about his school days. Even for Johann Hilten, reputed, at the time, to have been Luther's teacher and a martyr for the Reformation before the letter, the question people asked was, according to Engel, "From where did the good Hilten take his conjectures and prophecies?"[35]

If we recognize prophecy as a discourse operating under a particular set of rules that govern textual acts, prophetic authorship becomes, in turn, a way to identify a specific variety of those rules, just as Spenserian and Petrarchan sonnets are so called not because of the particular poet who composed them but by their allegiance to textual conventions. In the succession of texts ascribed to Wilhelm Friess, we can recognize a recurring pattern. First, Hans van Liesvelt had published prognostications for 1555 and 1556 by or attributed to Willem de Vriese. Frans Fraet then appropriated the name for a different prophecy in late 1557. An anonymous translator Germanized the prophecy and its author in 1558. Christian Müller of Strasbourg used the name for yet another prognostication (whose actual author was Nikolaus Caesareus) in 1562. For Müller, it seems, having a live German astrologer as author was not as useful as having a dead Dutch prophet. Finally a new prophecy under the same name was composed in Strasbourg in 1574 and began to appear in print in Basel and other cities in 1577.

It is uncertain whether the astrologer Willem de Vriese was ever a living human being, and the Antwerp trial documents do not treat him as such. It is even more doubtful that Wilhelm Friess ever enjoyed a human life before his often-cited death, a singular and punctual event that printers turned into a process lasting three decades. There is no doubt at all that Wilhelm Friess never wrote a prognostication that was actually written by Nikolaus Caesareus. The attribution of authorship to Wilhelm Friess or Willem de Vriese had little to do with the writing activity of some flesh-and-blood citizen of Maastricht in the sixteenth century. These texts do not share an author. What they have in common, instead, is a combination of astrology and prophecy that addressed the current situation and future prospects of Protestantism. The attribution of authorship to Friess was a way of legitimating particular textual acts in the minds of the text's composer and creating a set of expectations in the minds of a printer's customers. This kind of authorship does not convey information about the original composer of a text but, instead, identifies a particular way of speaking about the religious and political conditions of sixteenth-century society. Early modern authorship in the genre of prophecy, far from what modern conventions would lead us to expect, was one more way that a literary work identified the textual acts in which it was engaged.

Friess's name served the same function as that which Roger Chartier finds in authorial portraits in early modern books: to "reinforce the notion that the writing is the expression of an individuality that gives authenticity to the work."[36] Sixteenth-century readers of a prophecy by Wilhelm Friess had no knowledge of its origins beyond the authorial name, location, and manner of discovery offered by a pamphlet's title page. All the pamphlets claimed to contain the prophecies of the aged Wilhelm Friess of Maastricht that had been found with him after his recent death. In reality, the date of Friess's death was malleable, and the textual unity suggested by the alleged circumstances of discovery was equally fictional, but the flexibility with respect to biography and bibliography made Wilhelm Friess all the more useful as an author figure.

Rather than a permanent feature of a text and a key to its source, this kind of authorial identity could circulate among different texts of diverse origins. In similar fashion, a text once attributed to Friess could circulate under the names of Christian Engelmann, Paul Grebner, or Jerassemus van Eydenborch if the historical context changed. The authorship of Wilhelm Friess and his multiple prophecies arose in a specific historical context where readers desired a certain kind of literature, both readers and authorities demanded an authorial identity, and printers were anxious that someone else, even a fictive person, bore ultimate responsibility for the work.

Frans Fraet certainly would have been well served if responsibility for the seditious prognostication of Willem de Vriese had remained with its alleged author, but Fraet's attempt to remain anonymous failed. One might even say that Frans Fraet failed twice over. First and most obviously, he was unmasked as the source of the prophecy, which led to his arrest and execution. Following this came what would surely have been an even more bitter disappointment (had Fraet lived to see it), as the work he printed as an anti-Habsburg protest became a frequently reprinted reiteration and reinforcement of imperial narratives in Germany. Fraet had his posthumous revenge, however, in the second prophecy of Wilhelm Friess. If author figures enabled writers to express things that could not be said in other ways, then Fraet's creation of the first "Wilhelm Friess" helped make possible the second prophecy's radical vision of exit from empire and rejection of imperial narratives.

APPENDIXES

The First Prophecy of Wilhelm Friess

—————— ᭙ ——————

The following editions of "Friess I" and "Friess II" attempt to capture on paper the complex relationships between the various versions and editions of each text and its sources. As with the transcriptions of early modern printed texts in the notes, the editions presented here use modern values for i/j, u/v, and consonantal w. Round and tall s are not differentiated, umlauted vowels use modern orthographic conventions, and words begin with one capital at most. Spelling, capitalization, paragraph breaks, and punctuation are otherwise unchanged. Obvious typographical mistakes are corrected in square brackets. Abbreviations are expanded silently, and Latin digraphs are rendered as two letters. Blank lines are used to keep the texts roughly parallel to each other and do not reflect the layout of the printed editions.

The purpose of the editions presented here is to lay out the evidence for the textual historical arguments made in the chapters of this book (as well as the cases that call those arguments into question), to provide a convenient reading text, and to make available documents that would otherwise be obtainable only with considerable effort. These considerations influenced my choice of which texts to present here. For "Friess I," digital facsimiles of the one B edition and two L editions are, at the time of this writing, readily available online, as are several of Georg Kreydlein's editions. Readers interested in those editions will have no difficulty finding and reading them, so references to them are here relegated to the apparatus. The one edition of D is more difficult to find, however. For the N version, two early editions (N4 and N6) have equal textual historical value, as do the very late editions published in 1686–90 (N21–N26), but N6 has the additional significance of occupying a crucial place in the textual history of "Friess I," as it was the parent of the many Kreydlein editions and has not suffered the numerous deletions of the seventeenth-century N editions. The following edition provides the text of both D and N6, and the notes are limited to the most significant variant readings in other editions. Orthographic or dialectal variants of the same word are not distinguished in the apparatus. Unless otherwise marked, the base lemma in the apparatus is drawn from N6. This is explicitly stated when the reading of N6 is compared with other editions of the same family. If not otherwise noted, the other N editions can be assumed to substantially follow N6, while L3 can be assumed to follow the readings of L2. Most omissions and discrepancies of N22–N26 as compared to N21 are not noted. Citations to "Ferrari" identify particular lines from Barbara Ferrari's edition of the French *Vademecum* redaction in BAV Reg. lat. 1728, citations of "Brown" identify pages from Edward Brown's 1690 edition of the *Vademecum,* and citations of "Egenolff" refer to the extract from Grünpeck's *Speculum* as published by Christian Egenolff in his 1550 compilation of prophecies (VD16 P 5068).[1]

[a1r] PRONOSTICATIO.
Etliche setlzame Prophezei[u]ng /
geweissaget von dem alten M. Wilhelmo
Friesen / von Mastrich / welcher neulich
5 gestorben / die bey ihme gefunden nach
seinem tode / Von 1558. biss ins 63. jar sich
erstreckende / in denen sehr seltzame unnd
greuliche verenderung geweissaget werden.
10 Matthei am 6. Luce. 11. Acto. 21.
Dein wille geschehe / wie im Himmel also
auch auff Erden.

15 [a1v] Ich achte nichts bösers noch
ungelückseligers / denn so einer allezeit in
freuden lebet / unnd nye kein Creutze oder
widerstandt gehat / Denn der kann sich
selbst nicht erkennen. Ich achte den unselig
20 / der ohne anfechtung ist / denn das leben
des Menschens ist anders nicht / (als Job
spricht) Denn ein steter krieg mit dem
Teuffel. Darumb radt ich euch / meine
lieben freunde / das ihr euch willig ins
25 Creutze ergebet / Denn sieder das Gott die
Welt erschuff / ist nie so viel leidens
gewesen / als itzt ergehen wirdt in den
nachfolgenden fünff jaren / unnd solchs sol
gehen uber die gantze Christenheit / Odder
30 da Gott sein gerechtes Urtheil endern sol /
müssen wir uns zu Gott bekeren / als die
von Ninive theten / welcher Gott in seinem
zorn verschonet / Also würde Gott uber uns
/ sich auch erbarmen / da wir uns zu ihm
35 / von unsern Sünden bekerten inn dieser zeit
(welche gar böse sein wirdt) der fünff jare

[a1r] PRONOSTICATIO.
Gepracticeret van dem olden Meister
Wilhelm dem Fresen van Mastricht / de nu
kortes vorscheden unde na synem dode by
em befunden ys / Angande van dem Jar
M.D.LVIII. warende up dat LXIII. Jar.

Fiat voluntas Dei, sicut in coelo sic et in
terra.

[a1v] Der Minschen levendt ys nicht
anders (alse Job secht) denn ein stryd mit
dem Düvel / Darumme rade ick juw leven
Fründe / dat gy juw willich tho dem
lydende geven willen /

welckere dar nu komen schal / alle
Christenheit dorch / yn dessen nafolgenden
vyff yaren /

---

15 *nichts bösers noch ungelückseligers* N21 nichts unglückseli-
gers B nichts unseligers
17 *freuden* B friden
17 N4–N10 N21 *unnd nye kein* N12–N19 und kein
18 *widerstandt* N21 B Widerwärtigkeit L2 wedderstalth L3
wedderstandt
18 N4–N10 N21 *der* N12–N19 derselb
19 *Ich achte den unselig* B L2 darumb / acht ich den selben
ellendig
20 *anfechtung* B L2 armût
21 *anders nicht* N12–N15 nichts anders
21 *als Job spricht* B wie Job im vii. Capitel sagt
22 *spricht* L2 spricht D B sagt
23 *steter krieg mit dem Teuffel* D B streit mit dem Teuffel L2
Orgelwerck des Düvels
23–24 *meine lieben freunde* B mein geliebten L2 leven Christen
25 *Creutze* D B L2 leiden
25 *sieder* N21 B seit
26 *leidens* N21 B leiden
28 *fünff* B vier L2 twölff
29–35 Cf. D 45–54.

30 *Urtheil* D B L2 sententien; Ferrari 23 ne mue sa sentence
30 *endern* D L2 vorkeren B verandern
31 *müssen wir uns zu Gott bekeren* B auff das wir uns
kerten zů tugend L2 up dat wy unse herten tho
dögeden bekeren; Ferrari 24 se de noz pechiez nous
noz amendons
31 N4–N8 N21 *bekeren / als die von Ninive theten /
welcher Gott in seinem zorn verschonet* defective in N9–
N19; replaced by N9 verschönet N12 N13 verschönen
N10 N14 N15 versönen N16—N19 versöhnet
33 *verschonet* L2 *adds* deden bote penitentie vor ere
Sünden / strouweden Aschen up ere Höuede; Ferrari
27 ilz se mirent forment a penitence et a humilité
33 *Also . . . erbarmen* B also möcht der Herr auch mit uns
thůn L2 Also wert Godt uns ock don
35 N6 L2 *Sünden* D B sündtlichen leben
35 *bekerten* L2 betern und bekeren; Ferrari 31 nostre vie
voulons amender
35 *inn* D B zwischen
36 D N6 *sein wirdt* B ist

/ denn darnach sol alles besser werden. Alle
secten / welche unzelich sind / als Papisten
/ Calvinisten / Adiaphoristen / Maioristen /
40 Menianisten / Interemisten / unnd wie sie
ein namen haben / sollen inn der zeit
vereiniget werden / Denn die bösen /
verstockten Menschen / sollen mitler zeit
sterben / und also sol in den jaren 1563.
45 alles erfüllet werden was ich schreibe.

50

Die gantze Geistlicheit / sol gar
vernidert werden / und von grossem hunger
55 sehr betrengt / unnd geengstiget / die
Clöster sollen verstöret / und die Münch
unnd Pfaffen so darinnen sindt / sollen inn
grosser armuth verjaget werden / werden
nirgent keine stette haben / da sie können
60 sicher sein. Die Prelaten der Kirchen /
werden sich nicht kleiden mit Sammet /
scharlack / [a2r] punte Röcke / Denn mitler
zeit / sol der Hoff zu Rohm an allen örtern

unde wenn de vyff yar umme synt / so wert
ydt allthomal bether werden / wente alle
Secten der nu so vele syn /

schölen binnen der tydt alle eins syn /
Averst de bösen vorstockeden Minschen
schölen bynnen dessen vyff yaren ere ende
nemen.
Unde also schal dyth bynnen
M.D.LXIII. yaren vorfült werden wat ick
schryve / So wy uns averst worden van
unserm Sündtlicken leevende twyschen
desser tydt / welckere sehr quadt und böse
syn wert / bekeren / velichte mochte Godt
syne gerechte sententien vorkeren / und uns
yn synem torn alse Nynive sparen.
De Geistlicheit schal sehr vorneddert
werden / de Closters schölen werden
vorstöret / unde schölen vordreven werden
yn grotem armode / und nergent keinen
platz vinden sick tho vorbergen.
De Prelaten der Kercken / schölen nicht
gekledet syn mit scharlaken / edder bunten
kledern / denn bynnen dessen tyden / schal
de Hoff tho Rom scheiden van allen Platzen
/

36 D N6 *fünff* B vier L2 *omits*
37 *werden* L2 *adds* van Anno 61 schollen grote düre tide
kamen wenthe up dat Jar 66. so dat etlike lande kein sey
saeth hebben werden / unnde schollens holen laten in
andern landen und dar wert grote beangstinge und bangicheit werden / unde vele minschen werden vor armeth
warden / und wert keyne neringe syn / in den landen /
ock de lästen 4. Jaren werden ganß sere wünderlick syn /
alse van Anno 66. wenthe the 70. tho und in dessen jaren
schöllen im averlande grote gr[a]wsame Pestilentzien
kamen / so wert Godt vele Teiken unde mirakelen seen
lathen / beyde in der Lucht und up Erden / up dat wy uns
minschen van Sünden beteren und bote und Poenitentien
don / wenthe Gott de sprickt / Ick will nicht den Dodt
des Sünders / Sonder dat he sick betere und bekere / und
upsta van sinen sünden.
38 *welche unzelich sind* N B *der* jetzt so vil sein
38 *als Papisten . . . Interemisten* N4 N5 als Papisten /
Calvinisten / Adiaphoristen / Interemisten N7–N19 *omit*
L2 alse Papisten / Calvinisten / Jovisten / Weddertöpers
/ Sacramenterer etc.; Ferrari 63 Car les Juifz, Sarrazins,
Turcqz, Grecz et Tartarins; Brown 498 Judaeos, Saracenos,
Turcas, Tartaros, et Graecos
40 *unnd wie sie ein namen haben* D B L2 *omit*
41 *zeit* N21 *adds* mit uns
42 *vereiniget werden* L2 alle tho nicht syn / unnde ein gelove
syn und dat rechte Evangelium prediken und leren / und
schollen keyne Secten mehr upstaen /
42 *Denn* D Averst B aber; Ferrari 65 Maiz les pecheurs et

maulvais pechans et perseverans
42 *bösen / verstockten* L2 quaden upörschen unde
vorharden
44 *mitler zeit* D bynnen dessen vyff yaren B in disen vier
jaren L2 bynnen disser tidt
45 *sterben* B L2 umbkommen L2 *adds* ock wert Godt
deher slan mit mennigerley Kranckheit
45 *1563* N21 1690 L2 1570
45 *was ich schreibe* B L2 *omit*; Ferrari 68 Et sera ce que
dist acompli dedens l'an de l'Incarnation Nostre
Seigneur Mil IIII[c] LXX.
45–54 D Cf. N6 29–35.
53 *gantze* B ale; Ferrari 70 tout le clergié
53 *gar* D B sehr
56 *Clöster sollen verstöret* L2 Karcken und Closter schollen seer vordestrueret [L3: verstöret] und spoliereth
werden; Ferrari 240 les abbayes destruira
56 *und die Münch . . . sindt* D B *omit*
58 *verjaget* D B vertriben
59 N6 L2 *stette* D platz B ort
61 N6 *Sammet / scharlack / punte Röcke* D scharlaken /
edder bunten kledern N20 non serico, non purpura,
coccino, bysso, aut aliis preciosis vestibus B purpur
scharlach oder weychen Kleydern L2 Purpur edder
Scharlaken; Ferrari 76 non point vestus de pourpre, ne
d'escarlate, ne de nulz autrez riches draps
62 *mitler zeit* D L2 bynnen dessen tyden B inn disen
zeiten
63 *der Hoff zu Rohm . . . werden* B der stůl zů Rom
gestürtzt werden / und der Römisch Hoff zergehn

verschüchtert werden / Da soll wieder
65 Bapst nochl Cardinal / wieder Legat nochl
Bisschoff / noch jemandt von den grossen
Prelaten

(die inn aller Gotteslesterung unnd
70 scheusslicher unzucht leben)
in seinem regiment bleiben. Denn umb irer
hoffart / geitzes / und anderer grossen
sünden mehr / sollen sie verlieren / all ihr
reichthumb / Herrschafft unnd grosse
75 wohnung. Alle grosse Herrn / Fürsten / und
Könige / sollen grossen spott und ungenadt
wider sie uben / sollen sie berauben / aller
ihrer hoheit / pracht / gewalts und ubermuts
/ aller Geistlicher güter / klein unnd gross /
80 welche sie mit lügen unnd mordt zu sich
bracht haben / unnd sie so gar nacket
darstellen / das sie kaum haben werden / ein
geringes kleidt oder tuch / ihren leib damitn
zubedecken / darnach ihr verfolger ihnen
85 günstig sein / Denn sie sollen vertrieben /
unnd verspottet werden / sie sollen lauffen /
aus einem winckel inn den andern / zu
suchen ein stet da sie sich verbergen. Als
sie dann sehen und erfaren diese grosse
90 verachtung / plage unnd verfolgung / die
man ihn anthun wirdt / unnd gleichwol
nicht endern können / sondern leiden
müssen / So wirdt sie solchs vorstendig

Pawest / Cardinale / Bisschoffe / unde grote
Prelaten schölen lopen alle dwalende / und
mit groter pyne schölen se lopen tho söken
wor se blyven mögen.

Se schölen vorlesen alle ere rykedome /
Herschoppye unde schone waninge / wente
alle Försten unde grote Heren schölen
hebben grothen spott / unde unwerde up de
Geistlicheit unde up ere macht unde
rykedome / unde men wert en nehmen alle
ere gudt / groth unde klein / dat se van eren
beneficien hebben / unde men wert e
nouwe lathen ein par lynen [a2r] kleder

darna dat se gesinnet syn / de se quelen und
plagen schölen /

dyth schal enen geven vorstandt / unde se

---

66 *jemand von den grossen Prelaten* B alle grosse Prelaten;
    Ferrari 70 tout le clergié, le pape et ses cardinaulx, patri-
    arches, legatz et tous les prelatz de Saincte Esglise seront
    en ce temps abusez et abaissez

69 D *alle dwalende* L2 alse dulle [L3: affsinnige] Lüde N6 B
    omit

69 *die inn aller Gotteslesterung . . . leben* B die so vol boßheyt
    stecken D L2 *omit*

70 D *mit groter pyne* L2 mit groter smerten N6 B *omit*; Ferrari
    83 Et tous les autres clergiez pareillement s'en fuiront hors
    d'Avignon, querans lieu et place pour demourer, ce que a
    paine trouveront.

71 *in seinem regiment bleiben* L2 inn ere reiyrung nicht mehr
    so dominieren D B *omit*

71 *umb irer hoffart . . . sünden mehr* L2 umme ere grote
    Hovardie giricheyt / und mißbruck willen D B *omit*

74 *grosse* D schone B köstliche L2 herlike

76 *Könige* D B L2 *omit*

77 D B *up ere macht unde rykedome* N6 L2 *omit* B *adds* und
    ihrer grosser hoffart / und wercken die sie den leuten
    verkauffen L2 *adds* van wegen erer groten hoverdien / und
    guden warcken / de se hebben vorgegeven; Ferrari 87 et
    sur leurs possessions et sur la vie pompeuse

80 *welche sie . . . zu sich bracht haben* D B L2 dat se van eren

beneficien [B: Pfründen] hebben

84 *zubedecken* B *adds* und es mag dem einen besser gehen
    / dann dem anderen

84 *darnach . . . günstig sein* B darnach die sein / die
    gewalt uber sie haben

85 *Denn . . . verspottet werden* B dann sie werden sie
    vertreiben / und halten mit ihnen iren spott L2 se
    warden se vordriven und hebben eren spot mit
    enen L2 *adds* Wenthe se werden bedencken dat dar
    geschreven steyth / in Apocalipsis im 17. Cappit: Dar
    de grote Babilönische hore / up einen growsamen
    fennischen deste sith / mit synen sevem Höffeden /
    und einen süverliken Beker in erer handt / und hefft
    eine Krone up erem Hövede / Se wolde sick inde höge
    erheven / So hefft Godt de Here se neddergeslagenn
    und vorbrandt. Darümme dat se de grülike horerye
    bruckede / dat Godt im Hemmel vordraten hefft.

88 *Als sie dann sehen und erfaren* N4 N5 Wenn sie nu
    denn sehen und erfaren B Als sie nun werden hören
    L2 Und wen se nu seen werden; Ferrari 92 Maiz quant
    en ce point lesdits prelatz se verront

93 D *geven vorstandt* B geben einen verstand und
    demüt; Ferrari 94 leur mal et leur affliction leur don-
    nera entendement

machen / das sie mit demuth ihr sünde und
95 gebrechen / bekennen werden / unnd
werden mit weinenden augen unnd heissen
thranen den Herrn anruffen unnd sprechen /
O Herr es ist recht / das wir Creutze und
leiden haben / und diese grosse verfolgung
100 leiden / denn wir gröblich wider dich
gesündiget haben / inn grossem geitz /
hoffart und unkeuscheit / tragheit / und inn
andern unzelichen groben Sünden. Wenn
sie solchs bekennen / unnd ihnen ihr sünde
105 leidt sein lassen / wirdt Gott die Geistlicheit
in ihren ersten standt wider bringen / [a2v]
als sie war im anfanck der Apostoloischen
Kirchen / Man wird ihnen ein zimlichs
wider verschaffen / das sie Gottfürchtig und
110 ehrlich zur nodturfft davon leben können /
Aber grosse pfründe und renten / werden
wie nicht wider bekommen / Auch kein
gewalt odder tyranney / wider ihre Leuth zu
uben erlangen.
115 Es sol uber die Geistlichen / ein solche
plage und ungelück kommen / das es nicht
ausszureden odder zu schreiben ist. Es ist
zu rathen ihr wollet / das neunde Cap.
Ezechielis mit fleis ubersehen und
120 betrachten / da werdet ihr viel seltzame
Prophezeiung in finden / die uber die
Geistlichkeit kommen sollen.
Weiter lieben freunde / lasset euch
nicht bedüncken / das allein uber die
125 Geistlichen / solch angst und verfolgen
kommen werden / Ein jeder Mensch sol

schölen bekennen ere gebreken unde
schölen den Heren mit wenenden ogen
anropen unde seggen /

O Here ydt ys recht dat wy desse grote
vorvolgunge lyden / denn wy hebben sehr
gesündiget / in groter gyricheit /
hoverdicheit unde unküscheit etc.

Wenner se solckes bekennen / denn schal
Godt de Geistlicheit yn eren ersten standt
wedderumme stellen / alse ydt was in dem
anbeginne der Apostoloischen Kercken /
und men schal en einen temeliken standt
ordineren / up dat se Gödtlick unde ehrlick
leeven mögen / Averst ere Lehne / Rente
unde Herschoppie schölen se nicht wedder
krygen.

Desse angest unde tribulatie schal nicht
allene up de Geistlicheit vallen / sunder ein
yeder Minsche schal wol synen deil darvan

96–97 *heissen thranen* B L2 bittern trähern
98 N6 D B *recht* L2 gudt und recht; Ferrari 96 Biau Sire Dieu, c'est a bon droit que ces tourmens cy nous souffrons, car ainsi deservi l'avons par noz pechiez et maulvaise vie
98 *das wir Creutze und leiden haben / und diese grosse verfolgung leiden* N16–N19 das wir Creütz / leyden und grosse verfolgung leyden
102 *tragheit* N4 N5 faulheit
103 *unzelichen groben* B L2 schweren
104 *solchs* B L2 add alles
104 *unnd . . . leidt sein lassen* D omits B und in von gantzem hertzen leyd ist / alles was sie vorhin getriben haben L2 und ere schult bewenen
106 *bringen* D stellen B L2 setzen
108 *ein zimlichs wider verschaffen* D einen temeliken standt ordineren B einen zimlichen auffenthalt ordnen und verschaffen
111 *Aber . . . bekommen* B aber ihr zierde und grosse Herrschafft werden sie nit wider an sich bringen L2 men

ere Renthten so se vorhen gehat / werden si nicht wedder erlangen / noch keyne Herschopien
112–14 *Auch . . . erlangen* D B L2 omit
115 *Es sol . . . schreiben* ist N20 Tale infortunium spirituales manet, et brevi in eos redundaturum est, quod prolatu et consignatu αδύνατον est.
117–18 *Es ist zu rathen* B bedencket es wol was ich euch sag L2 Darümme
120 *seltzame Prophezeiung* B vil wunders L2 wunder; Ferrari 104 Et en ce chapitre IXe de l'Appocalipse, se vous voulez lire et regarder, monlt de merveilles y trouverez qui avenir doit tant sur le peuple baptisé comme sur l'Esglise.
123 *lieben freunde* B mein geliebten L2 Mein leven Christen
124 *bedüncken* L2 erfrouwen
125 *angst und verfolgen* D angest und tribulatie B jamer und trübsal; Ferrari 107 misere et tribulation
126 N6 B *kommen* D L2 vallen; Ferrari 107 venir

sein theil wol darvon bekommen / das
niemandt mit worten seines Gesellens
spotten mag / Dann es sol so viel leides /
130 jammers unnd ungelücks kommen / innen
den jaren / 60. 61. unnd folgendes / uber die
gantze Christenheit / das niemandt / wie
gros auch sein vernunfft und verstandt ist /
dasselbe recht gleuben kann / und auff das
135 die Welt busse thue / sollen geschehen /
grosse unleidliche / und unaussprechliche
zeichen.
Zum ersten / werden kommen würme /
die man meinet gar leicht zu uberwinden /
140 die sollen solche krafft und stercke
uberkommen / das sie werden anlauffen
unnd bey nahe tödten / Lewen / Wolffe /
Leoparden / Drachen / Beeren unnd Ochsen /
Die kleine vöglein / als Meisen / Fincken /
145 Sperling / Lerchen / Droscheln und Staren /
sollen anlauff thun unnd erwürgen mit
grossen hauffen / die Sperber / Falcken
/ Habichte und Greiffe. Dis ist ein gewis
zeichen und anzeigung / das in den
150 furgeschriebenen fünff jaren / alles volck
gar [a3r] traurig / beengstiget unnd betrübet
sein sol / des Creutzes und leidens halben.

krygen / also dat nemandt schal synen
Gesellen mit worden bespotten / wente ydt
schal so vele yammers unde unfals yn dem
LX. unde LXI. yare kamen / und
nafolgende aver de gantze Christenheit dat
nemandt dat sulfftige hedde können
gelöven.

In dem ersten schölen kamen Wörme /
de schölen hebben grote krafft unde
starckheit / unde schölen uplopen / unde
bina vele grote Deerte döden.

Dyth ys ein mercklick teken unde
bewysung / dat bynnen den vyff
vorschreven yaren / alle dat Volck schal
yammerlick bedrücket unde bedrövet

127 N6 B *bekommen* D L2 krygen; Ferrari 107 maiz sur chascun, petit et grant, noble, villain, riche et puissant doit
descendre pareillement
128 D N4–N19 *niemandt mit worten seines Gesellens* N21
niemand mit Worten ein den andern B der ein den andern
L2 de eine des andern
131 60. 61. N21 1687 L2 omits
132–35 *das niemandt . . . busse thue* B omits D L2 dat nemandts
scholde kůnnen gelöven
136 *grosse unleidliche / und unaussprechliche* B grausame und
unerhörte L2 dar so dans gescheen scholde / und darin
dem 70. jare schollen kamen / grusame erschrecklike und
unordentlike [L3: unerhörde] teiken in der Lucht / So dat
dem Minschen gruwen tzettern und bange sin schal so dat
de minschen dargegen nicht konnen den noch mit gelde
edder gudt / und de Riken schall so wol geplaget werden
alse de Armen; cf. Ferrari 107 at line 128.
138 N4–N6 N21 *werden kommen würme* N7–N19 Werden
Wůrme kommen L2 schollen darkamen grote Wörme
139 N4–N6 N21 *leicht* N7–N19 leichtlich
139 *die man . . . uberwinden* B von kleiner macht unnd gewalt
/ das man sie leichtlich kundt uberwinden L2 wunderliker
gestalt / de so licht schollen schinen aver dat Erdricke;
Ferrari 115 combien que de legier ilz seront a prendre et a
conquerir
141 N6 B *uberkommen* D L2 hebben; Ferrari 115 et telle force et
hardiment prenderont

142 *anlauffen* B umbbringen
142–43 *Lewen . . . Ochsen* B Lewen / Wölff / Leoparden /
Drachen / Beren L2 Löwen / Dracken / Wülve / Leoparden / Bern / und alle vehe / ock de Vögels under
dem Hemmel; Ferrari 116 les lyons, lieppars, griffons,
loups, ours, toreaulx
145 *Die kleine vöglein . . . Staren* B omits and adds instead
und auch werden sie umbbringen allerley gefögels
L2 de kleinen Vögels / alse Mesen / Vincken Sprene /
Lewercken / Drosselen Listeren; Ferrari 117 les petis
et menus oiseaulx, comme sont alouettes, merles,
faulvettes
146–47 *erwürgen mit grossen hauffen* B noch werden
sie mit grosser macht und freuden umbbringen L2
schollen sick vorgadderen im hupen / und mit erem
geschrey vorjagen
147 *die Sperber . . . Greiffe* B Griffionen / Habichen /
Falcken / Sperber / etc. L2 Valcken / Haffvick /
Sperver / Griphen / unnd alle groff [L3: graue] Vögel
/ etc.; Ferrari 118 les grans oiseaulx de proie, comme
espreviers, faucons, austours et griffons, et a grant joie
petit a petit les devoueront
148 *gewis* B sicher und gewiß L2 gewissen und sekere
150 *in den furgeschriebenen fünff jaren* B omits L2 binnen
den viff jaren
152 *des Creutzes und leidens halben* D van der qualinge
unde ungenochte N21 B *omit* L2 van wegen der groten
quale unnd ungenöchte

Under der Gemein / sol ein grosser
auffruhr wider die Herrn entstehen / Die
155 Eddelleut werden die vorreter ausskündien /
und zum Schwerdt uberantworten / werden
ihnen nehmen all ihr Gut und reichthumb /
und inn keinen schutz oder friede / hinfort
zu haben / zu lassen. In summa / kein
160 Mensch mag mit dem hertzen erreichen /
oder mit dem munde auff keinerley weis
aussprechen / das böse / verfolgung und den
jammer / der in den tagen / uber Fürsten
unnd Eddelleut kommen sol / Denn in der
165 warheit / ehe diese fünff jar zum ende
kommen / sol untrewe unnd verreterrey
unter den Menschen so sehr begangen
werden / unnd uberhandt nehmen / das
keiner ein gesellen oder compen finden
170 wird / dem er sich möge vertrawen. Noch
sollen dar kommen viel grosse und
erschreckliche plagen / uber die gantze
Welt / von den ungleubigen Sarracenen und
Türcken. Alles was dem Mahomet
175 anhengig ist / wird kommen unnd den
Christen anlauff thun / an allen örtern /
werden verwüsten viel Lande / und
sonderlich Italiam / Ungern / und ein gross
theil Deudtsch Landes. Noch sollen dar
180 kommen viel grosse / unnd unleidliche
plagen uber die gantze welt / darumb hebet
ewre hertzen zu Gott / denn zwischen dem
58. unnd 59. jar / sol uber all ein grosse
schwere Pestilentz / viel grösser denn von

werden / van der qualinge unde ungenochte
/ unde de gemeinte schal dorch einen grote
upror yegen ere Heren upstan / De eddelen
schölen de vorreders vordrengen / unde
thom Schwerde leveren / unde nehmen alle
ere gudt unde rykedome.

Nen Minsche mit dem munde wert uth
spreken dat böse unde vorvolginge dat yn
den dagen kamen schal / up Försten unde
Eddellüth /

und yn der warheit ehr desse vyff yar thom
ende ghan / so schal dar ein solck vordreyt
unde vorrederrye under de Minschen kamen
/ dat dar nemandt [a2v] schal vinden
Gesellen den he mach vortruwen.

Ock schal dar kamen noch vele mehr
vorvolginge yn de Werlt / denn de
ungelövigen Sarracenen unde Törcken
schölen kamen / unde den Christen an allen
syden uplop don / unde schölen ock
vorstören vele Lande / unde sonderlick
Italien / Ungern unde einen groten deel van
Düdeschem lande. Ock schal dar aver all /
eine grote schware pestilentie geschehen.

153 *Under der Gemein . . . entstehen* B und die gemeyn wirt in
grosser andacht den HERREN anrüffen L2 Ock wert sick
de gemeine van groter Raserie jegen ere Heren up heven
155 *die vorreter ausskündien* B acht haben auff alle verrähter /
und wa sie die selbigen bekommen L2 umme bringen
156 N6 B *uberantworten* D leveren L2 vordammen / wente en
schon leff edder leidt were
158 *und inn . . . zu lassen* B und nit mer erbarmung mit ihnen
haben / als wenn es hund weren L2 unnd nicht mehr
barmherticeit ene bewisenn efft hebben / alse mit einem
hunde; Ferrari 123 desquelz ne tiendront conte non plus
que de chiens, et ja pitié n'en auront
159 *In summa* B Nun was wölt ihr das ich euch mehr sag L2
Wat will ick mehr schriven; Ferrari 124 Que voulez vous
plus que je vous die?
163–64 *Fürsten unnd Eddelleut* N21 uns
164 *Denn* B unnd ich sag das L2 und gewisse
165 N6 D *fünff* B L2 vier; Ferrari 129 les V ans
166 *untrewe unnd verreterrey* D vordreyt unde vorrederrye B
jamer und verrähterey L2 jammer und elendt
169 N6–N19 *keiner ein gesellen oder compen* N4 N5 keiner
keinen gesellen N21 keiner keinen Menschen D nemandt

schal vinden Gesellen B keiner seinem Freündt / oder
gesellen L2 men keyne truw; Ferrari 151 Adoncques
courra fort traÿson, fraude, malice et deception, et
tant que ung seul compaignon on ne pourra trouver
ouquel on se puisse et ose hardiment fier.
172 *uber* D B in L2 *omits*
173 *Welt* N21 Reich
174 *Alles . . . anhengig ist* B und alles was von Mahomets
glauben ist L2 und dat van Machomets geloven is
175 N6 D *unnd den Christen* B *omits* L2 unter de Christen
176 N6 D *anlauff thun* B beängstigen L2 vordrengen /
und vorjagenn
176 *örtern* B enden D L2 syden
176 *an allen örtern / werden verwüsten viel Lande*
N16–N19 vil Lande und örther verwüsten
181 *darumb . . . Gott* B darumb fürchten den HERREN
von gantzem hertzen D L2 *omit*
182 *zwischen dem 58. unnd 59. jar* N21 zwischen den 88.
und 89. Jahr B in disen zeiten L2 twischen dem Lxviii.
jare wente thom Lxix
184 *schwere Pestilentz* B theüre zeit und Pestilentz
184 N6 *viel grösser . . . ergehen* L2 groter alse jemande
gehöret edder gedacht hefft D B *omit*

185 jemandt erdacht künte werden / ergehen.
Unnd von erst vorkündige ich euch ein
grosse theure zeit / darnach ein schrecklich
ungewitter / das niemandt / der von
mutterleib geboren ist / grösser gesehn hat.
190 Die Wasser sollen in vielen Stetten so gross
sein / das alle Menschen sich darüber
entsetzen werden. [a3v] Viel Lande und
Stette sollen gar uneinig unnd zweytrechtig
sein / und grosse angst leiden / sonderlich
195 in Italia und Franckreich / und auch ine
andern Landen / also / das viel Leute
dardurch inn gross armuth und gebrechen
kommen werden / die narung wird gar
vergehen / niemandt wird mit dem andern
200 mitleiden haben / welchs ein grosser
jammer sein wird. Diese plage von
Zweitracht / Krieg / Ungewitter und
Sterben / sol uber die gantze welt ergehen /
biss auff das 62. Jar / sie sol ihren anfang
205 nehmen zwischen Italien und Franckreich.
Darumb keret ewer hertzen zu Gott / alle
Menschen die ihr gnade begeret von dem
Herrn / denn von dem 59. jar / sol
Franckreich inn grosse noth kommen / das
210 (so fern unser Herr Gott seinen zorn nicht
abwendet) alle Fürsten / Graffen / Banner
Herr / Ritter und Eddelleut desselbigen
Königreichs / sollen in dieser zeit also
ernidriget unnd geschwechet werden / das
215 sie wider sich noch andere / mügen
beschützen oder verteidigen / denn die
Frantzosen sollen zu thun haben / wider
grosses und gewaltiges volck. Es ist nicht in
meinem vormügen / die verfolgung

Thom ersten segge ick juw eine grot
düre tydt / darna ein grot unwedder und
unstümicheit / dat nemandt mehr gesehen
hefft / de water schölen yn velen Steden
groth syn / dat alle Man / wo köne he ock
sy / sick des ock wert vorschrecken / vele
Lande unde Stede schölen ym groten
twydrachte syn / unde groten angst lyden /
Sonderlick yn Italia / Gallia / unde ock
andern landen / also dat vele dardorch tho
grotem armode kamen schölen / wente de
neringe schal gantz uth dem Lande syn /

unde desser plage unde twydrachte / kryge /
unwedder / schal de gantze Werlt dorch vol
syn / beth thom yare LXII.
Unde dyth ungelücke schal thom
allerersten geschehen twischen Italia unde
Franckryck /
Im yar LIX. schal dat Könickryke van
Franckryke yn groten nöden (krygeshalven)
syn / wenthe der eddelen Försten unde
Ridders macht unde gewalt ehre unde name
schal binnen desser tydt / dar se mede
vormehret syn / also vorneddert werden /
dat se sich sulvest edder andere nicht
mögen beschütten unde vordedigen / Wente
de Frantzosen schölen heben veel tho don
yegen eine grote macht van Volcke.
Idt ys yn mynem vormöge nicht dat ick
de tribulation alle beschryven möge /

---

187 *schrecklich* D B L2 gross
190 N6 D *gross sein* B hoch erheben L2 hoch und grot syn
190 D *wo köne he ock sy* B wie fromm sie auch seind N6
    L2 *omit*; Ferrari 157 et nul homme, tant soit hardy ne
    courageux, ne aussi fort et robuste, ne de grant cuer, qui
    n'en doie a les ouyr avoir grant hideur et grant paour, et
    trembler comme la feulle en l'arbre
197 *gebrechen* N21 Gefahr
199 *vergehen* L2 vor gan D uth dem Lande syn B auß den
    landen sein / also / das ir vil gezwungen werden in dz
    ellend zülauffen
204 *biss auff das 62. Jar* N21 biß auff das 89. Jahr L2 und gar
    dodt liggen
206 *keret . . . gnade begeret* N4 N5 N21 keret ewer hertzen zu
    Gott / alle menschen die gnade begeren B alle die gnad
    begeren / keret ewere hertzen zů dem Herren D L2 *omit*
206 *alle Menschen* N16–N19 *omit*
209 *Franckreich* D Köninckryke van Franckryck B Königreich
    Franckreich; Ferrari 165 dedens l'an LXV le royaulme de
    France sera en grant peril d'estre perdu et destruict

209 D *krygeshalven* L2 kriegshalben
210 *so fern . . . abwendet* D B L2 *omit*; Ferrari 166 se Dieu
    ne le garde
211 *alle Fürsten . . . verteidigen* B dann alle macht der
    edlen Baronen und Rittern / wirt gantz darnider ligen
    / also / das sie ihnen selbs nicht werden helffen kön-
    nen; Ferrari 166 Especialement car en ce temps la sera
    toute sa baronnie, sa force, puissance et chevalerie, sa
    prouesse et sa grant renommee si amendrie et ravalee,
    que l'un l'autre ne pourra aider, conseiller ne con-
    forter, ne les gens d'Esglise ne le clergé deffendre ne
    garder. . . . Car, se la puissance de France demouroit
    en estat, en honneur, en force et en vigueur, jamaiz
    le clergié de luy departir ne souffreroit, ne Antecrist
    aussi prescher ne regner ne le laisseroit.
219 *verfolgung* D tribulation B grosse angst und trübsal /
    die in Franckreich geschehn soll / Aber wölt ir lesen;
    Ferrari 179 Ne on ne pourroit dire ne escripre la grant
    tribulation et martire que es V ans aprez LX sur les
    François doit avenir. Maiz ce le chappitre VIIe de
    Ezechiel voulez lire

220 zubeschreiben / leset das 5. Capit.
Ezechielis / da werdet ihr inn finden / den
grossen jammer / der uber Franckreich
unnd die Frantzosen / inn diesen fünff jaren
/ wie vor geschrieben / ergehen sol.

225 Darnach sol kommen ein falscher
Hednischer Keyser / aus Nidergang mit
denen von Auffgang / unnd sol kommen
das gantze Landt niderwartz / Dieser sol die
Christen also martern und peinigen / mit

230 seiner grausamkeit / das er nichts
verschonen wird / sondern alles verwüsten
unnd zerbrechen / darüber er macht
bekümbt.

Alles leiden unnd verfolgung / von

235 anbegin der welt / [a4r] ist nicht
zuvorgleichen mit den plagen / die ergehen
sollen beim Regiment dieses Keysers / denn
keine Stadt odder Festung / wie gross unnd
starck sie auch sein / werden für ihme

240 können bleiben. Wenn man schreiben wird
1561. sol verwüstet werden / was
uberblieben ist / durch ungewitter unnd
krieg / welche die gantze welt durchziehen
sollen / so sol die welt in grossem leiden

245 sein / bis auffs 63. jar / Das ein iglicher
Mensch / wol wehr zubekleiden mit den
kleidern unnd waffen / der tugendt und
gedult / auff das er nicht inn verzweiffelung
falle.r

250 Nu habt ihr gehort / wie das die
Christen sollen geplaget werden mit
verfolgung / angst / hunger und kriege. Nu
wollet ihr auch hören / unnd lernen / die
erste Artzeney oder lehr / wie dieser

255 persecution odder verfolgung / zuentfliehen

sonder leset dat v. Capittel Ezechielis /
darynne schöle gy vinden de grote
vorvolginge / so yn Franckryck geschehen
schal up de Frantzosen bynnen dessen vyff
yaren vam LVIII. an wente LXIII.
Unde ydt schal kamen ein valsch
Heydensch Keiser uth Occident mit den van
Orient unde schal kamen alle dat [a3r]
Landt nedder / desse schal pynigen de
gantze Christenheit unde alle tho nichte
maken unde thobreken / so fern he de
macht hefft/

unde dewyle desse Keiser regert / kann nen
stadt edder Schlott wo starck se syn / vor
em bestan / unde alse men schryven wert
M.D.LXI. dat dar ys bestande bleven / schal
noch vort vorstört werden / dorch unwedde
kryg etc. dorch de gantzen Werlt / unde tho
dem yar LXIII. schal de Werlt yn grotem
lydenden syn / und yn dessen tyden scholde
wol ein yder Minsche sick mit dem wapen
und kledern der döget unde gedult kleden /
up dat he nicht yn twyvelinge kame.

Dewyle wy nu gehört hebben wo de
Christenheit schal mit angst van sterven /
hungers unde krygeshalven geplaget
werden / So höret nu ock unde vatet yn
yuwem herten dat erste remedium gegen
desse grote tribulation / wente Godt leret

226 *aus Nidergang mit denen von Auffgang* B mitten von Occident unnd Orient

229 *martern und peinigen* D pynigen B tribulieren L2 vorvol-
gen

230 N6–N19 *grausamkeit* N4 N5 Tyranney N21 Tyranney B
bosheyt L2 groter gewalt also dat he nemandt wert sparen
/ und alles slicht maken / dar tho en Godt geschicket hefft

234 Alles . . . *ergehen sollen* B Alles das leiden seit die Welt
gestanden / ist nicht zů vergleichen dem / das geschehn
wirt D L2 *omit*

237 *beim Regiment dieses Keysers* D dewyle desse Keiser regert
B weil diser Keyser Regieret

238 *Festung* D Schlott B Schlösser; Ferrari 257 Encores dit ledit
Cordelier que monlt de tres notables citez, des pays et des
royaulmes seront en peril de subversion et destruction

239 *werden für ihme können bleiben* N21 werden für einen auff-
steigenden grossen Monarchen sich kaum bergen können

241 *1561* N21 1689

245 *63* N21 91

245–49 *Das ein iglicher Mensch . . . falle* L2 Darůmme
waket up vam slape und wapet jw mit dögetsamheit /
unde vortwivelt nicht

252–53 *Nu wollet . . . zuentfliehen sey* D L2 Nu wöllet doch
vort hören und thoherten nemen / de erste Remedie
düsser vorvolging und tribulatien B *omits*; Ferrari 285
dont je vous prie que les remedes veuillez ouyr et en
voz cuers retenir. Pour eviter icelles afflictions et grans
persequtions, Dieu les nous aprent et monstre en
l'Euvangile: le premier remede si est que ung chascun
bien se doit garder que par autruy ne soit deceu

257 D *mit uprichtigem . . . und bote* L2 dat men ein upre-
cht herte und bote / van wegen unser sünde hebben /
des wil he nicht denn dodt des Sünders / sunder dat
he sick beker und leve B das wir zů ihm sollen rüffen
in der not / so wil er uns erhören

sey. Gott leret unns im Evangelio / das man
ihn sol anruffen mit demuth / im rechten
glauben / und mit auffhören von sünden /
das er uns wolle unsere sünde verzeihen /
260 unnd im Creutze und widerwertigkeit
gedult verleihen. Die andere lehr ist / das
ein jeder Mensche / der im vermügen ist /
sich vorradt auff fünff jar verschaffe / das
er sich hungers in den fünff zukomenden
265 jaren erwehren könne / Denn ihr solt wissen
/ (wie auch vor gesagt) das von dem 58. jar
biss zum 63. so grosse noth und gebrechen /
theurer zeit unnd hungers halben inn allen
landen sein wird / das vielleicht viel
270 Menschen / hungers und theurer zeit halben
sterben müssen / unnd werden alle
Menschen / sehr solcher theurer zeit halben
erschrecken. Der ist klug und recht
vorsichtig / der sein vorradt bis auffs 64. jar
275 machen wird / denn als dann sol alles
ungelück fur uber sein. Auch solt ihr wissen
das in Deudtschlandt / Burgundien und
Hispanien [a4v] gross erdtbiben geschehen
sol. Wenn wir inn solchem grossen leiden
280 sind / werden auch falsche Propheten
auffstehen / die sollen das volck / durch
ihre falsche lehr / wünderlicher ding
uberreden / Darumb sehet euch für / das ihr
euch auff ewer eigen vernunfft und
285 weissheit nicht verlasset / wenn ihr kommet
sie zu hören / oder ihr zeichen und
wunderwerck (die zie thun werden) zu
sehen / Denn Gott wird ihnen unser sünde
halben mancherley zulassen / der Teuffel
290 wird durch sie gar listig handeln / die Leute
zubetriegen unnd von Gott abzukeren /
Wehr derhalben mein radt / das die

uns yn dem Evangelio / dat wy schölen en
mit uprichtigem und othmödigem herten
anropen mit rechter warer ruwe und bote /
dat he uns will quyd schelden unse grote
Sünde und missedadt / und wolde uns
geven gedult yn unsem lydende.
Dat ander remedium ys / dat ein ytzlick
Minsche de jenige macht hefft / vorradt
schaffe V. yar / umme dat leevene tho
beholdende yegen desse thokamende lesten
V. yare vam LVIII. beth tho dem LXIII.
yare / wente binnen den vyff yaren schal so
grote noth unde gebreck van dürer tydt yn
allen Landen syn / dat sick alle Minschen
schölen entsetten /

Averst wenn men schryven wert LXIIII. so
schal ydt alles gedan unde vulendet syn /

---

256 *Gott leret unns im Evangelio* B Nun leret uns der HERR L2
Godt de Here lerth uns in dem Evangelio; cf. Ferrari 285 at
line 253

259 *das er . . . gedult verleihen* B darumb wil es von nöten sein
/ das wir fleißsig zům HERREN rüffen und bitten / er
möcht villeicht ettwas linderen / etc. L2 des wil he gerne
unse sünde und Missedhat vorgeven / so wy uns tho em
bekeren

267 D *wente binnen den vyff yaren* B Ehe dise vier jar für uber
sein

267 N6 *so grosse noth . . . erschrecken* D so grote noth unde
gebreck van dürer tydt yn allen Landen syn / dat sick alle
Minschen schölen entsetten N21 so grosse Noth / theure
Zeit und Hunger in allen Landen seyn wird / daß vielleicht viele Menschen hungers sterben müssen; Ferrari 292
sera si grant chiereté et si grant famine par tout le pays que

tout le monde en sera esbahy

274 N4–N8 N21 *bis auffs* N9–N19 auffs

276–83 N6 Cf. D 316–25.

277 *Deudtschlandt* D L2 Almanien; not in Ferrari (cf. 293–
94); Brown 504 Tertium remedium est considerare
signa quae Christus dat ibidem, scilicet, terribiles
terraemotus, qui fuereunt hoc ano in Alamania,
Burgundia et Hispania

279 *sol* L2 *adds* Nu hebben gy twe Remedien int erst
gehört

283 *uberreden* D L2 wyss maken

290 *gar listig handeln* D L2 sehr listich syn B grossen list
ankeren

292–97 *Wehr derhalben . . . zuentfliehen* D B L2 *omit;* Ferrari 300 Et pour ce vouldroie je bien conseiller sur ce
fait: que chascun s'en alast hors de la voie, et voulsist

Menschen (die nicht wollen vergifftet
werden mit derselbigen falschen lehre)
295 wollten dieselbigen meiden / heimliche
örter unnd winckel suchen / wo sie nur
könten / solchem bösen zuentfliehen. Die
dritte lehr solchem unglück zuentfliehen ist
/ das wir uns mit Gotes hülffe / von aller
300 wollust enthalten / unnd uns von allen
sünden bessern / nach unserm vermügen
mit warhafftiger rew und busse / Denn ihr
solt wissen / das alle verharte und
verstockte / die inn ihren sünden liegen
305 bleiben / sollen in grosser angst unnd noth
sterben / Es wird sie ihr gros vorradt nicht
helffen / den sie sich verschafft haben /
Denn es sollen nicht alle Menschen in
hunger / schwerdt oder kireg sterben /
310 sondern etliche auch durch mancherley
unfal / von der welt weg genommen werden
/ als durch gross ungewitter / durch
erhöhung und wachsung der wasser / oder
durch erdbibung / welche keines standes
315 schonen werden.

320

325
Zu derselbigen zeit als der unchristliche
Keyser und Tyran regieret / wird der H[e]rr
erwecken zwen fromme und heilige Menner

Darumme mögen wol alle Minschen
warhafftige poenitentien don / van eren
Sünden na unsem armen vormögen /
denn gy schölen weten / dat alle / de yn erer
bossheit vorblendet und vorhart syn / de
schölen all yn grotem armode und
bangicheit sterven / denn en schal nicht
mögen helpen alle ere vorsichticheit de se
don / wente se sterven nicht alle dorch dat
schwerdt / edder krygeshalven / sunder se
schölen nochdans dorch andere ungelücke /
unde tribulation sterven / als nömliken van
unwedder / effte averfloth [a3v] des waters
/ edder dorch Erdtbevinge / welckere noch
alle geschehen werden / wente gy schölen
mercken / dat yn Almanien / Burgundien
unde Hispanien schölen Erdtbevinge
geschehen.
In dessem groten lydende schölen
falsche Propheten ock upstan / de schölen
dar dem volcke uth Gades vorhencknis
dorch ere falsche lere wunderlike dinge
wyss maken / und de Düvel schal sehr
listich syn / umme de guden minschen tho
bedregende up dat se sick van Gade wenden
schölen /
Darna tho densulvigen tyden
wenn desse ungelövige Keyser und Tyranne
regeren schal / So schal de Here erwecken

querir trous, creux et cavernes et lieux secrez, comme
soubz terre, pour luy mucier et abscondre, et pour iceulx
Antecrizt fuir et eviter.

300 D *Darumme mögen . . . alle geschehen werden* L2 Vordan
dat ander Remedium / is dat syck ein minsche entholde
van aller unküscheit / Drunckenschop / Horerye / wenthe
de dat doen / schollen dath Rike Gades nicht besitten
/ alse geschreven stet dat wy van allen unsen sünden
affstan / wente gy söllen vorstan / alle de vorstockth unde
vorhardeth bliven / schollen in ehrer bossheit sterven /
So se nicht in Krige und Orloch umme kamenn / Sunst
werden se doch mit andern ungelücke van der Werlt wech
genamen werden

301 N4–N19 *bessern* N21 ablassen D poenitentien don L affstan; Ferrari 309 Le Ve remede est feable et bon: c'est que
de noz vices et de noz pechiez, desquelz nous sommes
monlt entechiez, nous abstenons; et que nostre vie cor-

rigons de toutes impietez et maulvaistié, de toutes ires,
rancunes, crimes, haynes. Et faice ung chascun penitence en vraie confession de ses pechiez et repentance

307 N6 *sich* N4 N5 N21 inen

310 *durch mancherley unfal / von der welt weg genommen
werden* L2 mit andern ungelücke van der Werlt wech
genamen werden D dorch andere ungelücke / unde
tribulation sterven; Ferrari 318 Et s'i ne finent par
guerre ou par bataille, c'est a dire par l'espee, si mour-
ront ilz par autre tribulascion

316–25 D cf. N6 276–83

326 *Zu derselbigen zeit* B Nun dieweil diß alles geschehen
soll D Darna tho densulvigen tyden L2 Darna tho den
sülven tiden

326 *der unchristliche Keyser und Tyran* B der Tyrannische
Keyser D desse ungelövige Keyser und Tyranne L2
düsse ungelövige Keyser und leres

/ die gekleidet sein werden mit tugenden
330 unnd heiligkeit / die sollen predigen / das
ware und reine wort Gottes / wieder die
fal[s]che Lehrer / sollen von [b1r] Gott
grosse macht haben / uber gut und uber
böse / Sie sollen nicht umbracht können
335 werden / durch eingerley sterbliche Creatur
oder menschen /
Uber dis alles / sollen sie von Gott grosse
macht haben / das ungleubige und
halstarrige volck zu schlagen und zu plagen
340 / wormit es ihnen belieben wird / gleichwol
wirdts niemandts fülen oder gewar werden /
Sie sollen von Gott dem Herrn haben macht
und gewalt / allerley zeichen zu thun / was
sie nur wollen / hier auff erden / darmit die
345 Menschen zu tugenden zuerwecken / sollen
also gar durch die Lender predigen und
verkündigen / den tag des Herrn / wider die
falsche lehrer / der da viel sollen sein.
Darnach sol einer aus den zwen
350 erwelet werden / von den rechten Christen
zu einem öbersten Bisschoff / der sol die
heilige Apostolische Kirchen widerumb
bestellen / die so lang ist verwüstet gewesen
/ Er wird sein leben in grosser heiligkeit zu
355 bringen / das er wird sein ein spiegel aller
tugent. Die geschickt und wirdig sind / sol
er underhalten / unnd ihnen zum
predigampt helffen. Darnach wird man
nicht gros achten Menschen gewalt / unnd
360 umb geldes willen / wird man keine grosse
pfründe und Bistumb besitzen / allein die es
wirdig sind / unnd das wort des Herrn
verkündigen können / sollen erwelet
werden wie im anfang der heiligen
365 Apostolischen Kirchen / wenn es auch die
aller geringsten fur der welt anzusehen

twe Godt früchtige und hillige Menner de
gekledet schölen syn / mit dögenden und
mit Godtfrüchtiger hillicheit / und se
schölen predigen dat warhafftige wordt
Gades yegen de falsche lerers und schölen
van Gade grote macht hebben aver gudt
unde quadt / se schölen nicht vordrücket
werden mögen / dorch yenige sterfflike
Creaturen edder Minschen / unde baven alle
dyth schölen se hebben van Gade grote
macht / dat ungelövige unde hartnackige
Volck tho schlan / wormit ydt en beleven
schal / unde nochtans schal nemandt weten
effte völen /

Darna schal ein van den twen gekaren
werden van den guden Christen tho einem
aversten Bisschoppe / de schal de hillige
Apostolische kercken wedder vorheven de
lange vorstöret ys gewest / Unde he schal
ein Speigel unde vorgenger syn yn allen
dögetlichen wercken / unde desulvigen so
es werdich syn / schal he underholden /
unde tho dem predichampte vorheven /
Darna schal men nicht vele holden van
veler groter Lüde macht / unde ydt schal
nemandt grothe pröven effte Bisschopdome
umme geldes willen besitten / sunder de
allene / de es werdich syn / unde dat wordt
des Heren vorkündigen / denn se schölen
gekaren werden / alse ym anfange der
hilligen Apostolischen Kercken /

329–30 *mit tugenden unnd heiligkeit* B mit tugendt D mit
    dögenden und mit Godtfrüchtiger hillicheit L2 mit wis-
    sheit und dögedenn / und Gads früchten; Ferrari 325 deux
    Cordeliers rempliz de saincte vie
331 *ware und reine* D B L2 warhafftige
333 *uber gut und uber böse* B omits D aver gudt unde quadt L
    aver gude und quade
334 *umbracht* D vordrücket L vordrucket B und niemand wirt
    sie können letzen; Ferrari 330 Et ne pourront estre de nul
    homme mortel empeschiez ne grevez
347 *tag* B zůkunfft L2 dat L3 omits
348 N6 L2 *lehrer* B Propheten
350 *rechten Christen* D L2 guden Christen B frommen
353 *bestellen* D vorheven B auffrichten L2 uprichten

355 *das er wird sein ein spiegel aller tugent* B L2 N16–N19
    omit
357 *underhalten* L2 vorvorderen
358 D *nicht vele holden van veler groter Lüde macht* L2
    nicht vele holden van groter lüden macht; Ferrari 343
    car pour ou ne pour argent que on sceut presenter ne
    donner, prebendes ne benefices nulz homs ne aura
363 N6 *sollen erwelet werden* N20 eligentur N21 B omit D
    schölen gekaren werden L2 sollen den geordineret
    werden; Ferrari 347 car le Sainct Pere ordonnera,
    comme il estoit en l'ancien temps, que les eveschiez
    seront esleuz des colleges et des esglises qui en def-
    fauldront et mestier en auront
365 *Kirchen* B adds unnd alle ding werden ordentlich
    zůgehen
365 *wenn es . . . anzusehen weren* D B L2 omit

weren / Ablas / Seelmessen unnd des
andern Teuffels drecks mehr / sollen gar
sterben / ein jeder sol sein Kirchenampt an
370 seinem ort aussrichten / sie werden nur
zimliche underhaltung haben.
Zu derselbigen zeit sol entstehen ein
Keyser / des gewalt sol sich strecken uber
die gantze Welt / derselbige wird so from
375 und Gottfürchtig sein / das er von [b1v]
jung und alt / reich unnd arm / geliebet wird.
werden / er sol auch keine Krone auff
seinem Heupt tragen / umb Christi willen /
der mit scharffen dörnen umb unser sünde
380 willen / gekrönet wardt / auch sol er der
heiligen Apostolischen Kirchen getrewe
sein / und sol alles volbringen / nach
seinem vermügen / was Gottes ehr belanget
/ und ist gewiss und war / das durch diese
385 zwo personen / als durch den Keyser unnd
Bisschoff die Welt (welche zuvor in grosser
angst und bekümmernis war) wider zu
ehren und frieden gebracht sol werden. Sie
sollen die ungleubigen Secten alle ausrotten
390 / es sey dann das sie sich bekehren / dann
sollen sie wider zu gnaden kommen. Der
merer theil wird seine falsche opinion

Afflate / Seelmissen etc.
schölen alle tho nichte werden / unde den
denst der Kerchen schal ein yeder don up
syne Landtsprake.

[a4r] Binnen densulvigen tyden schal
dar up stan ein Keiser unde syne macht
schal strecken aver de gantzen Werlt / de
schal ein sodan Förste syn / dat he schal
gelevet werden van Jungen unde Olden /
Ryck unde arm / unde he schal de krone up
syn Hövet umme Christus willen nicht
setten edder dragen /

unde he schal ydt alle vullenbringen na
synem vormögen / dat der ehre Gades
angheit etc.
By dessen twen werdigen Personen als
nömliken dem aversten Bisschop unde dem
Keyser schal de Werlt
wedder yn frede unde gelücke gestelt
werden / Se schölen de ungelövigen Secten
utroden unde tho nichte maken / ydt sy
denn dat se sick bekeren / als denn wert
men se yn gnaden gerne annemen.

367 *Ablas / Seelmessen . . . sterben* B und man wirt nit vil auff
Messen / Seelmeß / etc. halten L2 unde de meisten diel /
de in vortiden alse Mönick papen / und mit Villien und
Seelmessen hebben umme gan werden iren spot daruth
hebben
368 *des andern Teuffels drecks mehr* N16–N19 anders der
gleichen
369 N6–N15 *sterben* N16–N19 absterben N4 N5 vergehen N21
vergehen und auffhören
369 *ein jeder . . . underhaltung haben* B dann allein die das
wort Gottes rein und lauter predigen D unde den denst
der Kerchen schal ein yeder don up syne Landtsprake
L2 Den schal idt tho Nye syn / und wart dem denn dinst
Gades in allen landen / einen jeder up syne spracke na
older gewonheit / also se plegen in der Apostelen tiden
tho gebruken und predigen / uff dat hoff schal umme
getagen werden. So dat idt ein ander besitten schall / so
man list in dem Evangelio und in den warcken der Apostel
schreven stat / Alse de Aposteln den Heren fragden waner
de Jüngst dach solde sin do sprack Jesus tho ene / waner
gy seen dat de Figenboem begünneth tho knopende / so
wethe gy dat de Sommer harde by ist / und wan gy seen
teiken und mirakelen in der lucht / So sollen gy wethen /
dat de dach des Hern hard by ist / ock schollen gy seggen /
alse de Here sprickt / Dyn wille geschee wo im Hemmel /
also ock up Erden.
374–75 *so from und Gottfürchtig* D ein sodan Förste B ein
solcher Fürst L2 so dan ein printze; Ferrari 358 de monlt

377 *sol* B *adds* nimmer L2 *adds* nimmermehr; Ferrari
360 car jamais couronne sur son chief ne portera, en
l'onneur du roy Jhesus
378 *tragen* D setten edder dragen B setzen L2 dregen; cf.
Ferrari 360 at line 377
380 *der mit scharffen dörnen . . . gekrönet wardt* D *omits* B
der umb unsere sünden gekrönt ist worden / mit einer
dörnen kronen L2 De mit scharpen dornen Krone
umme unser aller sunde willen gekrönet is geworden
383 *belanget* D angheit L2 angeith
384 N4–N10 *und ist gewiss und war* N12–N19 Und es ist
gewiß und war L2 Und duth is warhafftigen war D B
omit
386 *Bisschoff* B obgemelter Bischoff D aversten Bisschop
L2 averste Bischkop
386 *welche zuvor . . . bekümmernis war* D B *omit*
387 *zu ehren und frieden* D yn frede unde gelücke B in
grosser einigkeyt L2 in freden und einicheit; Ferrari
368 mettera a delivrance, a paix et a seureté
389 *ausrotten* D utroden unde tho nichte maken B verfolgen L2 vordelgen und umme bringen laten
391 *zu gnaden kommen* D yn gnaden gerne annemen
B gern annemen L2 mit gnaden annemen; Ferrari
369 maiz se a Dieu se veullent retourner, et de leurs
pechiez amender, et leur faulse loy delaisser, tous
voulentiers les prendra a mercy391 *Der merer theil . . .
Tauffe entpfangen* B unnd die ungleubigen werden

saincte vie et de grant saincteté

verleugnen / Die ungleubigen sollen
Machomets Religion verleugnen / und von
395 den Christen die heilige Tauffe entpfangen.
Darnach im jar 1564. sol eine Religion
unnd Glaube sein / denn wird nicht mehr
nötig sein / einigerley wehr zutragen / Denn
vorgenanter Bisschoff und Keyser / sollen
400 eine ordinantie machen / das niemand
tragen solle einigerley waffen / darmit man
jemand tödten kann / unnd wer darwider
thut / den wird man umbbringen / mit
denselbigen waffen die man bey ihm findet
405 / sonder allerley appellation unnd
richtlichen process.
Die gantze Welt / sol zur einigkeit
geneiget sein / denn man wird inn rechten
verordenen hinfort zu allerzeit inn eintracht
410 zu bleiben / ja es sol ein solche einigkeit
sein / welcher gleich von der Welt
schöpffung nicht gewesen ist.
Darnach sol der Keyser ubers Mehr
ziehen / das gelobete landt eröbern / und
415 dar den Christlichen glauben verkündigen
lassen / wenn das ausgericht / sol er wider
kommen / unnd wird die Welt und sein
Keyserthumb [b2r] verlassen / er wird
darnach ein heilich leben füren. Er wird
420 nach sich lassen einen / der nach ihme das
landt weisslich regieren wird / aber es wird
nicht lang wehren. Sein regiment sol 15. jar
wehren / Der Oberste Bisschoff wird mit

Idt schal ym Jahre LXIIII. ein Gelove
unde ein Gesette syn / unde de
vorbenömede twe personen schölen maken
eine ordinantien / dat nemandt schal dragen
yennige wapen edder wehre / dar men
yemandt mochte mede döden /
unde wol wedder dat sulfftige dede / de
schal sterven mit dem sulven wapen / dat
bye em gefunden wert / sunder alle gnade
recht edder Statuten.

Darna schal de Keyser tehen aver dat Meer
unde gewinnen dat hillige Landt / unde
schal denn wedder keren unde de Werlt
sampt dem Keyserrick vorlathen /

Unde he wert einen na sick lathen / de na
eim dat landt wyssliken regeren wert /
averst ydt schal nicht lange waren / denn
syn regiment schal waren XV. Jar unde de

Mahomet verlassen / und keren sich zů Christo D L2 *omit*;
Ferrari 370 Desquelx monlt on trovera que la loy faulse de
Mahommet delaisseront et le sainct baptesme receveront
396 *jar* N12–N15 *omit*
396 *eine Religion unnd Glaube* D ein Gelove unde ein Gesette
B ein Gesetz und ein Glaub L2 ein Godt / ein Gelove;
Ferrari 372 et tant generalement que par tout le monde ne
sera que une loy et une creance, c'est assavoir une foy
401 N4–N6 *tragen solle* N7–N19 *omit*
403 *wird man umbbringen* B getödt werden D L2 sterven;
Ferrari 378 car le Sainct Pere et le sainct empereur roy
de France feront ensemble ung tel decret et une telle
ordonnance que nul ne portera armeures desquelles on
puisse grever, occirre ne tuer sus la mort, se nul estoit en
armeures trouvé ne seu, tant prestement sans enquerir ne
trouver autre jugement; Brown 506 praefatus repara-
tor, ad orbis pacificationem, constituet nova decreta
contra omnia vitia, non modicum dura hoc suo tempore,
secundum Hildegardis vaticinium, ad fovendam pacem
millennariam, ut quicunque arma bellica praesumpserit,
cum eisdem occidatur sine dispensatione quacunque

407 *Die gantze Welt . . . gewesen ist* B und es wirt als dann
ein grosse eintrechtigkeyt sein in der gantzen Welt
L2 und den schal de gantze Warlt geneyget syn tho
frede und einicheyt / und werden gude Pollicien mit
eindrechtigheit anrichten / alse idt van anfanck der
Werlt gewesen ist; Ferrari 382 Et encores feront ilz autre ordonnance, affin que, quant le monde sera rapaié,
paix soit par tout, concorde et tranquilité.
414 *das gelobete landt* L2 dat landt van geloffden D dat hillige Landt B dz heilige Landt; Ferrari 388 Lequel doit
conquester par force le royaulme de Jherusalem et de
la Saincte Terre d'Oultremer.
417 *die Welt und sein Keyserthumb* D de Werlt sampt dem
Keyserrick B das Keyserthumb L2 de Warlt; Ferrari
389 Et aprez ce que tout le royaulme du pays conquis
aura, tout le monde et mesmement son royaulme
deguerpira.
419 *Er wird . . . nicht lang wehren* B omits
422 N4–N8 *15* N9 N10 *25* N12–N19 *5*
423 *wehren* B *adds* und er wirt gůte regierer nach ihm lassen

dem Keyser nicht uber fünff jar leben /
425 dadurch denn die heilige Apostolische
Kirche in gros betrübnis kommen sol.
Denn sol fortan / die gantze Welt
durch / preiss / friede unnd freude sein / ohn
allerley uneinigkeit unnd zweytracht / die
430 Menschen sollen hinfort leben in rechter
warhafftiger lieb under einander / Denn ein
jeder Mensch wird verfüllet werden mit
tugenden / Als dann wird ein jeder /
verstandt und weisheit haben / gleich den
435 Aposteln / im anfang der Apostolischen
Kirchen. Sie sollen durch Gottes Geist / in
der heiligen schrifft erleuchtet werden / die
zuvor sehr lang verfinstert ist gewesen / sie
sollen auch verstehen alle prophezeiung
440 oder weissagung / so zuvor von den
Propheten geweissaget und beschrieben
sind. Es werden auch viel sein / die nicht
allein die Propheten verstehen werden /
sondern sollen auch selbst durch den
445 heiligen Geist / zukommene ding
verkündigen.
Es wird als dann niemandt macht
haben / einer den andern zubetriegen / oder
in böse falsche lehre / odder zur Hellen
450 zuvorführen. Aber zuvorkündigen von der
zeit / stundt und tage / wenn des menschen
Son kommen sol / spricht Christus Matthei.
am 24. Das von dem tage und stunde
niemandt wisse / auch nicht die Engel im
455 Himmel / denn allein der Vater / Darumb
last unns mit demütigem hertzen bitten /
unsern Herrn Jhesum Christum / der den

averst Bischop mit dem Keyser schal ock
nicht baven vyff Jahre leeven / dardorch
schal de hillige Apostolische Kerke sehr
bedrövet syn.

428 *preiss / friede unnd freude* B frid und einigkeyt L2 frede und einicheit; Ferrari 470 sera le monde tellement mué en saincteté et en bien vivre et en si grant prosperité et transquilité, que ce sera merveilles a ouyr recorder, de quoy chascun se doit bien esjouyr et donner liesse et cuer treshaultement429 *uneinigkeit unnd zweytracht* L2 bedroch und list B omits

430 N6–N19 *hinfort* N4 N5 N21 omit B fort an

432 N6 *verfüllet* N4 N5 N21 erfüllet B erfült L2 worvüllet

434 *verstandt und weisheit* B verstandt L2 vorstandt / und wisheit

434 *gleich* B wie L2 gelick

435 *Aposteln* B Apostelen L2 Discipulen; Ferrari 480 les sainctz apostres

435 *anfang* B L2 anbegin

435 *Apostolischen Kirchen* B Kirchen L2 hilligen Apostolischen Karcken

439 *verstehen* B außlegen L2 vorstan; Ferrari 483 entenderont

439 *prophezeiung oder weissagung* B Propheceien L2 prophesyen

441 *geweissaget und beschrieben* B Propheciert L2 geprophateret

449 N6 *in böse falsche lehre / odder zur Hellen* N21 in böse falsche Lehre oder sonsten B zů falschen leren L2 en de hellen alse vorhenne gedaenn hebben; Ferrari 486 de decevoir nulle personne ne de les mener ou puis d'enfer

455 *der Vater* B mein himlischer vatter L2 myn Vader im Hemmell

455 *Darumb last . . . gelitten hat* L2 Darümme möten wy uns van sünden bekerenn / und unsern Heren Jhesum Christum mit demödigen herten bidden / de vor uns armenn Sünder an dem stam des Crützes / den smeliken dodt / vor dat Minschlike geslecht geleden hefft

schendlichsten todt / für das Menschliche
geschlecht gelitten hat / das er unser
460 forsprach / für seinem Himlischen Vater
sein wolle / auff das wir ein gnedig urtheil
entpfangen / Amen.
[b2v] Beschluss.
465 Wachet auff ihr Christen leut vom
schlaff der sünden / thut auff ewre ohren /
scherfft ewre sinne unnd vornemet meine
wort. Darumb das ihr habt Gottes gebot /
unnd sein wort von euch geworffen / in die
470 pfützen der unreinigkeit / der vorgessenheit
unnd verachtung / und habt angefangen der
untugenden zu gebrauchen / ihr seid auch
inn der bossheit gantz weis / listig und
vorsichtig. Alle Erbarkeit vorkeret ihr / und
475 im blut und schweis der elenden Witwen
unnd Weysen / trinckt ihr euch truncken. Es
sind noch wenig tage vorhanden / das die
Christliche Stette zu grunde fallen sollen /
Darumb zihet an das kleidt der busse unnd
480 rewe / lauffet dem Herrn entgegen mit
weinen unnd klagen / do ihr das nicht thun
werdet / sollen die tage der trübsal gar
schnel erscheinen / für welchen ihr fliegen
werdet / biss an die ende des Meers / die
485 werdet ihr anruffen / das sie euch baldt und
leicht vom leben helffen. Auch sol ein solch
klagen unnd weinen under den Christen

464 *Beschluss* L2 Conclusia effte besluth
467 *vornemet* B L2 höret; for the text that follows, cf. Egenolff
124r–v: Erwachet ihr Christen Männer vom schlaffe der
sünden / und schneidet auff die bande ewers gehörs unnd
sinn / und verstehet meine wort mit fleiß. Darumb daß ihr
haben die gebott Gottes / und seine wort abgeworffen in
die grůben der unreynigkeit / der vergessenheit und verachtung / und haben angehaben zu brauchen die untugent
/ auch in der boßheit gantz weiß / listig und fürsichtig
seind / alle billigkeit zu verkeren / und in dem schweyß
und blůt der elenden betrübten witwen / und weysen
truncken zu werden
468 *Gottes gebot / unnd sein wort* L2 de gebade Gades / und
syn Wort B das reine wort Gottes
469 *in die pfützen der unreinigkeit / der vorgessenheit unnd
verachtung* L2 in de putte der unreinicheit / dorch vor-
getenheit und vorachtinge B in die stinckende brunnen
der vergessenheyt
470 N4–N6 N21 *unreinigkeit* N7–N19 uneinigkeit
471 *angefangen* B angenommen L2 angenamen
471 N6 *der untugenden zu gebrauchen* N21 der Untugend
und Laster zu gebrauchen B alle ungerechtigkeyt L2 tho
gebrucken de undogenden

472 *ihr seid . . . vorkeret ihr* B omits
475 *im blut und schweis* B von dem blůt L2 in dem Blodt
478 N6–N19 B L2 *Christliche* N4 N5 N21 Gottlosen; for
the text that follows, cf. Egenolff 124v: Es seind noch
wenig tag daß die Christlichen stett werden fallen zu
grunde / darumb kleydet euch mit dem kleyde der
Penitentzen und leyd / lauffend dem Herren entgegen
mit ewerm weynen und klagen / Und wo ir das nicht
thůn / so werden die tage der betrübtnuß / angst und
not schnelligklich erscheinen / von welchen ir fliehen
werden an die staden. Die flůß der wasser werden ihr
anrůffen / daß sie ewer leben gütlich empfahen
479 *busse unnd rewe* B Bůße L2 penetentien / unde draget
ruw und leidt
480 *lauffet* L2 lopet B unnd lauffet
483 N4–N6 *schnel erscheinen* N21 schnell über euch
erscheinen B plötzlich uber euch kommen L2 snel-
lichiken apenbar werden
483 *für welchen . . . ende des Meers* B so werden ir dann
kein platz der rhů finden
484 *ende des Meers* L2 Kanten der See effte watern
485 *das sie euch baldt und leicht vom leben helffen* B omits
L2 dat se iw levent sachticklich entfangen

sein / das einer zum andern sagen wird /
were es nicht besser gewest / wir weren in
490 unser Mutter leib gestorben? Darumb last
uns mit rewe unser sünden / den Herrn
demütig umb seine gnade bitten / das er dis
alles gnediglich von uns abwenden wolle /
unnd so uns Gott zum leiden beruffen hat /
495 last uns dasselbige zur straffe für unsere
sünde / gedüldig und willig tragen / auff das
wir von dem Herrn mögen belohnet werden
/ mit dem ewigen leben / welchs ewig leben
wolle uns unser lieber Herr Jhesus Christus
500 (es sey nach einer gelückseligen odder
ungelückseeligen zeit) gnediglich
mittheilen / welchem sey ehr und lob in   Soli Deo honor, nunc et in secula,
ewigkeit / Amen.   AMEN.

---

489 *in unser Mutter leib* L2 in unser moder live; cf. Egenolff
124v: Auch wirt es ein solichs weynen und schreien under
den Christen / daß einer zu dem andern sagen wirt: Were
es nicht besser / daß wir in mütterleib vertilget weren
worden?

490 *Darumb . . . abwenden wolle* B Hierumb laß uns nun den
Herren bitten das er dise trübsal von uns wenden wöl

491 *rewe* N21 *adds* und Leid

494 *unnd so uns . . . gnediglich mittheilen* B *omits and adds* in-

stead und wöl uns seinen heyligen Geyst senden / auff
das wir mögen wandeln in seiner gerechtigkeyt / dz
wir hernachmals ein gnedig urtheyl mögen empfahen
/ und mit im eingahn in sein ewig reich

502 *welchem sey ehr und lob in ewigkeit* D Soli Deo honor,
nunc et in secula B das hilff uns unser Herr Jesus L2
Dat gunne Juw und my Gott de Vader Got de Söne /
unnd Gott de hillige Geist

The Second Prophecy of Wilhelm Friess

———— ᭞ ————

For the edition of "Friess II" supplied here, I do not use F1, the 1639 edition that appears to be a descendant of the earliest version of the prophecy, as its language was significantly updated and altered in the seventeenth century. Similar reasons preclude use of F2, a seventeenth-century manuscript copy. Instead, for the base text, I use F3, the earliest printed edition (most likely to be dated to 1577), whose title page attests understanding of the original text. This edition is also the most complete, containing all the original text and all expansions. There is only one version of "Friess II," and F1 and numerous later editions are available online, so there is no need for a parallel text.

Unless otherwise marked, the base lemma in the apparatus is drawn from F3. Most omissions are not noted. "Altenburg" denotes the "Prophecy found in Altenburg" version of "Dietrich von Zengg," while "Lichtenberger" identifies the 1527 Wittenberg edition of Lichtenberger's *Prognosticatio*.[1] The additions to the original text (lines 88–108) appear in square brackets.

Ein Grausamme und Erschreckeliche Prophezeygung oder Weissagung uber Teuschlandt / Brabandt und Franckreich.

Diese Prophezeygung ist gefunden worden in Mastricht / bey einem Gottforchtigen Mann Wilhelm de Frieß nach seinem todt.

5   i. Thessalon. am v. Capit.

Den Geyst löschend nicht auß / die Prophecey verachtend nicht / Bewärend es alles / und behaltend das gut.

10   [a1v: blank]

[a2r] Ein Grausamme und Erschreckeliche Prophezeygung / oder Weissagung uber Theuschlandt / Brabandt und Franckreich.

15   ANNO M. D. LXXIIII. den xxiiii. Tag Aprilis / als ich in der Nacht umb zwölff uhren auff meim Beth lagh und wachte / da kam ein schöner Junger Mann zu mir / unnd sprach mich an / Sehe was geschehen soll / unnd merck fleißig auff / domals richte ich mich auff / unnd anstundt doucht mich daß ich auff einen hohen bergh mitten in Theutschlandt war. Daselbst sagte der Junger Mann zu mir: Wende dich gegen mitternacht / dann der Herr

20   wert dich weisen: Wie grausam er die Welt straffen wirdt / und ich thetes / da sahe ich ein groß folck hinein ziehen gegen Theutschlant: Dieselbigen hatten viel Fanen / Reutter und Fusfolck / ihre Fendlein waren schwartz / und hatten weisse Kreutze / u[n]d sie kammen an ein groß Wasser / da Reidt ein starcker Man vor / auff einem schwartzen Pferdt / sein kledt war eittel bluth / unnd hatte ein groß Horn in seiner Handt / und Er sprach zu seinem

25   Folcke: Ihr solt still stehn und warten biß wir unse mittgeselln rüffen das dieselbigen zu uns kommen / unnd Er bließ das Horn / unnd man hörte dasselbige weith und breith. Domals sprach der Junger Man zu mir: Kehrt euch gegen dem underganck / unnd ich thetes / daselbst [a2v] sahe ich ein grausam groß Folck kommen / unnd zogen gegen mitternacht / welche gar erschreckligh sahen / und hatten viel fanen wie die vorige Aber ihre fendlen

30   waren weiß und roth / und hatten ein roth Kreutz darein / unnd ihre Kleider waren auch also / und einer reitt vor in hin uff einem rothen Pferdt / derselbiger sahe wie ein böser Geist / Lewen und Beren folchden inen nach / und dreben dieselbige hefftig vort an / unnd die so ihnen lasterden / zerriessen sie von stundt an / unnd ein helle stimm gyngh under ihnen auß: Eylt euch sehr fleisch zu fressen Und ich erschrecket grausam / so das ich

35   beschwimmt und niderfallen woll / domals stercke mich der Junger Man und sprach: Sey getröst / und verzage nicht / dann ich wil dir mehr zeigen / unnd er sprach zu mir: Wende

---

15   F1 F3–F6 *ANNO M. D. LXXIIII. den xxiiii. Tag Aprilis* F2 Anno 1547. Den 24. Aprillis F7 Anno 1577. den 24. tag Aprilis F8 F9 ANNO M. D. LXX vii. den xxiiii. tag Septemberis F10 Anno M.D.LXXvii. den xxiiii. Aprilis F13 Anno M.D.LXXIX. den xxiiii. tag Julius F14 M.D.LXXIX. den xxiiii tag Hornung F16 Anno M.D.LXXXV. den 28. December F17 Anno Domini auff das 1588 und 89. biß in das 90. Jar F11 F15 *omit*

15   *zwölff uhren* F5–F17 *add* da

16   *Junger Mann* F1 F16 F17 Jüngling

16   *sprach mich an* F5–F17 *add* Er sprach zu mir

18   *anstundt* F1 also bald F2 von stundan F5–F6 F8–F14 von stunde F7 von stundt an F15–F17 stundan

19   F2–F4 *der Herr wert dich weisen* F1 der Herr wird dir Zeigen F5–F17 will ich dir zeigen

20   *er* F5–F17 Gott

23   *ein starcker* F5–F17 ein grosser starcker

24   seiner F17 *adds* rechten

25   *mittgeselln* F1 Dänische Gesellen

27   *underganck* F1 Abend (oder Westen) F5–F17 *add* der Sonnen

28   *daselbst* F1 F2 F7 F15 da

32   F2–F4 *hefftigh vort* F1 eilends forth F5–F17 hefftig

33   F2–F4 *ihnen lasterden* F1 sich verweileten oder zurück blieben F5 F6 so sie verhindertten F7–F17 so sich verhinderten

34   F2–F4 F7 F10–F14 *Eylt euch sehr fleisch zu fressen* F1 Eilet / daß ihr Fleisch fresset F5 F6 Eylt euch sehr fleiß zu fressen F8 F9 Eylt auch ser fleisch zu fressen F15 Eylet euch sehr fleißig zů fressen F16 F17 Eylet sehr ewr fleisch zufressen

34   F3–F6 F8–F14 *das ich beschwimmt* F1 dass ich ohnmechtig ward F2 mir geschwandt F7 das ich geschwind F15 das mir geschwand F17 das mir schier geschwand F16 das ich

36   *unnd er sprach* F1 F2 F15 und sprach

dich gegen den uffganck / unnd ich thet es / Daselbst sahe ich wederumb ein grausam folck
ziehen gegen mitternacht mit Reutter und fanen wie die vorigen / ihre fanen waren roth und
ein fewrich schwerdt darin / und ihre Kleider waren auch roth unnd mit bluth besprenget /
40 und ein gewaldiger geharnischter Mann zogh fur ihnen her / der so groß wahr das ich nie
mehr deßgleichen gesehen hab / und sein Harnisch glentzerett uber die maß / und daselbst
stunden viel gulden Buchstaben in. Und Ehr rieff sein Folck hefftigh an: eilet sehr / dan wir
willen ubergan und ihren Raet verstören. Da fragde ich den Jungen Man / Wer der Man
war / daruff antwortett ehr / Ehr ist der Verderber / da fragt ich ihm abermals: Was das fur
45 buchstaben waren an ihm geschrieben / daruff antwort Ehr mir: Alle pflagen unnd
straffungen die Ehr ußrichten soll. Und sie eilten und zogen gar schnel heran / da sie nun
zusamen kamen / da beschlossen sie eindrechtligh einen Rath / und wurden eins alle
Landen zu straffen und plagen. Unnd dasselbige war so ein unzalbar menichte folcks / das
mich verwunderet wie so viel menschen sein konden: Und sprach zu dem Junglingh: Wer
50 kuntt das folck zellen oder wie menigh sein der Fanen / da sprach Ehr: Des Folcks is[t] ein
grosse anzall / [a3r] aber der Fanen sein hundert und sechtzigh tausent unnd vier / unnd sie
rusteten sich geweldich dieweil sie an dem wasser waren. Und wie sie noch zusamen
stunden / kam ein grausamer erschrecklicher Man zwisschen dem uffganck und mittnacht
zu im / unnd hatt derselbe erschreckligh folck bey ihm / die theten eben wie Bärn / und bey
55 wem sie kamen den erwurgden sie / ußgescheiden von diesen obgenanten Leuten / welche
ohn zall waren. Und das folck zertheilde sich / und liessen denselbigen grausamen Man
mitten durch ziehen / und Ehr stallt sich vorn an die spitze / unnd hat einen gulden Kelch in
seiner rechter handtt / der voll bluts war / unnd in seiner lencker hant ein Junges
Kyndelein. Und Ehr dranck aus dem Kelch / und darnach aß Ehr ein zeit lanck von dem
60 Kynde / das dreib Ehr so langh / das Ehr den Kelch außdranck / unnd das Kyndlein uff fraß
/ biß an dem kopff. Darnach nam er den Kelch / und deß Kints kopff / und warffs under
daß folck / unnd sie zertraden dasselbige mitt füssen. Von stundt an ließ sich algemach ein
blutig Schwertt vom Himmell herab / unnd Ehr kriech dasselbige in die faust / und rieff
mit lauter stimmen / Wehe euch Teutschlandt / wehe euch Brabandt und Franckreich /
65 wehe euch alle Landen / wehe der Erden / dann glückselich is der / so auff euch nicht
geberet hatt / want ich dein Verderber komme / und verziehe nicht. Wehe deine Junge

41 *nie mehr deßgleichen* F1 F2 seines gleichen nie F15 dergleich mein tag nie kein
42 F2–F7 F10–F14 *rieff* F1 F15 schrie F8 F9 griffe F16 F17 rüffet
43 *ubergan und* F1 hinüber gehen unnd F2 fürüber gehen und F5–F17 *omit*
43 *verstören* F10 F11 *omit* F15 Eylet / eylet zum Rhat
47 *eindrechtligh* F8 F9 *omit*
49 *Und sprach* F1 F5–F17 Und ich sprach
50 *menigh* F1 F2 F5–F17 viel
51 F1 F3–F6 *hundert und sechtzig tausent unnd vier* F2 i. und 6000. und 40 F7–F17 Hundert und vier und Sechtzig Tausent
52 *noch zusamen stunden* F1 noch also bey einander waren F2 zusammen zugen F5–F17 nahe zusamen kamen
53 *erschrecklicher* F5–F17 *add* grosser
54 *derselbe* F1 F2 F5–F17 *add* ein
54 *theten eben wie Bärn* F1 theten gleich wie die Bähren F2 thetten wie Beren F15 gestelten sich wie wilde Bären
55 F2–F6 *bey wem sie kamen* F1 welchen sie antraffen F7–F17 zu wem sie kamen
55 *ußgescheiden* F2 ohne F1 F5–17 außgenomen
60 F3–F6 *so langh / das* F1 so lang und ferne, bis dass F2 bis F7–F17 so lang / biß
61 *warffs* F1 *adds* zusammen
62 *Darnach nam er den Kelch / und deß Kints kopff* F16 F17 *omit*
63 *blutigh* F1 bloß F16 F17 *omit*
63 *faust* F1 Hand F16 F17 *omit*
64 *Wehe euch . . . alle Landen* F1 Weh / Weh dir Teutschland / Weh euch allen Ländern F16 F17 *omit*
65 F3–F7 F10–F14 F15 *so auff euch nicht geberet hatt* F1 der auff dich nicht gebawet hat F2 der auf euch nit geboren hat F8 F9 nicht geberet hat F16 F17 so auß dir nicht geboren hat
66 *want* F1 F2 F5–17 Dann
66 *deine* F7–F15 den

gesellen / und Junge Dochteren / wehe deine stoltzen knab[en /] und Fursten / dan das
Landtt wirdtt mit meiner handtt erfullet werden: Und da Ehr solches außgesprochen hatt /
zohe Ehr vort an / und alle das folck mit Ihm / und Ehr erwurgett / und gyngh grausam
70   umb mit allen die so Ehr fandt / und dasselbige dreib Ehr so weith und breith / biß das
mich dauchte Ehr were hart bey mir domals fiel ich nider / unnd kam von mir selbst / und
weiß doch nicht wie lange ich an derselbigen platz gelegen hab. Do kam der Junger Man
und kreigh mich bey der hantt. unnd sprach / stehe auff / eß ist alleß furuber und ich thetes
/ unnd sahe sehr wei[t] umb mich her / und ich sahe keine lebendig mensch [a3v] mehr /
75   aber mich daucht das das ga[n]tze Erdreich alles blut war / von wegen das wurgen und
morden / so sie hatten gethan. Do sacht ich zu dem Jungen Man: Is[t] dan niemant mehr
der da lebt auff Erden / da sprach Er / Kere dich gegen mittag / und ich thetes. Daselbst
sahe ich ein klein haufflein Folcks gegen mir ziehen / in schwartzen Kleidern / sie drugen
auch etliche weisse Fanen. Und ein Erbar feiner Ma[n] ging fur inen hinein / und hat einen
80   grauwen Bardt / derselbigen hat ein gulden Buch in seinen linckerhandt / und ein gulden
Basune in der Rechterhandt / und er bließ dieselbe auff / und gab ein groß gelaut. Da
kamen auß den dicken Busschen und uber die hohe Bergen noch ein weinich folcks / die
uber blieben waren / under inen / und sie theten inen auch schwartze Kleider an / und sie
satzten sich zusamen an ein groß Wasser / wie der Rhein / und dauchte mich es ware umb
85   Straßburg. Und der Man / der das Buch hat / lerde sie aus demselbigen die Furcht Gottes /
unnd die verförten weiß er auff den wech Gottes. Und als er nun außgeleret hat / satzten sie
sich auff die knie unnd batten Gott an. Darnach stundt der Man mit allem folck auff / und
sprach: Laß uns von hinnen ziehen / unnd die Erde beklagen. [O du Welsche Welt nun
hebe an zu klagen und zu weinen / den grosser schmertz nahet dir / von deiner grossen

67   *deine* F7–F15 den
67   *Junge Dochteren* F1 Jungfrawen
67   *Fursten* F5–F17 grossen Herren
68   *handtt* F1 Reisigen Zeug
69   *vort an* F2 *omits* F1 F5–F17 fort
71   *fiel ich nider* F1 *adds* in eine ohnmacht
73   *ich thetes* F1 und ich that also F2 *omits* F15 da sahe ich auff
74   *unnd sahe* F1 F2 F5–17 und ich sahe
74   *sehr weit* F1 weit / ja sehr weit F2 weit
79   F3–F6 F8–F15 *Erbar feiner* F1 fein erbarer F2 feiner F7 Erbar weiser F16 F17 erbar
79   *hinein* F1 F2 F5–17 her
80   *Buch* F2 *omits* F16 külch
81   F3–F6 F8–F14 *und gab ein groß gelaut* F1 die gab einen sehr grossen Schall F2 daz Thonet weit F7 und gab ein gros gelauff
      F15 und es gab ein laut gethön F16 F17 und gab ein grossen schal
82   *Busschen* F15 Hürsten
83   *und sie theten inen auch schwartze Kleider an* F1 *omits*
84   *und dauchte mich es ware umb Straßburg* F5–F17 *omit*
86   *die verförten* F1 den Verirreten F2 die verstörten F15 die da irrten
87   *mit allem folck auff* F1 F2 F16 F17 auff mit allem volck
88   *ziehen* F16 F17 gehn
88   *O du Welsche Welt . . . wider recht* cf. Altenburg, a2r–v: O du Welsche welt nun heb an zů klagen unnd zů weinen / wann
      grosser schmertz nahet dir / vonn deiner grossen sünd wegen / wann der wind hat dz feür so vast entzündt / das es nit
      erlescht mag werden / mitt keiner weyß sicherlich. . . . Mancher meynt es gang in nit an / darumb das er sich helt an
      beiden teylen / doch so wirt im sein ruck gebogen / zů dem selbigen spil. Er gedenckt nit das die zeyt nahet / und das feür
      an in rüert / sie bedörffen wol eins kochs der in ir essen bereit; a3r: Ein grosses volck von Teütschen wirt sich versamlen
      / wann das feür begünnet an sie zů rüeren / unnd der rauch ist under inen. O wie groß blůt vergiessen werden sie thůn
      under denen / die da also herrschafft sůchen und herrschen wöllen wider recht; a3v: Es werden Graven noch Herren
      von dem Mör biß an den Rhein / keiner sicher / er würt empfinden / der winde des grossen ungewitters.
88   F3–F14 *Welsche* F2 F15 falsche F16 F17 böse
89   *zu klagen und zu weinen* F5–F6 F8–F17 zu klagen und weinen

90 sünde wegen / Denn der Windt hat das Fewer so vast entzündet / das es nicht erlescht mag
werden. Mancher meint es gehet im nit an / darumb das er sich helt an beiden theilen /
doch so wirt im sein rück gebogen / zu dem selbigen spil. Er gedenckt nicht das die zeit
nahet / und das fewr an in rüret / sie bedörffen wol eins kochs der in ihr essen bereit. Ein
grosses folck von Teutschen wird sich versamlen / wan das fewer an sie beginnet zu rüren /
95 Unnd der Rauch ist unter innen. Es werden Graven und Herrn von Meer biß an den Rhein /
keiner sicher / er würd empfinden von dem winde des grossen u[n]gewitters. O wie groß
blut vergiessen werden sie thun unter denen / die da herschafft suchen [a4r] und herschen
wölln wider recht.] [O Brabandt / O Franckreich / O Teutschlandt: schreyet und heulet ir
Hirten und Regierer / und thu die kleider der frieden von dir / bekleide dich mit Assche /
100 unnd zeuch ein Haren kleidt an / als uber ein angeboren / und sprich: Ich hab mir ein folck
aufferzogen / unnd erhöhet / aber es hat mich veracht. Es ist mir worden wie ein Löwe / der
jemandt nach stellet. O du armes folck / was ist vor ein fremdes folck under dier erstanden
/ es ist nicht ein Regierendt folck / sonder zerstörer / nicht Beschutzer / sonder
underdrucker der Weysen und Wittwen / durch gantz Teutschlandt. Es wirdt die Teutschen
105 duncken / es gehe sie nicht an. Also / daß das gemeyne folck sagen wirt / einer sonst der
ander so.] [Es werden sich auch die Leutersche Pfaffschap nach mitternacht so durch
hoffart unnd ergeitz auffgeblasen / und also grossen zweyspalt anrichten in Glaubens
sachen / aber in auff die lenge ubel bekommen. etc.]
Dann die ungerechtigkeit ist von in hin wech genommen / Laß uns auch begraben alle die
110 / so von den unsern umbkommen sein / Dan ihre Selen ruwen im frieden. Gelobet sey der
Herr unser Gott / dan sein urtheil ist gerecht. Da diese reden vollendet waren / fürde mich
der Junger Man wider auff meine Kammer / und da ich bey mir selber kam / hat die Klocke
vier uhren geschlagen.

93 *nahet* F15 *adds* und empfindt auch nicht das dz fewr so nahe
93 *bereit* F15 *adds* dann manchem das nit schmecken wirt
95 *Unnd der Rauch ist unter innen* F2 und der rauch under ihnen ist F5–F17 *omit*
95 *von Meer biß an den Rhein* F2 vom Möhr bis an den Rhein F5–F17 *omit*
96 *sicher* F2 F5–F17 *add* sein
96 *er würd* F5–F17 sie werden
98 *O Brabandt . . . einer sonst der ander so* cf. Lichtenberger, g4r: O Heilige mutter du Römische kirche / bis trawrig und
weyne / O Jungfrawe / du Reinstram / schreye / heulet yhr Hirten und Regirer am Reinstram / ynn Lothringen / yn West-
reich / ym Elsas / yn Schwaben / ynn Francken und ynn Ringawe. O du land der Jungfrawen / thue die kleider der frewde
von dir / bekleide dich mit asche und zeuch ein heeren kleid an / O Döringen / O Hessen / O Westerwald / O Wederaw /
nym an dich das heulen als uber ein eingepornen / und sprich / Ich hab mir ein volck aufferzogen und erhöhet / aber es
hat mich veracht / Es ist mir worden wie ein Lewe / der yemande nachstellet / darumb so ist mir meine frewde zu einem
bekümmernis geraten. O du armes volck / das du bisher ym kriege des gegenwertigen elendes gestanden bist / Was ist
doch fur ein newer könig unter dir erstanden? Er ist nicht ein regirer / sondern ein zurstörer der glewbigen / Nicht ein
tröster / sondern ein betrüber und rauber der geistlichen / nicht ein beschutzer / sondern ein unterdrucker der Waysen
und Widwen durch gantz Deudsch land. Es wird die Deudschen Fursten duncken / es kome daher ein newer zurstörer /
ein newer könig on runtzeln / also das das gemeine volck sagen wird / einer sonst / der ander so / der dritte aber anders;
cf. Höfler, *Geschichtschreiber der husitischen bewegung in Böhmen,* 6:417–18: O plebs misera huc usque in malicia praesen-
tis exilii posita, quoniam rex novus surrexit super terram, non gubernator sed desolator Christi fidelium, non extirpator
haeresium sed spoliator ecclesiarum omnium, non consolator sed depraedator monachorum et virginum; non protector
sed oppressor viduarum et orphanorum omnium
98 O Brabandt . . . mich veracht F16 F17 *omit*
100 F3–F14 *angeboren* F15 eingebornen F2 F16 F17 *omit*
104 *Teutschen* F16 F17 Weltweisen
105 *das gemeyne folck . . . einer sonst der ander so* F16 F17 unter dem gmeinen Volck / einer diß der ander das sagt
106 *Es werden sich . . . ubel bekommen. etc.* F1 F2 F5–F17 *omit*
109 *Dann die ungerechtigkeit . . . ist gerecht* F5–F17 *omit*

Following the end of the prophecy, all printed editions include additional material concerning the year 1588. The text appears in F3 as follows:

Kurtze Propheczeygung oder Weissagung von dem zu kommenden
/ M. D. LXXXVIII. Jahr
Dieses M. D. Lxxxviii. Jahr ist ein wunderbarlich Jahr dergleichen in
Tausent Jar nicht eins gewesen ist. Der Allmechtige gütige Gott
/ ein Vatter aller Barmhertzigkeit / wol alle ding zum besten
kehren. Denn es wirt ein grosser Cometstern gesehen werden.
Daruff werden grawsame und erschreckliche / zuvorn unerhörte
ding erfolgen. Darum die Alten nicht unbillich von diesem jahr
/ diese nachfolgende Verß gemacht haben.
Wenn man zellen wirdt 1580. und acht.
Das ist das Jahr das ich betracht.
Geht in dem die Welt nicht under.
So geschicht doch sonst mercklich groß Wunder.

In F4–F17, the last line omits the word *groß*, and additional material concerning 1588 follows. In F4–F7, the additional material closes with two short prophecies (omitted in F8–F17) attributed to a sybil and Birgitta of Sweden and drawn from Lichtenberger's *Prognosticatio*. They appear in F4 as follows:

Sybilla.
Wir sind die / auff welche kommen ist das end der Welt / Das böse
ist nahe bey dem guten. Erwölle das gute / und verwirff das böse.
Brigida.
Vertrawe auff Gott / und thu guts / bitte das alle ding zum besten
kommen / Denn Gott hat allein macht alles zukunfftige ungluck
gnediglich abzuwenden. Amen.

Editions Attributed to Wilhelm Friess

———— ✥ ————

Title transcriptions follow the same conventions used in appendixes 1 and 2: umlauted vowels are given modern orthography, *u*/*v* and *i*/*j* have their modern values, and abbreviations are resolved silently. Punctuation and spelling are otherwise unchanged. Titles that do not differ substantially from the preceding entry are given in shortened form. The dates of publication differ from the dates in VD16 or other catalogs in a few cases, where my research suggests that the previous dating is in error. The siglum provided for each edition corresponds to that used in the figures and text. The list includes only editions existing in libraries today or described in scholarly literature or historical records; it does not include editions that are assumed to exist for textual-historical reasons. Editions that were consulted in the original or in facsimile are marked with an asterisk. The libraries owning all known copies of the prophecies are listed at the end of each entry. For editions not listed in VD16, a library shelf mark has been provided where possible.

Prognostications of Willem de Vriese of Maastricht

V1 *Een vremde / ende wonderlijcke Pronosticatie /vanden Jare ons Heeren / M.D.L.v. Ghemaeckt ende ghecalculeert op den meridiaen der Stadt van Maestricht / duer den hoochgheleerden M. Willem de vriese / Doctoor der Medecijnen / ende der vrijer consten.* Antwerp: Hans van Liesvelt, for 1555.[1] *NB* 31227*. Brussels Koninklijke Bibliotheek

V2 *Prognosticatie vanden Jaere ons Heeren M.D. ende LVI. Gecalculeert opten*

Meridiaen der looflijcker stadt van Maestrich / gepractizeert door den vermaerden ende hoochgeleerden Meester Willem de Vriese den ouden / der Medecinen ende der vrijer consten Doctoor. Antwerp: Hans van Liesvelt, for 1556. *NB* 31228*. Brussels Koninklijke Bibliotheek

Prognostications and Calendars of *Willem de Vriese (the Younger?) of Maastricht*

V3   *Almanack ende Prognosticatie vanden Jaere ons Heeren Jheus Christi / Duysent vijfhondert ende LXXXI. Met die Jaermercten, Peerdemercten, van Brabant, Hollant, Zeelant, ende Vlaenderen, Noch is hier by ghevoecht die Historie ende nieuwe gheschiedenissen, soo over Brabandt, Hollandt, Zeelandt, ende Vlaenderen, nu onlancx gheschiet. Ghecalculeert op den Meridiaen der Stadt van Maestricht / ende de omligghende plaetsen / deur M. Willem de Vriese / der Medecijnen Doctoor.* Antwerp: Jan II van Ghelen, for 1581. *NB* 31230*. Antwerp Erfgoedbibliotheek Hendrik Conscience

V4   *Almanack ende Prognosticatie vanden Jaere ons Heeren. M.CCCCC. ende LXXXI. Ghecalculeert ende ghemaeckt / op den Meridiaen der Stadt van Maestricht / ende de omligghende plaetsen / deur M. Willem de Vriese der Medecijnen Doctoor.* Antwerp: Jan II van Ghelen, for 1581. *NB* 31231*. Antwerp Erfgoedbibliotheek Hendrik Conscience

V5   *Prognosticatie ende generale corte beschrijvinge / van desen tegenwoordighen Jaere ons Heeren Jesu Christi. M.D.LXXXI. Ghecalculeert ende ghemaect / op den Meridiaen der Stadt van Maestricht / ende de omligghende plaetsen / deur M. Willem de Vriese / der Medecijnen Doctoor.* Antwerp: Jan II van Ghelen, for 1581. *NB* 31232*. Antwerp Erfgoedbibliotheek Hendrik Conscience

V6   *Almanach oft Journael voor het Jaer ons Heeren M.D.XCVI. Ghecalculeert ende ghemaeckt op de Meridiaen der stadt van Maestricht.* Antwerp: Jacobus Mesens for Guislain Janssens, for 1596. *NB* 31233*. Antwerp Museum Plantin-Moretus/Prentenkabinet

The First Prophecy of Wilhelm Friess: *"Several Unusual Prophecies"/ "Etliche Seltzame Propheceiung"*

β   Unattested: [Antwerp: Frans Fraet, 1557 (Dutch?)].

B   *PROGNOSTICON. Das ist Ein sehr Warhafftige Prophecey / Practiciert durch den alten M. Wilhelm Frieß von Mastricht / Welche bey jhm erfunden nach seinem todt / und fahet an inn dem Jahr M. D. LIX. biß in das LXIII. Jar / in deren du gûthertziger Leser vil wunders finden wirst.* [N.p.: n.p., 1559]. VD16 ZV 26091*. Munich Bayerische Staatsbibliothek

D   *PRONOSTICATIO. Gepracticeret van dem olden Meister Wilhelm dem Fresen* *van Mastricht / de nu kortes vorscheiden unde na synem dode by em befunden ys / Angande van dem Jar M.D.LVIII. warende up dat LXIII. Jar.* [N.p.: n.p., 1558]. Not in VD16*. Düsseldorf Görres-Gymnasium

L1 *Prophecie vanden ouden meester Willem de Vriese van Maestricht, naer syn doot onder zijn hooft gevonden. Beginnende vanden jaere 58 totten jaere 70.* [N.p.: n.p.], 1566 (Dutch). *NB* 31229.

L2 *Pronosticatien. Eine wunderlike prophecie / gepracticeret van dem Olden Meister Wilhelm de frese van Mastricht / Doctor und Astronomus der sülvigen Stadt / welcker Kortes na synem dode under synem Höuet küssen gefunden ist geworden / welcker beginnende ys van 1558. wenhte up 1570. hir vann de lasten 4. Jaren seer wunderlick syn schöllen.* [Lübeck: Johann Balhorn the Elder, ca. 1566]. VD16 F 2844*. Berlin Staatsbibliothek Preußischer Kulturbesitz

L3 *Prognosticatio: Eine wunderlike Prophecie . . .* [Lübeck: Johann Balhorn the Elder], 1568. VD16 F 2845*. Berlin Staatsbibliothek Preußischer Kulturbesitz

N4 *PRONOSTICATIO. Etliche seltzame Prophezeiunge / Geweissaget von dem alten M. Wilhelmo Friesen / von Mastrich / welcher newlich gestorben / die bey ihm gefunden nach seinem tode / Vom M.D.LVIII. bis ins LXIII. Jar sich erstreckende / in welchem sehr selzame und greuliche verenderung geweissaget werden.* [N.p.: n.p.], 1558. VD16 ZV 17899*. Dresden Sächsische Landesbibliothek/Staats- und Universitätsbibliothek, Utrecht Antiquariaat Forum BV (offered for sale 2012).

N5 *PROGNOSTICATIO. Etliche seltzame Propheceyunge . . .* [N.p.: n.p.], 1558. VD16 ZV 21922*. Berlin Staatsbibliothek Preußischer Kulturbesitz

N6 *PRONOSTICATIO. Etliche seltzame Prophezeinng / geweissaget von dem alten M. Wilhelmo Friesen / von Mastrich / welcher neulich gestorben / die bey ihme gefunden nach seinem tode / Von 1558. biss ins 63. jar sich erstreckende / in denen sehr seltzame unnd greuliche verenderung geweissaget werden.* [N.p.: n.p. (Eisleben: Urban Gaubisch?), 1558]. VD16 F 2842*. Augsburg Staats- und Stadtbibliothek, Berlin Staatsbibliothek Preußischer Kulturbesitz, Wolfenbüttel Herzog August Bibliothek

N7 *PRONOSTICATIO. Etliche seltzame Prophezeiung . . .* [N.p.: n.p.], 1558. VD16 ZV 21923*. Berlin Staatsbibliothek Preußischer Kulturbesitz

N8 *PRONOSTICATIO. Etzliche seltzame Propheceyung . . .* [N.p.: n.p., 1558]. Not in VD16*. Frankfurt am Main Universitätsbibliothek (Flugschriftensammlung Gustav Freytag 5)

N9 *PRONOSTICATIO. Etliche seltzame Prophezeiung . . .* Nuremberg: Georg Kreydlein, [1558]. VD16 ZV 6208*. Frankfurt am Main Universitätsbibliothek (Flugschriftensammlung Gustav Freytag 4), Wolfenbüttel Herzog August Bibliothek

N10 *PRONOSTICATIO. Etliche seltzame Propheceiung / geweissaget von dem*

Alten M. Wilhelmo Friesen / von Mastricht / welcher newlich gestorben / die bey im gefunden nach seinem tode / Von 1558. biß ins 63. Jar sich erstreckende / in denen sehr seltzame und grewliche verenderung geweissaget werden. Königsberg (East Prussia): Johann Daubmann, [ca. 1558]. Not in VD16*. Leipzig Universitätsbibliothek NeueGesch.117

N12 *PRONOSTICATIO. Etliche seltzame Prophezeiung...* Nuremberg: Georg Kreydlein, [1558]. VD16 ZV 6209*. Munich Bayerische Staatsbibliothek, Stuttgart Württembergische Landesbibliothek, Wolfenbüttel Herzog August Bibliothek

N13 *PRONOSTICACIO. Etliche seltzame Prophezeiung...* Nuremberg: Georg Kreydlein, [1558]. VD16 ZV 27496*. Eichstätt Universitätsbibliothek (provenance: Capuchin monastery, Karlstadt a. M.)

N14 Printed with prognostication for 1559–65 of Nikolaus Caesareus: *PRONOSTICATIO. Etliche seltzame Propheceiung / geweissaget von dem alten M. Wilhelmo Friesen / von Mastrich / welcher newlich gestorben / die bey im gefunden nach seinem tode / Vom 1558. bis ins 63. jar sich erstreckende / in denen seer seltzame und grewliche verenderung geweissaget werden.* Nuremberg: Georg Kreydlein (or [Erfurt: n.p.?]), [1558]. VD16 F 2841*. Düsseldorf Görres-Gymnasium, Halle Universitäts- und Landesbibliothek, Munich Bayerische Staatsbibliothek, Wolfenbüttel Herzog August Bibliothek, Würzburg Universitätsbibliothek

N15 Printed with prognostication for 1559–65 of Nikolaus Caesareus: *Newe Propheceyung / Geweissaget von dem alten Wilhelm Friesen / von Mastrich / welcher newlich gestorben / die bey ihm gefunden nach seinem toodt / Vom 1558. biß ins 63. jar sich erstreckende / in denen seer seltzame und grewliche veränderung geweissaget werden.* [N.p.: n.p., 1558]. Not in VD16*. Frankfurt am Main Universitätsbibliothek (Flugschriftensammlung Gustav Freytag 103)

N16 *PROGNOSTICATIO. Etliche seltzame Propheceyung / geweyssaget von dem Allten M. Wilhelmo Friesen / von Mastrich / welcher newlich gestorben / die bey ime gefunden nach seinem Tode / von 1558. biß inns 63. Jar sich erstreckende / Inn denen sehr seltzame und gräwliche veränderung geweyssaget werden.* Nuremberg: Georg Kreydlein, [1558]. VD16 F 2843*. Augsburg Staats- und Stadtbibliothek, Jena Universitäts- und Landesbibliothek, Leipzig Universitätsbibliothek, Munich Bayerische Staatsbibliothek (2 copies), Wittenberg Lutherhalle, Wolfenbüttel Herzog August Bibliothek, Vienna Österreichische Nationalbibliothek, Zwickau Ratsschulbibliothek

N17 *PRONOSTICATIO. Etliche seltzame Propheceyung...* [Nuremberg: Georg Kreydlein, 1558]. VD16 ZV 6207*. Frankfurt am Main Universitätsbibliothek (Flugschriftensammlung Gustav Freytag 6), Wolfenbüttel Herzog August Bibliothek

N18 *PROGNOSTICATIO. Etliche seltzame Propheceyung*. . . [Nuremberg: Georg Kreydlein, 1558]. VD16 ZV 6206*. Dresden Sächsische Landesbibliothek/Staats- und Universitätsbibliothek

N19 *PROGNOSTICATIO. Etliche setzame Propheceyung*. . . [Nuremberg: Georg Kreydlein, 1558].[2] Not in VD16*. Erlangen Universitätsbibliothek Trew S 99

N20 Extract in Latin translation: Johann Wolf, *Lectionum Memorabilium et Reconditarum Centenarii XVI*. . . (Lauingen: Leonhard Rheinmichel, 1600), 1: 645*.

N21 Under pseudonym "Christian Engelmann": *Wunderbahre Propheceyung / So sich auff das Eintausend Sechshundert Sechs- und Achtzig / biß zu den 1691sten Jahr erstreckt / Darinnen Von einem der Welt wolbekanten hochgelarten Manne sehr grosse Veränderung entdecket werden*. Frankfurt: n.p., 1686. VD17 32:648152W*. Weimar Herzogin Anna Amalia Bibliothek

N22 *Wunderbahre Propheceyung / So sich auff das Eintausend Sechshundert Sechs- und Achtzig / biß zu dem 1691sten Jahr erstreckt* . . . [N.p.: n.p.], 1686. Not in VD17*. Duke University Library

N23 *Wunderbahre Propheceiung / So sich auf das 1686 biß zu den 1691sten Jahre erstreckt*. . . [N.p.: n.p.], 1686. VD17 1:063073H*. Berlin Staatsbibliothek Preußischer Kulturbesitz

N24 *Wunderbahre Propheceyung So sich auff das Eintausend Sechshundert Sechs- und Achtzig / bis zu den 1691sten Jahr erstreckt*. . . [N.p.: n.p.], 1686. VD17 12:121140B*. London British Library, Munich Bayerische Staatsbibliothek

N25 *Etliche Sonder- und Wunderbahre Merckwürdige Prophezeyung / So sich auff das 1680. biß zu dem 1700sten Jahr erstrecken / Darinnen Von denen Welt- wohlbekandten und Hochgelahrten Männern / alß von Johann Lichtenbergern schon Anno 1512. zu Wittenberg / und von Doct. Philippo Theophrasto Paracelso Anno 1546. zu Saltzburg und anderen unbekandten Authoren in diesen Seculo Grosse Veränderungen entdecket werden. Darbey auch des Seel. Martini Lutheri Meynung / was er von Johann Lichtenbergers Prophezeyung gehalten. Nebenst Einer wehemühtigen Klage und Bitte derer sämptlichen P[fa]ltzischen und Rheinischen ruinirten Ländern und Städten / an die Allerhöchste und unendlichste Majestät / wieder die allergrausamsten Proceduren Ludewigs des XIV. Königs von Frankreich. Zu diesen gefährlichen betrübten Zeiten wohlmeinend zum Druck befordert*. [N.p.: n.p.], 1689. VD17 1:088281P. Berlin Staatsbibliothek Preußischer Kulturbesitz, Wolfenbüttel Herzog August Bibliothek

N26 *Etliche Sonder- und Wunderbahre Merckwürdige Prophezeyungen So sich auf das 1680. biß zu dem 1700ten Jahr erstrecken. Darinnen Von denen Welt- wohlbekandten und Hochgelahrten Männern / alß von Johann Lichtenbergern* *schon Anno 1512. zu Wittenberg / und von Doct. Philippo Theophrasto Paracelso Anno 1546. zu Saltzburg und anderen unbekandten Authoren in diesen Seculo Grosse Veränderungen entdecket werden. Darbey auch des Seel. Doct. Martini Lutheri Meynung / was er von Johann Lichtenbergers Prophezeyhung gehalten. Nebenst Einer wehemühtigen Klage und Bitte derer sämptlichen Pfaltzischen und Rheinischen ruinirten Ländern und Städten / an die Allerhöchste und unendlichste Majestät / wieder die allergrausamsten Proceduren Ludewigs des XIV. Königs von Franckreich. Zu diesen gefährlichen betrübten Zeiten wohlmeinend auff vielfältiges Nachfragen / zum andern mahl zum Druck befordert. Und mit einer Explication der Obscuren Nahmen und Wö[r]ther verwahret.* [N.p.: n.p.], 1690. VD17 3:600599Z*. Halle Universitäts- und Landesbibliothek, Weimar Herzogin Anna Amalia Bibliothek, Wolfenbüttel Herzog August Bibliothek

Prognostication of Theodor Simitz for 1563–66, with the Prognostication of Nicolaus Caesareus for 1563–64 (ascribed to Wilhelm Friess)

Practica Teütsch / Gründtliche und warhafftige weissagung / uber das M.D.LXIII. LXIIII. LXV. unnd LXVI. Jar / Allen Christen zŭ trewer warnung / bŭß und besserug beschriben / Durch M. Theodoricum Simitz. Auch die Prophezeihung / welche von dem alten Wilhelm Friesen / von Mastrich / uber das 1563. 1564. Jar geweissaget ist / hinzŭ gethon. Strasbourg: Christian Müller the Elder, [1562]. VD16 S 6494/F 2846*. Munich Bayerische Staatsbibliothek

The Second Prophecy of Wilhelm Friess: "Terrible and Shocking Prophecy"/ "Grausame und erschreckliche Prophezeiung"

F1   *Eine grawsame und erschreckliche alte Prophezei oder VISION Uber Teutsch-Land / Welche ein Gottlibender Mann / wohnhafft in Embden auß einer alten Schrifft des Sehl. I. H. V. Notarii eigener Hand Anno 1623. den 19. Febr. extrahiret, und weil solche Vision oder Gesicht und Offenbarung nicht wenig importiret, auch Täglichen in erfüllung gerichtet wird / ist sie im verlauffenen 1638. Jahr zum Druck befordert / aber in Hollendischer Sprach / womit nicht jederman gedienet gewesen.* [N.p.: n.p.], 1639. VD17 39:140281T*. Gotha Forschungsbibliothek

F2   Manuscript (17th c.): Wolfenbüttel, Herzog August Bibliothek, Cod. Guelf. 31.8 Aug. 2°, 51r–55v*

F3   *Ein Grausame und Erschreckeliche Prophezeygung oder Weissagung uber Teuschlandt / Brabandt und Franckreich. Diese Prophezeygung ist gefunden worden in Mastricht / bey einem Gottforchtigen Mann Wilhelm de Frieß nach seinem todt.* [N.p.: n.p., ca. 1577]. VD16 F 2838*. Utrecht

Universiteetsbibliotheek, Wolfenbüttel Herzog August Bibliothek,
Zurich Zentralbibliothek (title page only)

F4 *Ein Grausame Und Erschreckeliche Prophezeygung.* . . [N.p.: n.p.], 1577.
VD16 ZV 21921*. Berlin Staatsbibliothek Preußischer Kulturbesitz,
Zurich Zentralbibliothek

F5 *Ein Grausame Unnd Erschreckeliche Prophezeygung.* . . [N.p.: n.p.], 1577.
VD16 ZV 17636*. Dresden Sächsische Landesbibliothek/Staats- und
Universitätsbibliothek, Soest Stadtarchiv

F6 *Ein Grausame Unnd Erschreckliche Prophezeygung.* . . [N.p.: n.p.], 1577.
VD16 ZV 6210*. Alberta University Library, Paris Bibliothèque
nationale de France, Wolfenbüttel Herzog August Bibliothek

F7 *Eine grausame und Erschröckliche Propheceyhung / oder Weissagunge / uber
Deutschlandt / Brabandt und Franckreich. Diese Propheceyhung ist gefunden
worden zu Mastrich / bey einem Gottsfürchtigen Manne / Wilhelm de Frieß /
nach seinem Tode / 1577.* Basel: Samuel Apiarius, 1577. Not in VD16*.
Utrecht Universiteetsbibliotheek Rariora oct. 94

F8 *Ein Grausame unnd Erschröckliche Propheceyhung / oder Weissagung uber
Pollerland und Teutschland / Braband und Franckreich. Diese Propheyhung
ist gefunden worden in Mastrich / bey einem Gottsförchtigen Mann Wilhelm
de Frieß / nach seinem Todt / 1577.* Basel: Samuel Apiarius, 1577.
VD16 F 2835*. Basel Universitätsbibliothek, Munich Bayerische
Staatsbibliothek, Poznan Biblioteka Kórnicka

F9 *Ein Grausame und Erschröckliche Propheceyung.* . . Basel: Samuel Apiarius,
1577. VD16 F 2836*. Munich Bayerische Staatsbibliothek

F10 *Ein Grawsame unnd Erschröckliche Propheceihung / oder weissagung uber
Teutschland / Braband unnd Franckreich. Dise Propheceyhung ist gefunden
worden / in Mastrich / bey einem Gottsfürchtigen Mann / Wilhelm de Frieß
/ nach seinem Todt / 1577.* Basel: Samuel Apiarius, 1578. VD16 ZV
6212*. Stuttgart Württembergische Landesbibliothek, Wolfenbüttel
Herzog August Bibliothek

F11 *Ein Grausame unnd Erschröckliche Prophezeyung.* . . [N.p.: n.p.], 1578.
Not in VD16*. Stuttgart Württembergische Landesbibliothek
Allg.G.qt.315–1588/1595

F13 *Ein Grausame und Erschröckliche Propheceyung.* . . [N.p.: n.p.], 1579
(f. a4v: "Erstlich gedruckt zů Basel"). VD16 ZV 25029*. Munich
Bayerische Staatsbibliothek

F14 *Ein Grausame unnd Erschröckliche Propheceyung / oder Weissagung uber
Teutschland / Braband und Franckreich. Dise Propheceyung ist gefunden
worden in Mastrich / bey ainem Gotsförchtigen Mann / Wilhelm de Frieß /
nach seinem tod. Anno 1579.* Basel: Samuel Apiarius, 1579. VD16 F
2837*. Wolfenbüttel Herzog August Bibliothek

F15 *Prophecey und Weissagung / Ein Vorwarnung dreier Frommen / fürsichtigen*

/ *Weysen Männern* / *gemeiner Christenheit zů gůtem* / *vor fünfftzig jaren*
/ *Durch Wilhelm Friessen von Mastrich* / *Johann Müllern von Eysleben*
/ *und Nicolaum Weissen auß der Graffschafft Mansfeld* / *an tag geben* /
etc. Erfurt: Johann Beck, 1586. VD16 ZV 16200*. Erfurt Stadt- und
Regionalbibliothek, Zurich Universitätsbibliothek

F16   *Ein Grausame unnd Erschröckliche Propheceyung oder Weissagung uber*
Teutschland / *Broband und Franckreich. Dise Propheceyung ist gefunden*
worden inn Mastrich / *bey einem Gottsförchtigen Mann Wilhelme de Frieß*
/ *nach seinem Todt* / *Anno 1586.* Basel: Samuel Apiarius, 1586. VD16
F 2839*. Munich Bayerische Staatsbibliothek, Wolfenbüttel Herzog
August Bibliothek, Yale University Library

F17   *Ein Grausame unnd Erschröckliche Pratica oder Propheceyung uber*
Teutschland / *Braband unnd Franckreich* / *und andere Länder mehr* /
etc. Dise Pratica oder Propheceyung ist gefunden worden inn Mastrich /
bey einem uralten und Gottsförchtigen Mann / *Wilhelm de Friess, der vor*
seinem Todt / *Geprophecyet unnd Gepratiziert hatt* / *auff das 88.und 89.*
Ja biß auff das 90. Jar. Basel: Samuel Apiarius, 1587. Also recorded as
[Augsburg: Josias Wörli, 1587]. VD16 F 2840*. Munich Bayerische
Staatsbibliothek, Wolfenbüttel Herzog August Bibliothek

F18   *Ein Grausame und Erschröckliche Propheceyhung* / *oder weissagung über*
Teütschland / *Braband und Franckreich. Diese Propheceyhung ist gefunden*
worden in Mastrich / *bey einem Gottsförchtigen Mann Wilhelm de Frieß* /
nach seinem Todt / *1577.* Basel: Samuel Apiarius, 1578. VD16 ZV 6211.
Stuttgart Württembergische Landesbibliothek, Wolfenbüttel Herzog
August Bibliothek

F19   *Ein Grausamme und Erschröckliche Propheceyung. . .* Basel:
Samuel Apiarius, 1580. Not in VD16. Luzern Zentral- und
Hochschulbibliothek

F20   *Ein Grausame und Erschröckliche Propheceyung oder Weissagung uber*
Teutschland / *Braband und Franckreich. Diese Propheceyung ist gefunden*
worden in Mastrich / *bey einem Gottsförchtigen Manne Wilhelm de Frieß* /
nach seinem Todt / *Anno 1583.* Basel: Samuel Apiarius, 1583. VD16 ZV
21920. Berlin Staatsbibliothek Preußischer Kulturbesitz

F21   *Ein Grausame unnd Erschröckliche Propheceyung. . .* Basel: Samuel
Apiarius, 1586. VD16 ZV 18206. Wolfenbüttel Herzog August
Bibliothek

F22   *Ein Grausame unnd Erschröckliche Propheceyung oder Weissagung uber*
Teutschland / *Braband und Franckreich. Dise Propheceyung ist gefunden*
worden inn Mastrich / *bey einem Gottsfrochtigen Mann Wilhelm de Frieß*
/ *nach seinem Todt* / *Anno 1585.* Basel: Samuel Apiarius, [1587].
Also recorded as [ca. 1585]. VD16 ZV 6205. Augsburg Staats- und
Stadtbibliothek, Regensburg Staatliche Bibliothek, Strasbourg

Bibliothèque nationale et universitaire (assignment of Strasbourg
copy to this edition is uncertain)

F23 *Bedencken Eines Hochgelehrten und fürtrefflichen Mathematici, von Ende
der Welt, und kuenfftiger veraenderung Weltlicher Policey* . . . *ausz dem lauff
der Natur desz jtztwerenden 87 jahrs bisz auff das 89 beschrieben: Item Drey
Propheceyungen und Vermahnungen dreyer* . . . *Männer Wilhelm Friesen von
Mastrich, Johann Muellern von Eiszleben und Nicolaum Weissen ausz* . . .
Manszfeld. [N.p.: n.p. ("Passfurt: Timotheus Wacker")] 1587. Not in
VD16. Basel Universitätsbibliothek FO IX 22:5

F24 *Newe Zeittung, Und erschreckliche Propheceyung, oder Weissagung uber
Teutschland, Polen, Niderlandt, Brabandt und Franckreich, so sich uffs
88. Jar anfangen werden zu geschehen, neben vormeldung, was für zeichen
fürm Jüngsten Tage hergehen werden, neben einem bericht was sich jtzt in
Franckreich zugetragen. Dies Propheceyung ist gefunden worden in Mastrich,
bey einem Gottsfürchtigen Mann, Wilhelm de Frieß, nach seinem Todt, Anno
1587.* Basel: Samuel Apiarius, 1587. VD16 N 807.[3]

F25 *Newe Zeitung / Und Erschröckliche Propheceyung oder Weissagung uber
Deutschland / Polen / Niderlandt / Brabandt / und Franckreich / so sich
uffs 88. Jar anfangen werden zugeschehen / neben vormeldung / was für
zeichen fürm Jüngsten Tage hergehen werden / neben einem bericht / was sich
jetzt in Franckreich zugetragen hat. Diese Propheceyung ist gefunden worden
in Mastrich / bey einem Gottsfürchtigen Mann / Wilhelm de Frieß / nach
seinem Tode / Anno 1587.* [N.p.: n.p., 1588] (f. a4v: "Erstlich gedruckt
zu Basel / durch Samuel Apiarium / Anno 1588"). Not in VD16*.[4]
Zittau Christian Weise Bibliothek Hist. 4° 949 (24)

F26 *Newe Zeitung, Und Erschreckliche Propheceyung oder Weissagung uber
Deutschlandt, Polen, Niderlandt, Brabandt und Franckreich, so sich uffs
88. Jahr anfangen werden zu geschehen, neben vormeldung, was für zeichen
fürm Jüngsten Tage hergehen werden, neben einem bericht, was sich jetzt
in Franckreich zugetragen hat. Diese Propheceyung ist gefunden worden in
Mastrich, bey einem Gottßfürtigen Mann, Wilhelm de Frieß, nach seinem
Todt, Anno 1587* . . . *Erstlich gedruckt zu Basel, durch Samuel Apiarium,
Anno 1587.* [N.p.: n.p.], 1587. VD16 N 806.[5] Berlin Staatsbibliothek
Preußischer Kulturbesitz (missing)

F27 *Kurtze Propheceyung oder Practica. Was sich Ungeferlich auff das
M.D.LXXXVII. und auff das M.D.LXXXXVIII. Jar zutragen soll / grosse
/ wichtige / schwäre / sörgliche / und schreckliche / und zuvor nie gehörte
wunder / und allen Ständen woll acht zunemen / damit ein jeder in dieser
geferlichsten und letzten zeitten sein Leben in Gott zu richten weiß / trewlich
angezeigt. Durch den erfaren Bilger Ruth im Waldt verborgen. Kauffs /
Ließ* . . . *Sampt einer Ander Prophetzeyung / ist gefunden worden / in
Mastrich / bey einem Gottsfürchtigen Mann / Wilhelm de Frieß / nach seinem*

Todt. Cologne: Nikolaus Schreiber, [1587]. VD16 ZV 28130*. Vienna Österreichische Nationalbibliothek, Zurich Zentralbibliothek

F28   *Corte Prophetie / van tgene int Jaer M.D.LXXXVIII. sal toedragen ende gheschieden / groote wichtighe sware / sorgelijcke / schrickelijcke ende onghehoorde wonderen / tot waerschouwinge ende bekeeringhe van alle menschen. Trouwelijcken gheschreven. Door den ervaren Pelgrum Ruth int Wout verborghen. Met noch een ander Prophetie, die welcke ghevonden is gheweest, tot Maestricht by eenen Godt-vruchtigen Man, ghenaemt Willem de Vries, nae zijn doot.* Amsterdam: Cornelius Claesz, [1588] (Dutch). *NB* 27073*. The Hague Koninklijke Bibliotheek, Dublin Trinity College, Leiden Universiteitsbibliotheek*

F29   Unattested: [N.p.: n.p.], 1638 (Dutch).

Dutch Hybrids of "Friess II" and Prophecies of Paul Grebner

G1   *EXTRACT Vande Prophecie / door eenen ghenaemt PAULUS SECUNDUS, der vrijer Consten Student / Uut een nacht Visioen / twelck hem gheopenbaert is / den 24. dach April / Anno 1601. Verkondighende van vele dinghen die gheschieden sullen. Met noch de Revolutien van Acht Jaren / gheduerende tot 1600. ende 8. Alles wat daer in geschieden ende sich toe dragen sal. Ghetranslateert uut de Hoochduytsche Tale.* Emden: Hans Wilrincx [pseudonym], 1601. STCN 124429874*. Leiden Universiteitsbibliotheek

G2   *Een wonderlijcke nieuwe Prophecije van de Nederlanden / ofte de seventhien Provintien door eenen hoochgeleerden Paulus Secundus der vrijer Conste Student in der Astronomie, Uut een nacht Visioen / twelck hem geopenbaert is den 24. dach Augustus des snachts ten xii. uren / Anno 1603. Vercondigende van vele toecomende wonderlijcke dingen / die int Jaer Duysent ses hondert ende thien geschieden sullen. Inhoudende op elck Jaer zijn Revolutien.* Breeda: Peeter Gevaerts, 1604. STCN 12266941X*. Leiden Universiteitsbibliotheek

G3   Under pseudonym "Jerrassemus van Eydenborch," combined with a vision of Paul Grebner: *Een wonderlicke nieuwe Prophecije vande Nederlanden oft seventhien Provintien / Door eenen Hoch-geleerden Jerassemus van Eydenborch, der vrijer Consten Student inder Astronomie, uut een Nacht Visioen twelck hem geopenbaert is den 25. dach December des snachts ten 12. uyren Anno 1604. Vercondighe van veel toecomende wonderlicke dingen die int Jaer ses hondert ende vijf / tot den Jare ses hondert ende elf gheschieden sullen / in houdende elck Jaer sijn Revolutie. Uut de Hoochduytsche Tale in onse Nederlantsche spraecke gehtrouwelijck overgheset.* Emden: Frans de Vlamingh [pseudonym], 1605. STCN 831631287*. Amsterdam Universiteitsbibliotheek, Bern Universitätsbibliothek, The Hague

Koninklijke Bibliotheek, Ghent Universiteitsbibliotheek, Groningen Universiteitsbibliotheek, Leiden Universiteitsbibliotheek

G4 Under pseudonym "Jerrassemus van Eydenborch": *Een wonderlicke nieuwe Prophecije vande Nederlanden* . . . Delft: Bruyn Harmansz Schinckel, 1605. STCN 831631414. The Hague Koninklijke Bibliotheek, Leiden Universiteitsbibliotheek

G5 Under pseudonym "Johannes Ulpus": *Wonderbaerlicjcke nieuwe Prophetie vande seventhien Provincien / door den hoochgeleerden D. Johannem Ulpus / vrijer Consten Student inde Astronomie.* Middelborch: Cornelis Jacobsz, [1607] ("Gedruckt tot Middelborch / nae de Copije van Kuelen"). Not in STCN*. Ghent Universiteitsbibliotheek Bib. Meul. 001094

Notes

Introduction

1. Barnes, *Prophecy and Gnosis*, 2.

2. McGinn, *Antichrist*, 277.

3. Many of these figures have been addressed by entire scholarly books, including McGinn, *Antichrist*; Möhring, *Der Weltkaiser der Endzeit*; Petersen, *Preaching in the Last Days*.

4. Smoller, *History, Prophecy, and the Stars*, 105–6.

5. See Leppin, *Antichrist und Jüngster Tag*, 179–82 (or, more extensively, 179–205).

6. Virdung, *Practica von dem Entcrist* (VD16 V 1302), 8v: "dar umb wan wir sehen das dise ding kumen alß sich leyder yntzunt ir vil erzeigenn / nemlich mit den durcken und den geistlichen und dem opffer und emptern der kirchen etc. so wissen wir dan das der Entcrist und die letzt zeit nohe ist." Throughout, transcriptions from unedited sources follow the principles of transcription described in appendix 1, and a double virgule divides lines of verse. Translations are my own.

7. Pettegree, *Book in the Renaissance*, 72.

8. The account here of astrology and prophecy in print summarizes the more extensive discussion in Green, *Printing and Prophecy*.

9. Kurze, *Johannes Lichtenberger*, 68.

10. The numbers of editions given here and elsewhere are based on careful scrutiny of VD16 and library catalogs, verified wherever possible through consulting facsimiles. On Luther's prophetic profile after his death, see Kolb, *Martin Luther as Prophet, Teacher, and Hero*.

11. Apart from brief mention in Barnes, *Prophecy and Gnosis*, and Leppin, *Antichrist und Jüngster Tag*, secondary literature is quite sparse on Severus, Jordan, Füger's excerpt of Lactantius, and the prophecy that circulated under Hilten's name in the later sixteenth century.

12. The most extensive treatment of Friess to date is Barnes, *Prophecy and Gnosis*,

81–82, 234, 285 n. 57. Friess is otherwise referred to only briefly in Freytag, *Bilder aus der deutschen Vergangenheit*, 1:5; Sandblad, *De eskatologiska föreställningarna*, 135; Efron, "Nature, Human Nature, and Jewish Nature in Early Modern Europe," 40 n. 18; Dixon, "Popular Astrology and Lutheran Propaganda in Reformation Germany," 404, 405–6; Leppin, *Antichrist und Jüngster Tag*, 65 n. 51; Beyer, "George Reichard und Laurentius Matthaei," 306 n. 30; Green, *Printing and Prophecy*, 67, 154, 219 n. 19.

Chapter 1

1. The description here of Jacob van Liesvelt's death follows Francois, "Jacob van Liesvelt," 341–55.

2. Führer, *Die Kirchen- und die antireformatorische Religionspolitik Kaiser Karls V.*, 347–52.

3. This account of Antwerp's history follows Marnef, *Antwerp in the Age of Reformation*, 3–22.

4. Francois, "Jacob van Liesvelt," 355.

5. Francois, "Jacob van Liesvelt," 351–52. The Bible edition in question is *NB* 3704.

6. Francois, "Jacob van Liesvelt," 353. Kronenberg (*Verboden boeken en opstandige drukkers in de Hervormingstijd*, 135) describes the *Troostinge der goddelycker scryft* as a work of the German theologian Caspar Huberinus.

7. Olthoff, *De boekdrukkers, boekverkoopers en uitgevers in Antwerpen*, 2, 63.

8. Smit, *Kalliope in de Nederlanden*, 2:253–54.

9. Marnef, *Antwerp in the Age of Reformation*, 178, 181.

10. Scott, *Domination and the Arts of Resistance*, 4.

11. See Duke, *Dissident Identities in the Early Modern Low Countries*, 161–62; Scott, *Domination and the Arts of Resistance*, 140–52.

12. Pettegree, *Emden and the Dutch Revolt*, 20. Nierop's "Censorship and Illicit Printing" provides an overview of censorship in the Netherlands in the sixteenth century.

13. Marnef, *Antwerp in the Age of Reformation*, 24–25, 188.

14. Duke, *Dissident Identities in the Early Modern Low Countries*, 158; Marnef, *Antwerp in the Age of Reformation*, 43.

15. Duke, *Dissident Identities in the Early Modern Low Countries*, 162; Scott, *Domination and the Arts of Resistance*, 152.

16. See Müller, "Zensurforschung," 334.

17. Scott, *Domination and the Arts of Resistance*, 158, 184.

18. Jaspers, *Savonarola (1452–1498) in de Nederlanden*, 60.

19. Doedes, "Nieuw merkwaardigheden uit den oude-boeken-schat," 224–42. The 1548 edition of *Historien ende prophecien uut der Heyligher Schriftueren verciert met suyverlike beeldinghen ende devote ghebeden* is *NB* 3925, while the 1555 edition is unrecorded.

20. Doedes, "Nieuw merkwaardigheden uit den oude-boeken-schat," 230: "Si crijghen doverhant dye ghene, die uwen Cristum hier verdrucken in sinen litmaten"; "Mer sie vervolgen ooc nu den genen, die hen lieden die warachticheyt seggen derf . . . ende si verstootense (namelijk: die boden van uwer waerheyt) en verachtense waer si connen. Die ander vangense, sie hangense, ende hen wort soo veel verdriets aengedaen, datter schier niemant meer spreken en derf . . ." (ellipses as found in Doedes's quotation); "Siet doch neder, alder miltste Heere, hoe men die boose conin-

gen te gemoet gaet ende hoemen haer spreect na haren mont, ende daer en is bicaus niemant, die sinen hals derf avontueren om dye glorie dijns naems. Niemant en wil met Paulo gebonden worden ende dat leven te voren geven."

21. Pettegree, *Emden and the Dutch Revolt*, 135–36. On Goossens, see Diekmann-Dröge, "Van den Eerwerdigen Meester Jan Goosens."

22. Gerdes, *Introductio in historiam evangelii seculo XVI*, 44.

23. Haer, *Francisci Haraei Annales ducum seu principum Brabantiae totiusque Belgii tomus tertius*, 35–36. On the "Compromise of the Nobility," see Gelderen, *Political Thought of the Dutch Revolt*, 110–15; Kossmann and Mellink, *Texts Concerning the Revolt of the Netherlands*, 59–62; Marnef, *Antwerp in the Age of Reformation*, 88; Pettegree, *Emden and the Dutch Revolt*, 112. The authorship remains uncertain, however. Putnam (*William the Silent*, 161) speculates that Philips van Marnix was the author of the "Compromise of the Nobility."

24. Duke, *Dissident Identities in the Early Modern Low Countries*, 147.

25. The rise in astrological printing was first noted in Broeckx, "Lettre a M. le docteur P. J. van Meerbeeck," 14. According to the USTC, "Prognosticatie" editions in the Low Countries jump from a few per decade into the range of one to two dozen beginning in the 1550s.

26. For an overview of astrological prognostications in the German-speaking regions of Europe, see Green, *Printing and Prophecy*, 109–23, or the expanded version in Green, "Printing the Future."

27. Copp, *Was auff diß Dreyundzwayntzigest und zum tail vyerundzwayntzigest jar. Des himels lauff künfftig sein* (VD16 C 5026), a1v, b1r: "Ich sag dir dast nit gern hörst // Ja ob du noch so gwaltig wörst // Glaub mir ich habs nit thon auß neyd // Dann deyn schad ist mir gar kain freüd"; "Aber die Finsternus so diß xxiii. Jar am andern sontag in der fasten ist gewesen wirt meins bedunckens vil übels bedeütten / als grossen kryeg / vil blůt vergyessen / brand / unainigkayt unnd auffrůr zwyschen dem gemainen man unnd der pfaffhayt / Ist auch zů besorgen ain bundtschůch der gemayn wider die herschaft und nemlich wider die Bischoff und alle pfaffen."

28. See Green, *Printing and Prophecy*, 126–28; Talkenberger, *Sintflut*, 224–35. The "clearer" edition of 1523 is VD16 C 5023.

29. Vriese, *Een vremde ende wonderlijcke Pronosticatie vanden Jare ons Heeren M.D.lv* (*NB* 31227), a1r: "duer den hoochgheleerden M. Willem de vriese / Doctoor der Medecijnen / ende der vrijer consten." See also the edition of this booklet in Kampen, *Het zal koud zijn in't water als't vriest*, 203–8.

30. Vriese, *Een vremde ende wonderlijcke Pronosticatie vanden Jare ons Heeren M.D.lv* (*NB* 31227), a3r: "Si sullen wonderlijcke dingen willen ordineren teghen haer overheyt ende regenten / si sullen claghen van lasten ende gravamina die si niet ghedraghen en connen / si sullen nieuwe politien ende statuyten eysscht na haren eyghen sin / jae oock schier met foortsen die eysschen Si sullen murmureren / mompelen / susureren ende achterclappen van haren regenten / ende die selve geerne in haet ende nijt brenghen waert moghelijck / Soo dat die heeren regenten ende voorstaenders der landen ende steden wel wijsen raet moghen ghebruycken / ende haer ghemeynten peyselijc regeren / soo si dat voor God ende alle die werelt willen verantwoorden." See Kampen, *Het zal koud zijn in't water als't vriest*, 27–28.

31. Vriese, *Een vremde ende wonderlijcke Pronosticatie vanden Jare ons Heeren M.D.lv* (*NB* 31227), a2v: "Duytslant en sal in geen der manieren in rusten sijn / maer sullen hier ende daer heerscharen ruyters ende knechten vergadert worden / ende niemant

172 · Notes to Pages 19–20

en sal weten / waer si henen sullen willen. Den eenen heer en sal den anderen niet
betrouwen / noch die eene stadt der anderen / maer si sullen tegen malcanderen
opstaen ende malcanderen verderven / diesghelijcke salder ooc krijch ende twist sijn
in gheheel Europa / want een yegelijc sal hem besorgen verheert te worden / ende
in meerder servituit ende subjectien ghebracht te worden / daerom sal een yege-
lijck soecken om haer liberteyt te vindiceren ende vryheyt te vercrijgen tot dat hi ten
lesten gheheel sal uutbersten ende so gheweldich branden dat gheheel Europa die
voncken jae die colen ghevoelen sal."

32. Vriese, *Een vremde ende wonderlijcke Pronosticatie vanden Jare ons Heeren M.D.lv* (*NB*
31227), a2v–a3r: "Jupiter retrogradus en sal in sijnder revolutien noch in sine ret-
rogressie den geestelijcken staet niet connen beschermen voor die furien ende dat
grimmen van mars ende Saturnus / want veel tegenspoets ende contrarieteyten sullen die geestelijcke persoonen lijden / is ooc dat si eenen grooten val / vercleyninge
ende vernederinge sullen hebben / huere Prelaten ende grootste hoofden sullen
in sommige landen tegen den onderganck der sonnen afghesedt / verjaecht ende
verdreven worden. In duytslant sullen sommige Bisschoppen dat weerlijck regiment
selve overgeven ende verlaten. Sommige gheestelijcke ende religieuse mannen sullen
haer plaetsen ende woonsteden verloopen ende verlaten. Nyet wetende van yeman-
den diese vervolghen sal oft dreyghen wil / dan alleen uut vreesen / ende vertwijfelt-
heyt. Sommige sullen haer veynsen datse niet geestelijck en zijn vercleedende ende
veranderende haer leven. Die ander sullen meynen vaste vrije gestadige plaetsen in
sommighe landen te hebben / maer tsal verre van daer zijn / si sullen haest uut haren
ghehoopte plaetsen moeten scheyden. In summa grooten druck / ancxt ende lijden
sal haer overcomen. Ick en weet niet oft dit gheschieden sal meer uut quaetwillicheyt
van sommige verkeerde menschen / oft duer haer eyghen schult / daerom behoordtn
die gheestelijcheyt ons wel voor te gaen in goet leven / ende ghetrouwe leeringhe des
woort Gods / op dat God sine gramschap van hen ende van ons ghenadelijck keere."

33. Montag, *Birgitta von Schweden*, 327: "Auch hat der apt Joachim von Callabria,
ein stiffter eins closters zu Florencz, der zu den selben gezeiten war, geschriben in
seiner glos über den propheten Jeremiam, daz zukünftig ist ein groses trübsal über
die cristenheit von den keczern, haiden und den bösen cristen, und daz die güter von
den priestern genomen werden, darzu vil stet und slösser zustört werden, alz daz auch
vor gesagt hat sant Hildigart, und sie werden verjagt aus einem land in daz ander.
Darumb ir vil in die wüstung werden gen und füren werden ein armlich leben."

34. Honemann, "Ferrer, Vincenz," 726–27.

35. Ferrer, *Ain wunderbarlich Büechlin und prophecei / des heiligen Manns Sant Vincentz
von Valentz* (VD16 V 1210), d3r–v: "Dergleichen auch werden die Gaistlichen / davon
Ich oben gemellt hab / so auch in die wüestin werden fliehen / in grossem ellend
und armůt leben. Sie werden Ire gaistliche claider verkern / kain platten tragen /
kain gaistlichen wandl füeren / sie werden sich nit merckhen lassen / das sie lesen
khünden / werden weder Cappelln / Betheüser / noch Altar haben / sonder mor-
gens in aller frůe / werden die / denen es erlaubt wirdt sein / auff aim stain oder
stockh zůerichten / unnd eyllendts Meß lesen. . . . Und so sie Meß glesen haben /
so werden sie die Kelch / Klaider und annders darzůe ghörig / eyllenndts verbergen
/ allso das sie khainer in disen kurtzen jarn fur priester erkennen wirdet / und das
werden die schweigendte khnecht sein. . . . Und dises wirt got verhengen damit die
Sün Levi gerainigt werden / von ihrer boßhait / davon sie sich selbst willigclich nit
rainigen haben wöllen."

36. Vriese, *Een vremde ende wonderlijcke Pronosticatie vanden Jare ons Heeren M.D.lv* (*NB* 31227), a4r: "Die borghers ende inwoonders sullen somtijts twistich zijn ende tweedracht / som tijts om nieuwe policien / ende sullen ander begheeren. Somwijlen oock in die sake van die religie."

37. Vriese, *Prognosticatie vanden Jaere ons Heeren M.D. ende LVI* (*NB* 31228), a3r: "Item het gemeyne volc sal in dit jaer seer oproerich ende tweedrachtich wesen / om der religien wille / sy en sullen met haren leeraers / ende sielensorgers niet te vreden wesen / sullen clagen / dat haer dz broot des Godlicken woorts niet te recht uutghedeylt en wort / misschien niet sonder oorsake ende redene / om dat sy veel gebreken inden Geestelijcken staet culperen sullen / ende die eer sien ende aenmercken sullen eer sy haer eygen gebreken mercken / om welcke gebreken ende sonden wille / haer Hypocrijten tot regenten ende ongeleerde boose leeraers gegeven worden."

38. Vriese, *Prognosticatie vanden Jaere ons Heeren M.D. ende LVI* (*NB* 31228), a2v: "Soo stelt hem dan dit Jaer ende die regerende Planeten desselfs recht aen / gelijck ofter een groote ende sonderlinge reformatie soude comen onder die Gheestelijck-heyt. . . . Haer schatten ende vergaderde goeden / die sie over lange Jaren versamelt hebben. die mochten wel dit jaer seer smelten ende in der weerlijcker Heeren ende Princen handen geraken want billich die alderopperste regent / en wil niet by den onrechtveerdighen Mammon ghedient wesen."

39. Vriese, *Prognosticatie vanden Jaere ons Heeren M.D. ende LVI* (*NB* 31228), a3r: "Voort soo mochten wel dit jaer veel Prophecien vervult worden / die voor langen tijt gepropheteert sijn."

40. Vriese, *Prognosticatie vanden Jaere ons Heeren M.D. ende LVI* (*NB* 31228), a2v: "Daerom ghy herders van Isarel siet wel toe daer zijnder onder u lieden / die heyme-like conspiracie dit Jaer sullen willen maken ende muyterije sullen willen stichten / ja ooc tweedracht ende viantschap saeyen ende dit alreede begonst hebben te doen tegen Princen ende Potentaten der weerlt / ende tusschen Christen Princen."

41. Wieder, *Schriftuurlijke liedekens*, 73.

42. Vriese, *Prognosticatie vanden Jaere ons Heeren M.D. ende LVI* (*NB* 31228), a3v: "Dese vorst mocht wel eenighe reformatie ende renovatie maken ende aevrechten in die Cristelijcke religie ende sal oock een groot accoort maken met den Duytschen vorsten tot beyder welvaert."

43. Duke, *Dissident Identities in the Early Modern Low Countries*, 101; Marnef, *Antwerp in the Age of Reformation*, 82–85.

44. Vriese, *Prognosticatie vanden Jaere ons Heeren M.D. ende LVI* (*NB* 31228), a3v–a4r: "Vanden Prince der slaven ghenaemt Esau Pharmona"; "Nochtans heeft hi allenthenen veel groote ende geweldige vianden / als Solomannum / Ottomann der Turcken keyser / den grooten Cham / den heer der Moscoviten / den Sophi."

45. Vriese, *Prognosticatie vanden Jaere ons Heeren M.D. ende LVI* (*NB* 31228), a4r: "ende die ondersaten in grooten servituyt gehouden / so datter niemant int lant tegen zijn tyrannije seggen oft spreken en mach op verlies van sijnen lijve."

46. Howorth, *History of the Mongols*, 1034–35.

47. Strick's name appears as a signatory, for example, in a 1556 royal decree of Philip II, published in *Kronyk der stad Alkmaer*, 395.

48. Report by the pensionary of Antwerp, as cited in Valkema Blouw, "Van Old-enborch and Vanden Merberghe Pseudonyms," 265: "zekere zeer quade opruerige pronosticatie opten naem van eenen Meester Willem de Vriese."

Chapter 2

1. See, for example, Roose, "De Antwerpse hervormingsgezinde rederijker Frans Fraet," 95–98.

2. The editions printed by Maria Ancxt are *NB* 17744 and 17745. For the other edition, unrecorded in *NB*, see "Frans Fraet" in Frederiks and Branden, *Biographisch woordenboek der Noord- en Zuidnederlandsche letterkunde.*

3. Marnef, *Antwerp in the Age of Reformation*, 29–33; Waite, *Reformers on Stage*, 74.

4. Valkema Blouw, "Van Oldenborch and Vanden Merberghe Pseudonyms," 245–49.

5. Hofman, "Liederen en refreinen van Frans Fraet," 227–28; Valkema Blouw, "Van Oldenborch and Vanden Merberghe Pseudonyms," 246.

6. Letter from Philip II to the Margrave of Antwerp, as cited in Valkema Blouw, "Van Oldenborch and Vanden Merberghe Pseudonyms," 266.

7. Haemstede and Gysius, *Historie der martelaren*, 326r: "een bloetgierigh mensche"; Marnef, *Antwerp in the Age of Reformation*, 19.

8. Génard, "Personen te Antwerpen in de XVIe eeuw, voor het 'feit van religie' gerechtelijk vervolgd," 441: "midts dat den verweerdere diverssche seditieuse boecken, als prononsticatien ende andere op versierde ende gefingeerde namen gedruct, vercocht ende verspreyt heeft."

9. Report by the pensionary of Antwerp, as cited in Valkema Blouw, "Van Oldenborch and Vanden Merberghe Pseudonyms," 265: "die vande poorterye vercleerden ter contrarien dat zy in nyet en volchden de opinien vande scepenen noch oudescepenen noch daerinne en consenteerden"; Marnef, *Antwerp in the Age of Reformation*, 86.

10. Letter from Philip II to the Margrave of Antwerp, as cited in Valkema Blouw, "Van Oldenborch and Vanden Merberghe Pseudonyms," 266: "datter materie ende stoffe meer dan ghenough is om den voirsz gevanghene te bringhen ende legghen ter scerper examinatien, desen nochtans nyet tegenstaende verstaen dat die vanden derde leden vanden voirsz stadt difficulteijt ende zwaricheijt daerinne souden vinden ende maken."

11. Génard, "Personen te Antwerpen in de XVIe eeuw, voor het 'feit van religie' gerechtelijk vervolgd," 442.

12. Jan van Immerseel's reply is cited in Valkema Blouw, "Van Oldenborch and Vanden Merberghe Pseudonyms," 266: "Lequel at este le lendemain execute, nayant sostenu ne debatu aucune mauuaise opinion, et en article dela mort publicquement a declare nauoir aulcum mauuais sentiment, ains quil morut volentiers et bon XPien, pour ces oeuures quil disoit auoir fect pour lentretenement de ces femme et enfans."

13. Génard, "Personen te Antwerpen in de XVIe eeuw, voor het 'feit van religie' gerechtelijk vervolgd," 442–43, 445.

14. Hofman, "De Antwerpse drukker Frans Fraeten," 73: "De reden: hij heeft onder verschillende pseudoniemen ketterse boeken gedrukt, verkocht en verspreid."

15. Marnef, *Antwerp in the Age of Reformation*, 40, 82, 87; Nierop, "Censorship and Illicit Printing," 34, 35, 37–38.

16. Nierop, "Censorship and Illicit Printing," 40.

17. Report by the pensionary of Antwerp, as cited in Valkema Blouw, "Van Oldenborch and Vanden Merberghe Pseudonyms," 245–46 n. 78, 265: "noch hadde gedruct op andere namen date ende plaetsen verscheyden quade boecken innehoudende quade secten ende leeringen tenderende tot oproericheyt ende seditien ende besunderen oick nu onlancx versiert ende gefabriceert zekere zeer quade opruerige

pronosticatie opten naem van eenen Meester Willem de Vriese / tenderende tot commotie van zeer quaden exemple ende consequentien."

18. Report by the pensionary of Antwerp, as cited in Valkema Blouw, "Van Oldenborch and Vanden Merberghe Pseudonyms," 265: "de voers. pronosticatie vele saken was innehoudende grootelyck doende tegen de weereldlycke ende oic geestelycke overheyt"; "nadyen oic der poorteryen het verlyt ende pronosticatie gelesen waeren metten titelen vande boecken by hem gedruct"; letter from Philip II to the Margrave of Antwerp, as cited in Valkema Blouw, "Van Oldenborch and Vanden Merberghe Pseudonyms," 266: "een valsche schandeleuse ende seditieuse pronosticatie, oft prophecie, Ruerende alle geestelijcke ende weerlycke princen ende potentaten, ende oick gemeyne volcke, de selue verweckende tot seditie oft desperatie."

19. Hofman, "De Antwerpse drukker Frans Fraeten," 74; Valkema Blouw, "Van Oldenborch and Vanden Merberghe Pseudonyms," 245–46 n. 79.

20. Valkema Blouw, "Van Oldenborch and Vanden Merberghe Pseudonyms," 245–46 n. 78.

21. Letter from Philip II to the Margrave of Antwerp, 4 January [1558], as cited and edited in Valkema Blouw, "Van Oldenborch and Vanden Merberghe Pseudonyms," 266: "Ende gemerct dat de voirsz getuigen tselue alleene nijet en heeft kunnen gedoen, maer hem sonder twyffel beholpen heeft met quade valsche ende opruerige gheesten, mogelijck hijmelyck verstandt hebbende met onsen viant sulcx datter materie ende stoffe meer dan ghenough is om den voirsz gevanghene te bringhen ende legghen ter scerper examinatien."

22. Pettegree, *Book in the Renaissance*, 206; Pettegree, *Emden and the Dutch Revolt*, 139.

23. Hofman, "De Antwerpse drukker Frans Fraeten," 73; Valkema Blouw, "Van Oldenborch and Vanden Merberghe Pseudonyms," 245–46 n. 78.

24. Bots, Matthey, and Meyer, *Noordbrabantse studenten 1550–1750*, 747, no. 5681. For bringing this record to my attention and for their generous assistance with interpreting the biographical information on Willem de Vriese, I wish to thank Dr. Annelies van Gijsen and Prof. Dr. Willem Frijoff.

25. Dr. L. Wiggers, director, Regionaal Historisch Centrum Limburg, e-mail message to author, 30 July 2012.

26. Report by the pensionary of Antwerp, as cited in Valkema Blouw, "Van Oldenborch and Vanden Merberghe Pseudonyms," 265: "ende besunderen oick nu onlancx versiert ende gefabriceert zekere zeer quade opruerige pronosticatie opten naem van eenen Meester Willem de Vriese"; Jan van Immerseel's reply to Philip II, as cited in Valkema Blouw, "Van Oldenborch and Vanden Merberghe Pseudonyms," 266: "certaines prognostications par luy forgees et imprimes." I thank Dr. Annelies van Gijsen for bringing this wording to my attention.

27. Valkema Blouw, "Van Oldenborch and Vanden Merberghe Pseudonyms," 267–69.

28. Prof. Dr. Willem Frijhoff, e-mail message to author, 11 July 2012.

29. The base text for the translation is provided by the edition N16 (VD16 F 2843), the most widespread form of the most popular version of the prophecy.

Chapter 3

1. The following discussion of Rupescissa's life follows Robert Lerner's historical introduction to Rupescissa, *Liber secretorum eventuum*, 15–36, 83–85.

2. Rupescissa, *Liber secretorum eventuum*, 214: "nolo ut nomen prophete michi, qui ut dixi *propheta non sum*, ascribatur." Cf. Amos 7:14.

3. DeVun, *Prophecy, Alchemy, and the End of Time*, 46, 132.

4. Brown, *Fasciculus rerum expetendarum et fugiendarum*, 2:499, 507: "Confusa hic sunt omnia, *excriptoris* partim vitio; partim vero ipsius *authoris* crassa inscitia et judicio pravo"; "Misere hic corrumpitur textus ob egregiam scribae vel transcriptoris inscitiam: siquid ex laceris verbis sensus possis elicere, bene est: vide autem interea, Lector, quantum damni patiuntur authores, cum amanuenses stulti, qui manuscripta antiqua nesciunt legere, eorum opera excribenda in se recipiunt. *Dulcissima musica asini ad lyram.*" On Brown's edition, see Bignami-Odier, *Études sur Jean de Roquetaillade*, 157 n. 6.

5. Brown, *Fasciculus rerum expetendarum et fugiendarum*, 2:499.

6. Herkommer, "Johannes de Rupescissa," 724–25. The previously unrecognized verse rendition of the *Vademecum* is found in Ambach, *Vom Ende der Welt* (VD16 A 2161), 11v–L4r.

7. Ferrari, "Un petit traictié extrait," 308. On this manuscript, see Bignami-Odier, *Études sur Jean de Roquetaillade*, 246; Grange, *Histoire littéraire de la France*, 41:233–34.

8. Ferrari, "Un petit traictié extrait," 305, 303: "Il s'agit en effet, plus que d'une traduction, d'une véritable réécriture, caractérisée non seulement par des ajouts, des suppressions et des modifications importantes par rapport à la source, mais aussi par une réorganisation profonde de la matière."

9. Ferrari, "Le Vade mecum," 228; Ferrari, "Un petit traictié extrait," 306.

10. Vauchez, "Bilan des recherches," 33.

11. Leppin, *Antichrist und Jüngster Tag*, 65 n. 51.

12. Hofman, "Liederen en refreinen van Frans Fraet," 248.

13. A prediction that weapons would be forbidden and violators hoisted on their own petards is found in all four versions of "Wilhelm Friess"; in the prophecy of "Dietrich von Zengg" (see chapter 5), using somewhat different language; and in the prophecy of pseudo-Jakob Pflaum, a disorganized compilation of well-known end-time tropes that was printed seven times in southern Germany between 1522 and 1534. See Lerner, *Powers of Prophecy*, 159–62.

14. Scott, *Domination and the Arts of Resistance*, 157.

15. On this passage in the *Vademecum*, see Lerner, "Popular Justice." The motif of smaller things rebelling against larger ones is also found in *Prophecey Wunderbarlicher zůkünftiger ding* (VD16 P 5064).

16. Scott, *Domination and the Arts of Resistance*, 105, 158.

17. Hofman, "De Antwerpse drukker Frans Fraeten," 75.

18. Maas, *Textual Criticism*, 42–54.

19. See Greetham, *Textual Scholarship*, 326–28.

20. See Schmieder, "Letteratura profetica," 7.

21. See Hofman, "Liederen en refreinen van Frans Fraet," 253.

22. Cf. the texts in Egenolff's 1550 *Propheceien und Weissagungen* (VD16 P 5068), 4r, 5v (Paracelsus), 113v–114r (*Extract of Various Prophecies*). The Latin "Prophecia antiqua" reads: "Anno Sexagesimo caveat sibi omnis homo."

23. Grünpeck, *Speculum naturalis coelestis et propheticae visionis* (VD16 G 3641), a6r; Grünpeck, *Spiegel der naturlichen himlischen und prophetischen sehungen* (VD16 G 3642), a5r–v.

24. Grünpeck, *Spiegel der naturlichen himlischen und prophetischen sehungen* (VD16 G

3642), a5r: "und habt angefangen in der übung der tugent narrisch und nachlessig / aber in der boßheyt gantz weyß / listig / und fursichtig zesein."

25. On Grünpeck, see Talkenberger, *Sintflut*, 110–45. On Lichtenberger, see Kurze, *Johannes Lichtenberger*, Talkenberger, *Sintflut*, 55–110. On the *Extract of Various Prophecies*, see Talkenberger, *Sintflut*, 145–53. On the Dutch pamphlet and for an extensive edition of the text, see Faems, "Deynde der werelt naket."

26. For a fuller account of the development of Egenolff's prophetic compilation, see Green, *Printing and Prophecy*, 102–8.

27. On these controversies, see Dingel, "Culture of Conflict," 19–43; Nischan, "Germany after 1550," 387–92.

28. Green, *Printing and Prophecy*, 96–99; Reeves, *Influence of Prophecy*, 453–62; Stöllinger-Löser, "Vaticinia de summis pontificibus," 1595–1600.

29. Flacius, *Duae veteres prophetiae* (VD16 P 5061). On Flacius, see Preger, "Flacius Illyricus, Matthias"; Moldaenke, "Flacius Illyricus, Matthias."

30. On Flacius and this work, see Hartmann, *Humanismus und Kirchenkritik*.

31. Lazius, *Fragmentum vaticinii* (VD16 ZV 9507), h5r–h6r.

32. Flacius, *Catalogus testium veritatis* (VD16 F 1293), 897: "Johannes de Rupescissa monachus vixit circa annum 1340. reprehendit spirituales de multis gravißimis sceleribus, et officii sui extrema neglectione: ob eamque causam fuit in carcerem coniectus. In quodam veteri codice legi, eum etiam asseruisse, ecclesiam Romanam esse meretricem, Papam esse Antichristi ministrum, et Cardinales esse pseudoprophetas. In carcere conposuit libellum propheticum, tituolo Vade mecum in tribulationem, in quo praedixit imminentem spiritualibus afflictionem et tribulationem: et clare indicavit fore, ut Deus repurget clerum, habeatque sacerdotes pauperes, pios, et fideliter gregem Domini pascentes: bona vero Ecclesiasticae ad laicos revertantur. Quae omnia iam reipsa compleri, perficique cernimus."

33. Hofman, "De Antwerpse drukker Frans Fraeten," 76–78.

34. On this element of the *Vademecum*, see Lerner, "Popular Justice."

Chapter 4

1. Wolf, *Lectionum memorabilium et reconditarum centenarii xvi* (VD16 W 4210), 645. On Wolf's collection, see Schmolinsky, "Prophetia in der Bibliothek."

2. I am grateful to Dr. Oliver Duntze of the Gesamtkatalog der Wiegendrucke for pointing out the similarity to Gaubisch's types.

3. Bumke, "Fluid Text," 107–8.

4. Reske and Benzing, *Buchdrucker des 16. und 17. Jahrhunderts*, 684–85, 686–87.

5. Friess and Caesareus, *Etliche seltzame Propheceiung* (VD16 F 2841/C 84), c3r: "Sie werden aber gewaltiglich darnider gelegt werden / und wird solchen auffrhürischen gleicher mas ergehen / wie den Bawren im Bawrenkrieg / vor drey und dreissig Jaren."

6. Butler, "Liturgical Music in Sixteenth-Century Nürnberg," 263–304, 326–32, 338–51.

7. Leppin, *Antichrist und Jüngster Tag*, 212–13.

8. Schanze, "Der Buchdruck eine Medienrevolution?" 297; Zedler, "Sibyllenweissagung," 35.

9. Marginal notes in a copy of N10 indicate that "Wilhelm Friess" continued to find readers at least into the 1570s. On the blank verso of the final leaf, a reader

copied down a prophecy of events for the years 1570–80 that is found throughout Europe from the 1570s onward and in updated form as late as the nineteenth century. To my knowledge, the various versions of this unnamed prophecy have never been systematically collected or studied. Brief notes concerning one of the versions of this prophecy can be found in Frijhoff, *Embodied Belief,* 165–66, and in Lecanu, *Dictionnaire des prophéties et des miracles,* 2:715–16, which compares earlier and later versions. In the copy of N10 (Leipzig UB NeueGesch. 117, b2v), the prophecy appears as follows:

Prophetia.
In quodam antiquo libro repertum. Anno . . .
70. Ferraria tremet.
71. Cyprus a Syone recedet.
72. Pastor non erit.
73. Ira Dei super nos.
74. A paucis cognoscetur Christus.
75. Proelium magnum in universa terra.
76. Affrica ardebit.
77. Surget maximus vir.
78. Europa trepidabit.
79. Fames erit super universam terram.
80. Fiet unum Ovile et unus Pastor.

10. Cf. Leppin, *Antichrist und Jüngster Tag,* 267 n. 13, for a similar list of frequently reprinted apocalyptic works.

11. VD16 S 6138–6146, ZV 14383–14385, 17939, 18248, and 20089. Two more editions, VD16 S 6147 and ZV 27759, followed in 1567 and 1569. Literature on Severus is slight, consisting only of a few passing references in Hoffmann-Krayer and Baechtold-Staeubli, *Handwörterbuch des deutschen Aberglaubens,* 817; Leppin, *Antichrist und Jüngster Tag,* 102 n. 241, 116 n. 319, 118 n. 335, 135 n. 36, 181 n. 81; Mauer and Hörmann, *Medien und Weltbilder im Wandel der frühen Neuzeit,* 140 n. 10; Zinner, *Geschichte und Bibliographie der astronomischen Literatur,* 60.

12. Severus, *Von der bedeutung die da folgen werden / aus dem obgemelten Constellation / und der Finsternissen* (VD16 ZV 14383), a2v: "der Babst mit den seinen wird den stuel zu Rom verlassen / unnd für grossen engsten in die Wüsten fliehen / daselbst sicher zu wonen / unnd wirdt der stuel zu Rom auffgehaben werden / unnd wirdt kein Babst mehr sein / Auch werden allenthalben in Deutschen Landen kirchen und klöster zustört / unnd die Geistlichen verjagt und vertrieben werden / und werden keine pfründe mehr haben / und wird under den Geistlichen gross wehe Clagens allenthalben in Deutschlanden sein."

13. Severus, *Von der bedeutung die da folgen werden / aus dem obgemelten Constellation / und der Finsternissen* (VD16 ZV 14383), a3v, a4v.

14. Severus, *Von der bedeutung die da folgen werden / aus dem obgemelten Constellation / und der Finsternissen* (VD16 ZV 14383), a3r–v.

15. Cf. Severus, *Von der bedeutung die da folgen werden / aus dem obgemelten Constellation / und der Finsternissen* (VD16 ZV 14383), a1v. a4r; Nagel, *Himmels Zeichen. Grosse Coniunctiones Planetarum superiorum, und newer Wunderstern / so Anno 1604. den 29. Septembris erschienen* (VD17 3:002506P), c3r, d1r. On Nagel, see Barnes, *Prophecy and*

Gnosis, 177–80, 212–14, and two recent articles by Leigh T. I. Penman, "Repulsive Blasphemies" and "Climbing Jacob's Ladder."

16. Simitz and Caesareus, *Practica Teütsch / Gründtlich und warhafftige weissagung* (VD16 S 6494/F 2846), a1r: "Auch die Prophezeihung / welche von dem alten Wilhelm Friesen / von Mastrich / uber das 1563. 1564. Jar geweissaget ist / hinzů gethon." On Müller, see Reske and Benzing, *Buchdrucker des 16. und 17. Jahrhunderts*, 891.

17. Simitz and Caesareus, *Practica Teütsch / Gründtlich und warhafftige weissagung* (VD16 S 6494/F 2846), c3r: "Nun kommen erst die böse und erschröckliche Jar / nemlich das 1563. 1564. und 1565. Jar / Dann in disen jaren werden sich die grossen verenderungen im Reich zůtragen / welches gleichen in hundert jaren nit geschehen ist."

18. Simitz and Caesareus, *Practica Teütsch / Gründtlich und warhafftige weissagung* (VD16 S 6494/F 2846), c3v–c4r: "Dieweil dann nun in disen jaren Saturnus / Jupiter / und Mars zůhauff kommen / so bedeuts auch / das sich vil seltzame Secten erheben werden / grosse verenderung der Reich und Religion / verwüstung viler Land und stett / und wirt in der warheyt der Geystlich stand hart angefochten werden / und wirt Mars sampt Saturno sein bosheyt genügsam ausgiessen / durch rauben / mörden / und brennen / unnd werden den gemeynen pöfel zů krieg und auffrhůr wider ir oberkeyt / und wider die Geistlichen hetzen / das sie die auffs feindlichste verfolgen / sie an ihren ehren und gütern berauben / und schaden zůfügen / Sie werden aber gewaltigklich darnider gelegt werden / und wirt solchen Auffrhürischen gleichermasz ergehn / wie den Bauren im Bawrenkrieg vor dreyen und dreissig Jaren."

19. Bruin, *De Statenbijbel en zijn voorgangers*, 213–19.

20. Reske and Benzing, *Buchdrucker des 16. und 17. Jahrhunderts*, 563, 565.

21. Valkema Blouw, *Typographia Batava*, 617, no. 5396; *NB* 31229.

22. Kuttner, *Het hongerjaar 1566*. On Kuttner's work, see Duke, *Dissident Identities in the Early Modern Low Countries*, 180.

23. Pettegree, *Emden and the Dutch Revolt*, 186. Cf. Valkema Blouw, "Van Oldenborch and Vanden Merberghe Pseudonyms," 245–46 n. 78.

Chapter 5

1. Pettegree, *Emden and the Dutch Revolt*, 109–42; Duke, *Dissident Identities in the Early Modern Low Countries*, 157.

2. Van Haecht, *Kroniek over de troebelen van 1565 tot 1574 te Antwerpen en elders*, 1:48; Duke, *Dissident Identities in the Early Modern Low Countries*, 173.

3. Duke, *Dissident Identities in the Early Modern Low Countries*, 138.

4. Duke, *Dissident Identities in the Early Modern Low Countries*, 157.

5. Marnef, *Antwerp in the Age of Reformation*, 102–3.

6. Van Haecht, *Kroniek over de troebelen van 1565 tot 1574 te Antwerpen en elders*, 1:122: "Maer daerom seyden de calvinisten, dat sy daer gelyck de papen eenen afgodt afmaeckten. . . . 'Gy syt vleescheters en bloetdrinckers'"; Marnef, *Antwerp in the Age of Reformation*, 102.

7. Van Haecht, *Kroniek over de troebelen van 1565 tot 1574 te Antwerpen en elders*, 1:191.

8. Van Haecht, *Kroniek over de troebelen van 1565 tot 1574 te Antwerpen en elders*, 1:194, 197.

9. Van Haecht, *Kroniek over de troebelen van 1565 tot 1574 te Antwerpen en elders*, 1:198–201.

10. *Antorffischer Empörung so sich zwischen den Papisten / und den Geusen . . . nechst den 13. 14. und 15. tag Martii zůgetragen / kurtzer Bericht* (VD16 A 2981), a3r.

11. Van Haecht, *Kroniek over de troebelen van 1565 tot 1574 te Antwerpen en elders*, 1:202; Loosjes, *Geschiedenis der Luthersche kerk in de Nederlanden*, 46; Marnef, *Antwerp in the Age of Reformation*, 103, 105; Olson, "Matthias Flacius Faces the Netherlands Revolt," 109.

12. Flacius, *Excusatio Matthiae Flacii Illyrici contra calumnias adversariorum quod praesentium calamitatum ecclesiae Brabantiae causa fuerit* (VD16 F 1391), 3v: "Et tamen quid aliud tandem tumultuando contra Magistratum effecerunt, nisi ut in Maiores calamitates inciderint, Evangelium Christi omnesque illas Ecclesias tetro seditionis nomine oneraverint, et demum persequutoribus tanto plausibiliorem speciem saeviendi dederint?" On the spread of news from the Netherlands to Germany, see Duke, *Dissident Identities in the Early Modern Low Countries*, 120. One example concerning events in Antwerp is *Antorffischer Empörung so sich zwischen den Papisten / und den Geusen . . . nechst den 13. 14. und 15. tag Martii zůgetragen / kurtzer Bericht* (VD16 A 2981).

13. On Apiarius, see Reske and Benzing, *Buchdrucker des 16. und 17. Jahrhunderts*, 85–86; Ehrstine, *Theater, Culture, and Community in Reformation Bern*, 62–63.

14. All editions supplement "Friess II" with prophecies concerning the year 1588, a date that had attracted the attention of prognosticators since at least 1553. Prognostications for the year 1588 had previously appeared in connection with "Friess I" in N14, the edition that was printed together with the prognostication of Nikolaus Caesareus, where the 1588 material, including a well-known quatrain, forms an appendix to Caesareus's prognostication. Caesareus attributes the quatrain about 1588 to the ephemerides of Cyprian Leowitz, which had been published the previous year: "Ex Ephemeridibus Cypriani. Tausent fünffhundert achtzig acht // Das ist das Jar das ich betracht. // Gehet in dem die Welt nicht under // So gschicht doch sonst gros mercklich wunder" (Friess and Caesareus, *Etliche seltzame Propheceiung* [VD16 F 2841/C 84], c3v). On this quatrain, see Thorndike, *History of Magic and Experimental Science*, 5:374–75 n. 190; Barnes, *Prophecy and Gnosis*, 81, 120–23, 161–67, 232–36; Leppin, *Antichrist und Jüngster Tag*, 139–49; Zinner, *Johannes Müller von Königsberg*, 154–55. The quatrain in question appears in 1557 in Leowitz, *Ephemeridum novum* (VD16 L 1263), cc10v, where Leowitz attributes it to Regiomontanus and writes that he remembers once hearing it from Johannes Schöner. Two Latin versions of the same verse are found in Leowitz's 1564 work *De coniunctionibus magnis insignioribus superiorum planetarum, solis defectionibus et cometis* (VD16 L 1268), n3v. The earliest printed source is Engelbert of Admont and Brusch, *Hodoeporicon Bavaricum* (VD16 E 1211/B 8765), 6, 144.

15. Barnes, *Prophecy and Gnosis*, 81.

16. Schmitt, "Bruder Dietrich (von Zengg)."

17. Green, *Printing and Prophecy*, 197–98; Talkenberger, *Sintflut*, 468.

18. Höfler, *Geschichtschreiber der husitischen bewegung in Böhmen*, 6:416: "Idcirco ego innominabilis timens iram daemonis in occulto sermone nitor laborare et ex communi fama quasi apis argumentose colligere simul in unum bona et mala." Lichtenberger borrowed this passage to build a pseudonymous authorial identity as the "Pilgrim Ruth" in the *Prognosticatio*. On the authorship by a Bohemian Catholic, see Leidinger, *Andreas von Regensburg, sämtliche Werke*, 379 n. 4–5.

19. See the complete title formulation of this edition (F1) in appendix 3. On

Emden, see Pettegree, *Emden and the Dutch Revolt.* Beyer ("George Reichard und Laurentius Matthaei," 306 n. 30) correctly recognizes this edition as a prophecy attributed to Wilhelm Friess and notes similarities with the seventeenth-century prophecies of Georg Reichard.

20. *Grawsame und erschreckliche alte Prophezei* (VD17 39:140281T), a1v: "Mehr wisse der Leser / daß mir von einem glaubwürdigen Mann dem ich diese Vision communiciret / zugeschrieben / daß er selbige schon vor 10. Jahren in hochteutscher Sprach gelesen / unnd daß sie mit dieser / was den sensum unnd das Hauptwerck anlangen thut / gar fein concordire unnd übereinstimme / daß man also desto mehr versichert ist / daß es eine warhafftige Vision / ob es gleich im übrigen wegen des vielfeltigen abschriebens und mißverstandes der Copiisten nicht concordiren möchte."

21. Heinemann, *Kataloge der Herzog-August-Bibliothek Wolfenbüttel*, 327–34.

22. On the contrast of *lutherisch* and *leutherisch*, see Wander, *Deutsches Sprichwörter-Lexikon*, 3:295, which cites Valerius Herberger's Hertz-Postilla, a work that went through numerous sixteenth- and seventeenth-century editions.

23. Someren (*Pamfletten*, 1:28, 34, 38, nos. 101, 124, 138) ascribes the title woodcut of F3 to the same workshop as the title woodcut of *Kurtze Relation / wie die Statt Grave beschossen*, printed by von Kempen in 1586 (not in VD16). That woodcut had already appeared on the title page of an anonymously printed pamphlet concerning events in Antwerp in 1583. Someren in turn compares this second woodcut ascribed to the same workshop to a woodcut used to illustrate a Dutch edition of the prophecies of Paul Grebner (illustrated in Burger and Moes, *Amsterdamsche boekdrukkers*, 3:350–53, nos. 599–600), which shows Mars, Saturn, and Mercury, an eclipsed sun and moon, and two winds, within a complex scene that is highly reminiscent of the title page of F3. Like "Friess II," Grebner's work also addressed religious implications of Henry III's migration from Poland to France in 1574. For what little is known of Gerhard von Kempen, see Reske and Benzing, *Buchdrucker des 16. und 17. Jahrhunderts*, 454–55.

24. See Warburg, *Heidnisch-antike Weissagung*, 25–27.

25. Frell, *Sechß und dreyssig Zeichen Vor dem jüngsten Tag* (VD16 ZV 21238), a2r. For extensive discussion on the debates over the supernova of 1572, see Weichenhan, *Ergo perit coelum.*

26. Magirus, *Prognostication oder Practica . . . auff das Jahr . . . M. D. LXVIII* (VD16 ZV 10243), a1r.

27. Leowitz, *Ephemeridum novum* (VD16 L 1263), T3r.

28. Winckler, *Summarische Practic* (VD16 W 3428), b1v–b2r, b3r: "In solchem allem / werden wir viel leydigs elends und wunders erfaren. . . . Solche Finsternuß macht am andern / bey den verstendigen Göttlichs Wort / welche dem Zwilling unterworffen / abermals mehr / dann mir / oder andern zu schreiben zimlich sein wollen"; "Derwegen viel der gelehrten / diese künfftige Jar / der zeit / so dem tag des Gerichts Gottes vorgehen soll / zu vergleichen / oder solche für das end dieser welt / selbst zu achten / seind verursacht worden."

29. Leowitz, *Ephemeridum novum* (VD16 L 1263), L8r, dd1r.

30. Leowitz and Eisenmenger, *Warhafftige weissagung der fürnemsten dingen so vom M. D. LXIIII. Jar biß auff das 1607. sich zůtragen werden* (VD16 ZV 25875), f2v: "jedoch so wird es anreitzen und erwecken / etlich feindschafft und haß für nachvolgende Jar / Unnd das von wegen der Finsternuß des Mons / so sein wird den viii. Decembris in gemeldtem 1574.[sic] jar / und welche ir würckung / in nach gehenden 1574. jar wird erzeigen."

31. Leowitz, *De coniunctionibus magnis insignioribus superiorum planetarum, solis defectionibus et cometis* (VD16 L 1268), n2r: "Ceterum anno Domini 1573. et 1574. fiet Oppositio magna superiorum planetarum in Scorpione ac Tauro, item in Sagittario et Geminis: cui etiam Eclipsis Solis satis tetra in Sagittario commiscebitur, quae tamen apud occidentales populos potissimum efficaciam suam exercebit: atque eandem in duos sequentes annos producet. Ego ex hac Oppositione magna, et Eclipsi Solis, iudico inusitatum aeris calorem, et siccitatem: deinde vehementes dissensiones inter fratres, agnatos et affines: frequentes exactiones, ac graves expilationes, quibus subditos suos domini passim gravabunt, atque ad conspirationes clandestinas, et seditiones impellent. Pars procerum ac nobilium defectionem meditabitur. In negotiis matrimonialibus, vel de dote mulierum, veterisque iuris dominio, aut reconventione pactorum, altercationes incident. Motus bellici atroces erunt: item conflagrationes, depopulationes ac direptiones agrorum, oppidorum, arcium et Civitatum. Principum ac magnatum decessus luctuosus ostenditur. Mutationes insignes tam in religione, quam politiis ingruent. Praecipue vero caveat sibi Hispania, cum eius regna Sagittario subiaceant."

32. The decorative initial that marks the beginning of the text of the F3 edition is in a style that became popular only after 1576. One would expect that a text that gives such a significant role to Strasbourg would be printed in that city, and a Strasbourg printer, Bernhard Jobin, did use typefaces and decorative initials of the same style, but Jobin used them only in 1584 and later.

33. Schönfeld, *Prognosticon astrologicum* (VD16 S 3718), a1r.

Chapter 6

1. Taylor, *Political Prophecy*, 3–4.

2. Barnes, *Prophecy and Gnosis*, 285.

3. On "Gamaleon," see Kurze, "Johann von Wünschelburg," 821. The best analysis of the textual history and context of "Gamaleon" is Courtney Kneupper's 2011 dissertation, "Crafting Religious and National Identity: The Use of Prophecy in Late Medieval Germany" (Northwestern University).

4. Deppermann, *Melchior Hoffman*, 227.

5. Derksen, *From Radicals to Survivors*, 70.

6. Jost, *Prophetische gesicht und Offenbarung* (VD16 J 993), a8r: "und in der nacht umb eins ongeferdt / da sahe ich in dem schein des herren ein grosse schar volcks / und mitten under der schar hab ich gesehen ein mans bild / der selbig trůg an ein roten mantel / und in seiner seiten ein wundzeichen. Und ich hab weiter gesehen / daz nach diser obgemelten schar / ist kummen gerant ein grosse schar reuter / und ein hauffen reyßigs zeügs / die selbigen hatten alle uffgesteckte pfahenfedern / die selbigen federn hingen yhn von den hütten auff den rucken Weiter hab ich gesehen / das nach disen obgemelten scharen / ist kummen ein grosser man / der selbig thet mit grossem starckem plast auß plasen / windt und wasser."

7. Jost, *Prophetische gesicht und Offenbarung* (VD16 J 993), c5r: "Weiter hab ich gesehen im schein des herren / das einer ist kummen reiten uff einem weissen pferd / der selbig war eitel schwartz / und ich sahe das er ward zů einer wag / darnach sahe ich das er wider ward zů einem menschen / und das er sich mit harnscht bekleidet / und ich sahe zwen neben im stan / die schmirten im den harnischt schwartz und dunckel / uff das er mocht sein wandel sicher füren durch alle landt."

8. Jost, *Prophetische gesicht und Offenbarung* (VD16 J 993), c3v: "da hab ich gesehen

ein man der war gantz greülich groß unnd schwartz / unnd ward uß dem selben man ein einige finsterniß / und ließ sich die uff die erden / unnd schinnen dem man unnd der selben finsterniß finstere tunckele tranen nach / und schwebeten die selben tranen voller Ostien brot."

9. Derksen, *From Radicals to Survivors*, 144–50.

10. *Ein Warhfftige prophecey uber Teuschland unnd anderen Königreich von Sachsen / funden in einem Barfusser Closter in der Liberey geschrieben / anno Tausendt dreyhundert* (VD16 ZV 25981), a2v.

11. Hofmann, *Luther und die Johannes-Apokalypse*, 417–18.

12. Luther, *Etliche warhafftige weissagung / und fürneme spruche des Ehrwirdigen Vaters / Hern Doctor Martini Luthers* (VD16 L 3474), b4r–v: "Weil aber wir der nicht achten / unnd Gott für solche tewre gaben nicht dancken / Sondern unns mehr an gelt / reichthumb / gewalt unnd wollust / auff welche wir all unsern vleiss / mühe / und arbeit setzen / lassen gelegen sein / müssen derhalben der Türck / Bapst / und andere unzeliche Teuffeln aus Welschlandt / Hispania / und aus allen örtern der Welt kommen / die uns von wegen unserer unaussprechlicher und schentlicher undanckbarckeit weidelich herumb rücken / kür machen und schlachten werden." On Timann's collection and similar collections, see Kolb, *Martin Luther as Prophet, Teacher, and Hero*, 178–83.

13. Luther, *D. Martin Luthers Werke: Kritische Gesamtausgabe*, 40:139–40: "Nos Iudaei sumus quasi ultima fex orbis et minima hominum portio. Insurgunt autem contra nos hominess, hoc est Reges, Principes, Divites, Sapientes, et quicquid in hoc seculo potens et magnum est, hi omnes non adversantur nobis nec oderunt nos communi modo, sic contra nos insurgunt, ut conentur plane nos delere et opprimere. Si enim ad Orientem, ad Aquilonem, ad Septentrionem et Meridiem te vertas et consyderes, quot et quam ampla regna nos cingant, quae omnia capitali odio contra nos incensa sunt, plane iudicabimur similes oviculae, quam centum lupi circumstant et omni momento irruere et vorare eam conantur."

14. Schindling, *Humanistische Hochschule und freie Reichsstadt*, 130–44.

15. Duke, *Dissident Identities in the Early Modern Low Countries*, 231–32; Rathgeber, *Strassburg im sechzehnten Jahrhundert*, 399–402.

16. Luther, *Dr. Martin Luther's Briefwechsel*, 9:139: "Judicium Dei nunc secundo videmus, semel in Munzero, nunc in Zwinglio. Propheta fui, qui dixi: Deum non laturum diu istas rabidas et furiosas blasphemias, quibus illi pleni erant, irridentes Deum nostrum impanatum, vocantes nos carnivoras et sanguibibas et cruentos, et aliis horrendis nominibus appellantes."

17. van Haecht, *Kroniek over de troebelen van 1565 tot 1574 te Antwerpen en elders*, 1:122.

18. On the use of this image in sacramental polemics, see Duke, *Dissident Identities in the Early Modern Low Countries*, 191–93.

19. Nischan, "Confessionalism and Absolutism," 190–91, 195–96.

20. Wieder, *Schriftuurlijke liedekens*, 73: "Dat was het 'klein hoopken,' de 'klein vergadering der uitverkorenen,' de 'gemeente overdekt met bloed,' die uit stad en land verdreven werd en waar nergens een woonplaats voor was, die uit het land moest vluchten en in ballingschap verkeeren."

21. Duke, *Dissident Identities in the Early Modern Low Countries*, 50, 155; van Haecht, *Kroniek over de troebelen van 1565 tot 1574 te Antwerpen en elders*, 1:202; Marnef, *Antwerp in the Age of Reformation*, 199.

22. Warburg, *Heidnisch-antike Weissagung*, 32–33.

184 · Notes to Pages 101–5

23. Nischan, "Confessionalism and Absolutism," 190.

24. Guise, *Des Cardinals von Lotthringen Römische practicken / von den Ketzern in Deudschland aus zurotten* (VD16 ZV 2936), a2r–v; see also VD16 ZV 2937, 2938, 27953.

25. Cf. Balodis, *Väld och frihet*, 204–5.

26. Zittau Christian Weise Bibliothek Hist. 4° 949 (24), a1v (F25). Further annotations on folio a2r calculate that the number of banners mentioned in the prophecy multiplied by 500 soldiers each would yield an army of 82 million combatants, and the annotations add some chronological context: "anno 1590. hab ich gehört den 10 aprilis das der Turk horaus wil mitt 60 mol hundert tausent Turken das ist mitt 6 000 000 sex tausent mol tausent man quid est 19 mol mer dan er vor wien hatte. anno. der houschreken waren one Zaall auch."

27. *Warhaffte und eigentliche Beschreibung* (VD16 W 470), a1v: "Daß vor Hundert Jahren der jetzig fall in Franckreich / unnd wie es mit dem König zugangen / also geweißsagt und propheceyet ist worden. Wie folgt. Dum Rex Henricus regnabit origine natus // Hic Rex bis factus, tam re quam nomine dictus, // Lilia vir fortis propriis evellet ab hortis, // Rex cadet, et vulgus, militia Francica, clerus, // Peste, fameque, siti ferro, flammaque, peribunt. // Diese Prophecey ist in S. Victors Bibliothecken ausser Pariß / vor langen Jahren / durch ihr viele daselbst gesehen / und gelesen worden." See also VD16 W 470, ZV 4614.

28. Halbronn, *Le texte prophétique en France*, 2:490–92.

29. Solikowski, *Probi et Galliae ac Poloniae amantis viri, ad Gallos et Sarmatas oratio* (VD16 ZV 23084), 24r–27v.

30. Arnold, *Unparteyische Kirchen- und Ketzer-Historie*, 1–2:332.

31. Gillespie, *Echoland*, 124.

32. Nischan, *Lutherans and Calvinists in the Age of Confessionalism*, VII, 11.

33. Fischart, *Grundliche und Warhaffte beschreibung / Wie die Reformirte Religion in Franckreych / von Henrico II. dem Vatter / demnach Francisco II. Und Carolo IX. Seinen Sönen / biß auff gegenwürtige zeit verfolget worden / sampt deren heimlichen / biß anhehr unbewüsten list und Practicken / Auß den Dialogis Eusebii Philadelphi Cosmopolitae, und anderen historien / gezogen. Demnach wie Henricus / Hertzog von Angiers / König in Polen erwelet / gekrönet / widerumb entwichen / und gen Venedig ankommen* (VD16 G 3531).

34. Hotman, *Memoirs of Gaspar de Colligny*, 200–201.

35. Barnaud, *Reveille Matin* (VD16 B 395), *7r–v: "das in der gantzen Welt kain Haus oder Geschlecht seie / welches mit so schandlicher untreu und verrätterei beflekt / als eben dises Haus Valois. Weiter auch um des willen / das E.G. und ir dazumal ain solchs abscheuen / solcher Morthat halben getragen / das sie vil liber etwan ainen Kühirten / oder ainen Eseltreiber / zu irem König erwölet hetten / denn diser Mörder oder bluthund ainen."

36. Kühlmann, "Johann Fischart," 590–92.

37. Hoffmann, "Bücher und Autographen von Johann Fischart," 504.

38. Hauffen, "Fischarts Bildungsreise und seine philosophischen Studien in Paris und Straßburg," 598, 600.

39. Hauffen, "Fischarts Bildungsreise und seine philosophischen Studien in Paris und Straßburg," 333–36.

40. Kleinschmidt, "Gelehrtentum und Volkssprache in der fruhneuzeitlichen Stadt," 136–37.

41. Hoffmann, "Bücher und Autographen von Johann Fischart," 504.

42. Olson, "Matthias Flacius Faces the Netherlands Revolt," 103–9.

43. Englert, "Zu Fischarts bilderreimen," 391.

44. The title of the broadside in question is *Effigies brevisque notatio vitae reverendi viri D. M. Mathiae Flacii Illyrici.*

45. Hoffmann, "Bücher und Autographen von Johann Fischart," 531; Kleinschmidt, "Gelehrtentum und Volkssprache in der fruhneuzeitlichen Stadt," 141–42; Kühlmann, "Johann Fischart," 601, 611 n. 49.

46. Rührmund, *Johann Fischart als Protestant,* 52–53.

47. Weber, "Welt begeret allezeit Wunder," 275: "gläubiger calvinistischer Protestant"; Kühlmann, "Johann Fischart," 596, 597: "entschiedener Parteigänger der Calvinisten."

48. Hauffen, *Neue Fischart-Studien,* 225–26: "Und drum der Hurenkelch draus würd, // Welcher dem Antichrist gebürt." Ernst Rührmund (*Johann Fischart als Protestant,* 42) disputed Hauffen's view.

49. Hauffen, "Die Verdeutschungen politischer Flugschriften aus Frankreich, den Niederlanden und der Schweiz," 544–53; Hauffen, "Die Verdeutschungen politischer Flugschriften aus Frankreich, der Schweiz und den Niederlanden," 650; Hauffen, "Fischarts Bildungsreise und seine philosophischen Studien in Paris und Straßburg," 350.

50. Gillespie, *Echoland,* 124.

51. Weber, "Welt begeret allezeit Wunder," 283, nos. 24–25.

52. Fischart, *Aller Practick Großmutter* (VD16 F 1133), a2r–v.

53. Fischart, *Affenteurliche und Ungeheurliche Geschichtschrift Vom Leben / rhaten und Thaten der . . . Helden und Herrn Grandgusier / Gargantoa / und Pantagruel* (VD16 F 1127), bb5r: "ain Mercurischen Rorpfeiffer der den huntertäugigen Argo entschläft."

54. Seelbach, "Fremde Federn," 543; Fischart, *Catalogus catalogorum,* 11, 12, 22, nos. 98, 122, 304. The Strasbourg editions of Luginsland are VD16 L 3199–200.

55. Weber, "Welt begeret allezeit Wunder," 283, no. 22; Hauffen, *Neue Fischart-Studien,* 190–92.

56. Reprinted in Weber, "Welt begeret allezeit Wunder," 276, 289, no. 58: "Solcher Wunderprediger hat uns Gott kürtzlich viel nach einander geschicket / als nämlich / das der Mon zweimal ist verfinstert worden / erstlich den 2. Aprilis / darnach den 27. Septembris des ablauffenden 77. Jars: Darauff hat bald gefolget das Wundergestirn oder die fewerige Rut des Cometens: das ich nun der zwen starcken und weitraichenden Erdbidem / deßgleichen der Sterben und Pestilentzischen Suchten / so sich hin und wider erzaigen / und der Krieg und deß Kriegsgeschreies geschweige."

57. Reprinted in Weber, "Welt begeret allezeit Wunder," 276: "Auß disem Wölcklin ist erschinen ein schwartz gekleydet Volck / wie ein groser Krigshaufen zu Roß und Fuß / das ist allgemächlich und sittig durch obgemelte Sonn hindurch gegen Aufgang gezogen: und unter disem Volck hat hinden ein hohe lange Mannsperson / welche weit über alle andere gereichet / nachgefolgt. . . . Sondern bald nach durchgezogen ein Kriegsvolck mit lauterem Blut überzogen / dermassen / das nicht allein die Sonn / sondern auch der Himmel Blutrot / scheutzlich und schröcklich anzusehen gewesen. . . . Was nun dises Wunderzeichen und andere dergleichen für anzeigungen seien / kan ein jeder / der sich nur ein wenig inn der Welt umbsihet / bei im selbs erachten / das es warlich nichts anders dann trewe Warnungen des Trewen Gottes / und Träwungen seiner Strafen seien. Gott gebe das wir inn bußfertigkeyt solche erkennen."

58. Dasypodius (*Warhafftige Außlegung des Astronomischen Uhrwercks zu Straßburg*

[VD16 D 235], c4v) gives the date of completion as the feast of St. John the Baptist (June 24). Schade ("Spätrenaissance am Oberrhein") surveys literary treatments of the astronomical clock.

59. Fischart, *Aigentliche Fürbildung und Beschreibung deß Neuen Kunstlichen Astronomischen Urwerckes.*

60. Kühlmann, "Johann Fischart," 597; Schuler, *Strassburger Münster*, 90–91.

61. Dasypodius, *Warhafftige Außlegung des Astronomischen Uhrwercks zu Straßburg* (VD16 D 235), e2v.

62. Oestmann, *Die astronomische Uhr*, 54–55.

63. Dasypodius, *Warhafftige Außlegung des Astronomischen Uhrwercks zu Straßburg* (VD16 D 235), e2r.

64. Fischart, *Affenteurliche und Ungeheurliche Geschichtschrift Vom Leben / rhaten und Thaten der . . . Helden und Herrn Grandgusier / Gargantoa / und Pantagruel* (VD16 F 1127), a6r–v: "Was solt die kumpfgelegen nas auf Sibillisch die Marien der Semele vergleichen / die den Bachum bisgenitum erzihet? er ist noch nit mit dem Gansfůß durch den Bach gewattet"; "Wa ir dan diß Lichtenbergisch traumdeiten nicht glaubt / warum wolten ir nicht eben so vil von diser kurzweiligen zeitung und neuen Chronich halten / die euch vileicht eben so vil räterst als jenes fabuliren kan aufgeben."

65. Hoffmann, "Bücher und Autographen von Johann Fischart," 563; Moser, "Sprachliche Studien zu Fischart," 106; Weber, "Welt begeret allezeit Wunder," 521.

66. Hauffen, *Neue Fischart-Studien*, 39; Meusebach, *Fischartstudien*, 286; Fischart, *Catalogus catalogorum*, 26, no. 375: "Prophecey von der Japetischen Sprach gegen Nord / daß dieselb kurtz vor dem End der Welt der gantzen Welt werde Gesatz und Maß geben und vorschreiben: Auch daß die Monarcheien allzeit von Sud gegen Mitternacht gewandert haben: erklärt durch D. Wickartum de Moguntiaco."

67. Englert, "Zu Fischarts bilderreimen," 539–40; Honegger, *Die Schiltburgerchronik und ihr Verfasser Johann Fischart*, 80; Kühlmann, "Johann Fischart," 596. On the "Jobinsche Orthographie," see Kleinschmidt, "Gelehrtentum und Volkssprache in der fruhneuzeitlichen Stadt," 137 n. 33.

68. Kleinschmidt, "Gelehrtentum und Volkssprache in der fruhneuzeitlichen Stadt," 137–43, 143 n. 60; Kühlmann, "Johann Fischart," 589–90.

69. Kleinschmidt, "Gelehrtentum und Volkssprache in der fruhneuzeitlichen Stadt," 143: "Die 'Lebhaftigkeit' als Prinzip des Fischartschen Stils, die in der Erzählerprofilierung ebenso wie im spontanen Aufführungscharakter der literarischen Fiktion zu ausgeprägten Strukturmustern ausgebaut erscheint."

70. As cited in Hauffen, *Neue Fischart-Studien*, 30: "Scripsit item alia plura, quae aut suppresso suo nomine aut permutato, edita sunt."

71. Müller, "Texte aus Texten," 75: "Die meisten sind aus Texten anderer gemacht, durch Übersetzung, Paraphrase, Amplifikation, Parodie, Anspielung, Zitat und anderes, meist—doch nicht immer—in komischer Verzerrung."

72. Hoffmann, "Bücher und Autographen von Johann Fischart," 558; Weber, "Welt begeret allezeit Wunder," 283, nos. 24–25; Weller, "Zur Fischart-Literatur," 10–11.

73. Fischart, *Von erwölung des Königs in Poln* (VD16 ZV 15315), a1v–a4r.

74. Fischart, *Von erwölung des Königs in Poln* (VD16 ZV 15315), a4r–v: "Dir in dein Landt nein bringen // Kriegsvolck und was zu solchen dingen // Gehöret und notturfftig ist // Von harnisch / wehren / schilt und spieß."

75. Fischart, *Von erwölung des Königs in Poln* (VD16 ZV 15315), a6v–a7r, a8r: "Und ehe man sich recht umbgewendt // Wurden sie vorher ihm rennen // Dir dein gantzes Landt außbrennen // Nider würgen beid weib und man."

76. Fischart, *Von erwölung des Königs in Poln* (VD16 ZV 15315), b1r: "Wenn er aber sehe das du wirst arm // Mit dir zugieng das Gott erbarm // So wurd er nicht der letzte sein // Der dir fiehle in dein Landt hinein."

77. Fischart, *Von erwölung des Königs in Poln* (VD16 ZV 15315), b2v: "Und anstellen an allem endt // Den brauch der Hochwirdigen Sacrament // Nach des Herren Christi bevehl."

78. Fischart, *Von erwölung des Königs in Poln* (VD16 ZV 15315), b3r–v.

79. Prof. Dr. Ulrich Seelbach, e-mail message to author, 16 May 2013.

Chapter 7

1. Barnes, *Prophecy and Gnosis*, 52–53.

2. Nischan, "Confessionalism and Absolutism," 189.

3. See Leppin, *Antichrist und Jüngster Tag*, 45–46, 181; Nischan, "Confessionalism and Absolutism," 189–90.

4. Leppin, *Antichrist und Jüngster Tag*, 46 n. 5; Schottenloher, "Untergang des Hauses Habsburg," 131–32.

5. Nischan, "Confessionalism and Absolutism," 204.

6. Duke, *Dissident Identities in the Early Modern Low Countries*, 24.

7. Schoppe, *Christliche unnd Nötige Warnung für dem erdichten Lügen-Geist der falschen Propheten* (VD16 S 3867), L1v: "Es pfleget der Satan seine Weissagungen auch gemeinlich also zuversaltzen / das man seine klawen und lügen maul leichtlich mercket / wenn man nur gute achtung drauff gibt und mit reinem augen ansicht und Christlich erweget. Als für etlichen und dreissig jahren wurden gesprenget etliche Weissagungen des alten Wilhelms Friesen von nastrich / von den fellen so sich vom 1558. biß ins 1563. zutragen würden / das an viel gefehlet / uber das gab er unter andern für / es würde in der zeit ein frommer und Gottfürchtiger Keyser kommen / und viel guts thun / und dem Obersten reinen Bischoffe helffen die Welt wider zu recht bringen / und die ungleubigen secten alle ausrotten / auch das gelobte Land wider eröbern und den Christlichen glauben alda verkündigen lassen / aber hernach würde er sein Keyserthum verlassen und ein heilig leben führen / etc. Wer spüret hie nit den Geist des irthumbs. Denn ein Weltlicher Regent so from / Gottfürchtig / friedsam und friedfertig / dazu ein trewer pfleger / ernerer und schützer der waren Kirchen und religion ist / wie kan der ein heiligers leben führen / als wenn er in seinem stand bleibet / und darin und mit Gott und Menschen / nach seinen beruff recht dienet?" See Barnes, *Prophecy and Gnosis*, 234.

8. Valkema Blouw, *Typographia Batava*, 502, no. 4427.

9. Kurze, *Johannes Lichtenberger*, 69.

10. Mentgen, *Astrologie und Öffentlichkeit im Mittelalter*, 127, 135.

11. For the version attributed to Johannes Doleta, see Mentgen, *Astrologie und Öffentlichkeit im Mittelalter*, 111. The editions include the two "Friess II" editions previously mentioned as well as VD16 ZV 4633 and ZV 22756. An unrecorded edition is *Kurtze Propheceyung oder Practica* (not in VD16 [Utrecht UL, F qu 269 dl 9]). For the broadside editions, see Harms and Schilling, *Sammlung der Zentralbibliothek Zurich*, 6–7:314–15, 334–35. *Prognosticon: So mit vornehmer Astronomorum Calculation, auff das 1629. Jahr gerichtet* (VD17 23:332291K) is an edition of the "Toledo Letter" printed in 1629.

12. Neuheuser, *Victoria Christianorum verissimorum universalis* (VD17 14:006754K), 32: "So hat auch einer mit namen Wilhelm von Mastrich der Christlichen Kirchen zerrüttung / von der Bäpstler Lateinischen Kirchen beschehen / verstanden / wie-

derumb wissentliche *Vaticinia* oder Andeutunge gemacht / wie es mit Römischer Kirchen gehen / wie sie die Christliche Kirche unnd wahres Christen Volck / darauß wieder scheiden / und endlich die überhand under einer grossen weissen Fahnen erhalten werde / darinnen vielleicht das Zeichen *Tau* geführet wird / wie sich die Exempel im Niderland schon angefangen haben."

13. Kose, *Warhafftige / gründliche und Göttliche Offenbarung* (VD17 23:323699T), a3r–v.

14. Jansz, *Copye Van een Brieff / geschreven uyt Frieslandt / door Inthie Jansz*, a1v–a2v. On this prophecy, see Frijhoff, *Embodied Belief*, 144, 161; Dupont-Bouchat, Frijhoff, and Muchembled, *Prophètes et sorciers dans les Pays-Bas, XVIe-XVIIIe siècle*, 279–83. Frijhoff lists over twenty editions from the seventeenth century into the early twentieth (*Wegen van Evert Willemsz*, 375 n. 46; see also 370–77, 424–26.

15. Arnold, *Unparteyische Kirchen- und Ketzer-Historie*, 3–4:246.

16. Arnold, *Unparteyische Kirchen- und Ketzer-Historie*, 3–4:257: "Den 23 Julii, in der mitternacht-stunden, da ward ich wieder verzückt, da kam der engel Gottes zu mir, und bracht mich auf eine grosse heyden in das Polner land, da sahe ich 2 grosse heere als Tartarn und Cossacken, und sahe auf eine halbe stunde zu, biß sich die völcker zusammen führten, nach diesem stritten sie wider die Polen 2 stunden; ich sahe ihnen zu, und die Polen verlohren den sieg, und der engel Gottes sprach zu mir zweymal: Verflucht bist du von Gott, Polner-land, und durch dieses land soll der Türck in Teutschland kommen."

17. Arnold, *Unparteyische Kirchen- und Ketzer-Historie*, 3–4:257.

18. Rohr, *Prophezeiung von der Entscheidungsschlacht des Europäischen Krieges am Birkenbaum*, 10–11.

19. Bauer ("Die Rezeption mittelalterlicher Prophezeiungen im 17. und 18. Jahrhundert," 125 nn. 23–24) cites this edition but does not connect it to the name of Wilhelm Friess.

20. Weimar Herzogin Anna Amalia Bibliothek 4° XXV: 138 (12c).

21. *Etliche Sonder- und Wunderbahre Merckwürdige Prophezeyungen So sich auf das 1680. biß zu dem 1700ten Jahr erstrecken* (VD17 3:600599Z), a1r: "Nebenst Einer wehemühtigen Klage und Bitte derer sämptlichen Pfaltzischen und Rheinischen ruinirten Ländern und Städten / an die Allerhöchste und unendlichste Majestät / wieder die allergrausamsten Proceduren Ludewigs des XIV. Königs von Franckreich. Zu diesen gefährlichen betrübten Zeiten wohlmeinend auff vielfältiges Nachfragen / zum andern mahl zum Druck befordert. Und mit einer Explication der Obscuren Nahmen und Wö[r]ther verwahret."

22. Kurze, *Johannes Lichtenberger*, 71.

23. On the "Lion of the North" prophecy, see Hotson, *Paradise Postponed*, 56–60.

24. Kurze, *Johannes Lichtenberger*, 33–38.

25. On the flood controversy, see Green, *Printing and Prophecy*, 131–50; Mentgen, *Astrologie und Öffentlichkeit im Mittelalter*, 135–55; Talkenberger, *Sintflut*, 154–335.

26. See Scott, *Domination and the Arts of Resistance*, 167–71.

27. Green, *Printing and Prophecy*, 106–7.

28. Niccoli, *Prophecy and People in Renaissance Italy*, 4.

29. Lerner, *Powers of Prophecy*, 187; Coote, *Prophecy and Public Affairs in Later Medieval England*, 15.

30. Moynihan, "The Development of the 'Pseudo-Joachim' Commentary 'Super Hieremiam,'" 134.

31. Robert Lerner cautiously attributes both early redactions of the *Vademecum* to

Rupescissa and notes another case of "extracts from extracts" from the same work ("Popular Justice," 39–40 n. 2, 48).

32. Coote, *Prophecy and Public Affairs in Later Medieval England*, 15.

33. Cf. Lerner, *Powers of Prophecy*, 188.

34. Leppin, *Antichrist und Jüngster Tag*, 28–29, 287, 292; Seebaß, "Die Bedeutung der Apokalyptik für die Geschichte des Protestantismus," 104: "Die apokalyptischen Traditionen haben stets auch dazu angehalten, mit der Identifizierung des Antichrists den Ort der eigenen Zeit in der Gesamtgeschichte zu bestimmen."

35. Engel, *Kurtzer / Jedoch gewisser und gründtlicher Bericht / von Johan Hilten / und seinen Weissagungen* (VD16 ZV 5013), a2r-v: "da ich noch ein Junger Knab und also unter meiner lieben *Praeceptorum Disciplin* zu Straussberg gewesen / sind mir und meinen andern *Condiscipulis*, neben andern Biblischen und Weltlichen Historien / auch des Gelahrten und frommen Mönchs *Johannis Hiltenii* / so des Herrn D. Martini Lutheri Praeceptor zu Eysenach in Düringen gewesen / Weissagungen zu Deutschen Argumenten (wie mans in Schulen nennet) auffgegeben worden / dieselbige ins Latein *styli exercendi gratia*, zubringen"; "auch zuvor von vielen gehöret das sie gerne wissen möchten / woraus doch der gute *Hiltenius* seine *conjecturas* und Weissagungen genommen." On Hilten, see Hofmann, *Luther und die Johannes-Apokalypse*, 662–72.

36. Chartier, *Order of Books*, 52.

Appendix 1

1. Ferrari, "Un petit traictié extrait," 308–19; Brown, *Fasciculus rerum expetendarum et fugiendarum*, 2:496–508; *Propheceien und Weissagungen* (VD16 P 5068).

Appendix 2

1. *Dise prophecy ist funden worden in Osterreich uff einem Schloß das heißt Altenburg* (VD16 D 1458); Lichtenberger, *Die weissagunge Johannis Lichtenbergers deudsch* (VD16 L 1597).

Appendix 3

1. Edited in Kampen, *Het zal koud zijn in't water als't vriest*, 203–8.

2. The attributions of N17–N19 to Kreydlein are my own, based on the use of identical type and title woodcuts and very similar page layouts, but with enough differences to determine that these are not identical to other Kreydlein editions.

3. This edition is listed in Weller, *Die ersten deutschen Zeitungen*, 304–5, no. 656, with a copy in Nuremberg known to Weller. The present location of this copy is unknown.

4. This edition is identified as distinct from the previous one in Weller, *Die ersten deutschen Zeitungen*, 305, no. 656, although the editions are listed under the same entry.

5. Heyer, "Zweite Nachlese zu Weller," 222, no. 35 identifies this edition as separate from the prior two, which were listed by Weller. A copy was known to Heyer from the Breslau Stadtbibliothek, but no copy is currently found in the Wroclaw University Library catalog.

Bibliography

Sources: Editions and Early Printed Books
(Not Including Wilhelm Friess Editions)

Ambach, Melchior. *Vom Ende der Welt / Und zukunfft des Endtchrists. Wie es vorm Jungsten tag in der Welt / ergehn werde. Alte und newe Propheceyen / Auff diese letzste böse zeit . . . in rheumen gestelt.* Frankfurt am Main: Hermann Gülfferich, [ca. 1548]. VD16 A 2161.

Antorffischer Empörung so sich zwischen den Papisten / und den Geusen . . . nechst den 13. 14. und 15. tag Martij zůgetragen / kurtzer Bericht etc. Deszgleichen auch die Artickel / Der Vergleichung / Welche . . . zwischen bayden Partheyen / nach gestillter Empörung / Auffgerichtet. Augsburg: Hans Zimmermann, 1567. VD16 A 2981.

Arnold, Gottfrid. *Gottfried Arnolds Fortsetzung und Erläuterung Oder Dritter und Vierdter Theil der unpartheyischen Kirchen- und Ketzer-Historie Bestehend In Beschreibung der noch übrigen Streitigkeiten im XVIIIden Jahrhundert. Nebst den Supplementis und Emendationibus über alle vier Theile.* Vols. 3–4. Frankfurt am Main: Thomas Fritsch heirs, 1729.

Arnold, Gottfrid. *Gottfrid Arnolds Unparteyische Kirchen- und Ketzer-Historie / von Anfang des Neuen Testaments biß auff das Jahr Christi 1688.* Vols. 1–2. Frankfurt am Main: Thomas Fritsch, 1699.

Barnaud, Nicolas. *Reveille matin: Oder Wacht frü auf. Das ist. Sumarischer / und Warhafter Bericht von den verschinenen / auch gegenwärtigen beschwärlichen händeln in Frankreich / den Franzosen und andern genachbarten Nationen zu gutem / Gesprächweis gestellet und verfasset.* Translated by Johann Fischart. Strasbourg: Bernhard Jobin, 1575. VD16 B 395.

Brown, Edward. *Fasciculus rerum expetendarum et fugiendarum.* Vol. 2. London: Richard Chiswell, 1690.

Copp, Johannes. *Was auff diß Dreyundzwayntzigest und zum tail vyerundzwayntzigest jar. Des himels lauff künfftig sein / Auß weyß Doctoris Johannis Copp urtayl.* Augsburg: Heinrich Steiner, 1522. VD16 C 5026.

Dasypodius, Konrad. *Warhafftige Außlegung des Astronomischen Uhrwercks zu Straßburg / beschriben Durch M. Cunradum Dasypodium / des solches Astronomische Uhrwerck anfenglichs erfunden / und angeben.* Strasbourg: Nikolaus Wiriot, 1578. VD16 D 235.

Dise prophecy ist funden worden in Osterreich uff einem Schloß das heißt Altenburg. Ist gemacht von einem Münich Carmeliten ordens von Prag. Da man zalt nach der geburt Christi / Vierhundert / Zweyundsechtzig Jare. Freiburg im Breisgau: Johann Wörlin, 1522. VD16 D 1458.

Effigies brevisque notatio vitae reverendi viri D. M. Mathiae Flacii Illyrici. Strasbourg: Bernhard Jobin, 1577.

Ein Warhfftige prophecey uber Teuschland unnd anderen Königreich von Sachsen / funden in einem Barfusser Closter in der Liberey geschrieben / anno Tausendt dreyhundert / und sind der Copeien 24. gewest. Freiburg: Christian Mundanus [pseudonym], 1573. VD16 ZV 25981.

Engel, Andreas. *Kurtzer / Jedoch gewisser und gründtlicher Bericht / von Johan Hilten / und seinen Weissagungen. Da denn insonderheit auch zufinden / woraus solche Weissagungen genomen / und wie sie albereit am meisten erfüllet worden: Sampt etlichen andern Weissagungen und conjecturen von stürtzung des Babsthumbs / und untergang des Türckischen Reichs.* Frankfurt a. d. Oder: Johann Hartmann and Friedrich Hartmann, 1597. VD16 ZV 5013.

Engelbert of Admont and Kaspar Brusch. *Engelberti Abbatis Admontensis, qui sub Rudolpho Habspurgio floruit, de Ortu et fine Romani Imperii Liber. Cum Gasparis Bruschii Poetae laureati Praefatione. Accessit eiusdem Bruschij Hodoeporicon Bavaricum, in quo et Regiomontani vaticinium quoddam explicatur, et varia de die extremo conjiciuntur.* Basel: Johann Oporinus, 1553. VD16 E 1211/B 8765.

Ferrer, pseudo-Vincent. *Ain wunderbarlich Büechlin und prophecei / des heiligen Manns Sant Vincentz von Valentz / Prediger ordens / von den letsten zeitten und dem endt der welt / Newlich durch ain Gotseligen der Kirchen liebhaber / gaistlichem und weltlichem Standt zů ainer bösserung / verteütscht unnd in druckh geben.* Munich: Andreas Schobser, 1540. VD16 V 1210.

Fischart, Johann. *Affenteurliche und Ungeheurliche Geschichtschrift Vom Leben / rhaten und Thaten der . . . Helden und Herrn Grandgusier / Gargantoa / und Pantagruel / Königen inn Utopien und Ninenreich. Etwan von M. Francisco Rabelais Französisch entworfen.* [Strasbourg: Bernhard Jobin], 1575. VD16 F 1127.

Fischart, Johann. *Aigentliche Fürbildung und Beschreibung deß Neuen Kunstlichen Astronomischen Urwerckes / zu Straßburg im Mönster / das M. D. LXXIIII. Jar vollendet / zusehen.* Strasbourg: Bernhard Jobin, 1574.

Fischart, Johann. *Aller Practick Großmutter. Die dickgeprockte Pantagruelinische Btrug dicke Prockdick / oder Pruchnastickatz / Laßtafel / Baurenregel unnd Wetterbüchlin / auff alle Jar und Land gerechnet und gericht.* Strasbourg: Bernhard Jobin, 1593. VD16 F 1133.

Fischart, Johann. *Catalogus catalogorum perpetuo durabilis (1590).* Edited by Michael Schilling. Tübingen: Niemeyer, 1993.

Fischart, Johann. *Grundliche und Warhaffte beschreibung / Wie die Reformirte Religion in Franckreych / von Henrico II. dem Vatter / demnach Francisco II. Und Carolo IX. Seinen Sönen / biß auff gegenwürtige zeit verfolget worden / sampt deren heimlichen / biß anhehr unbewüsten list und Practicken / Auß den Dialogis Eusebii Philadelphi Cosmopolitae, und anderen historien / gezogen. Demnach wie Henricus / Hertzog von Angiers / König in Polen erwelet / gekrönet / widerumb entwichen / und gen Venedig ankommen.* 1574. VD16 G 3531.

Fischart, Johann. *Von erwölung des Königs in Poln / samt kleiner weissagung ihres nachgestelten erholten dancks. Durch den außgesünderten desselbigen Landes mit behertzen gestelt.* Strasbourg: Bernhard Jobin, 1574. VD16 ZV 15315.

Flacius, Matthias. *Catalogus testium veritatis, qui ante nostram aetatem reclamarunt Papae.* Basel: Michael Martin Stella for Johannes Oporinus, 1556. VD16 F 1293.

Flacius, Matthias. *Duae veteres prophetiae de pia Ecclesiae Dei instaturatione, ad nostra tempora pertinentes.* Magdeburg: Michael Lotter, 1550. VD16 P 5061.

Flacius, Matthias. *Excusatio Matthiae Flacii Illyrici contra calumnias adversariorum quod praesentium calamitatum ecclesiae Brabantiae causa fuerit.* N.p.: n.p., 1568. VD16 F 1391.

Frell, Joerg. *Sechß und dreyssig Zeichen Vor dem jüngsten Tag so vorher lauffen werden / unnd die Zeyt eröffnen / unnd anzeigen / das Er vorhanden sey / unnd die zukünfft Christi zum gericht verkündende auffs aller kürzest zur warnung angezeigt.* N.p.: n.p., 1580. VD16 ZV 21238.

Génard, Pierre, ed. "Personen te Antwerpen in de XVIe eeuw, voor het 'feit van religie' gerechtelijk vervolgd: Lijst en ambtelijke bijhoorige stukken." *Antwerpsch archievenblad* 8 (1877): 322–472.

Gerdes, Daniel. *Introductio in historiam evangelii seculo XVI. passim per Europam renovati docrinaeque reformatae. Accedunt varia quibus ipsa historia illustratur, monumenta pietatis atque rei literariae.* Groningen and Bremen: Hajo Spandaw and Gerhard Wilhelm Rump, 1749.

Grünpeck, Joseph. *Ein spiegel der naturlichen himlischen und prophetischen sehungen aller trübsalen / angst / und not / die uber alle stende / geschlechte / und gemaynden der Christenheyt / sunderbar so dem Krebsen under geworffen sein / und in dem sibenden Clima begriffen / in kurtzen tagen geen werden.* Nuremberg: Georg Stuchs, 1508. VD16 G 3642.

Grünpeck, Joseph. *Speculum naturalis coelestis et propheticae visionis: omnium calamitatum tribulationum et anxietatum: quae super omnes status: stirpes et nationes christianae reipublice: presertim quae cancro et septimo climati subiecte sunt: proximis temporibus venture sunt.* Nuremberg: Georg Stuchs, 1508. VD16 G 3641.

Guise, Charles de. *Des Cardinals von Lotthringen Römische practicken / von den Ketzern in Deudschland aus zurotten. Dem Frantzösischen Legaten in Polen mitgetheilet. Aus des Cardinals Eigen Handschriefft auffgefasset . . . Aus einem gedrucktem Lateinischen Exemplar trewlich Verdeudschet.* N.p.: n.p., 1573. VD16 ZV 2936.

Haecht, Godevaert van. *Kroniek over de troebelen van 1565 tot 1574 te Antwerpen en elders.* Edited by Rob van Roosbroeck. 2 vols. Antwerp: De Sikkel, 1929.

Haemstede, Adriaen Cornelisz van, and Johannes Gysius. *Historie der martelaren, die om het getuygenisse der Evangelischer waerheydt haer bloedt gestort hebben, van de tijden Christi onses Salighmakers aftot den jare sesthien hondert vijf-en-vijftigh toe.* Dordrecht: Jacob Braat for Jacobus Savry, 1659.

Haer, Franciscus van der. *Francisci Haraei Annales ducum seu principum Brabantiae totiusque Belgii tomus tertius: quo tumultus Belgici, ab anno MDLX usque ad Inducias MDCIX pactas, enarrantur, cum brevi rerum per Europam illustrium narratione.* Antwerp: Plantin, 1623.

Höfler, Karl Adolf Constantin von, ed. *Geschichtschreiber der husitischen bewegung in Böhmen.* Vol. 6. Fontes rerum austriacarum: Oesterreichische Geschichts-Quellen 1. Vienna: Hof- und Staatsdruckerei, 1865.

Hotman, François. *Memoirs of Gaspar de Colligny, Admiral of France. With an account of the Massacre of St. Bartholomew's Day, August 24, 1572.* Edinburgh: W. Oliphant and Sons, 1844.

Jansz, Intje. *Copye Van een Brieff / geschreven uyt Frieslandt / door Inthie Jansz. Ouderlinck der Ghemeente jesu Christi tot Ooster-Zee / ende Echten.* Leeuwarden: n.p., 1623.

Jost, Ursula. *Prophetische gesicht und Offenbarung / der götlichen würckung zu diser letsten zeit / die vom. xxiiii. jar biß in dz. xxx. einer gottes liebhaberin durch den heiligen geist geoffenbart seind / welcher hie in disem büchlin. lxxvii. verzeichnet seindt.* [Strasbourg: Balthasar Beck], 1530. VD16 J 993.

Kose, Johann. *Warhafftige / gründliche und Göttliche Offenbarung: So durch die krefftigen und durchdringenden Wort Gottes . . . einer Christlichen Person in einem Gesichte im Jahr 1591. und im 1599. Jahr widerumb ist gezeiget worden.* Erfurt: Esaias Mechler, 1601. VD17 23:323699T.

Kronyk der stad Alkmaer, Met desselfs omgeleegene dorpen, heerlykheeden, en adelyke gebouwen; Waar in verhaald worden de voornaamste Oorlogen, en onlusten der Kenmers, en Westvriesen: Beneevens de voornaamste Previlegien, Handvesten, Costumen, en Ordonnantien. Amsterdam: E. en J. Visscher, H. Bosch, S. Schouten; Leiden: J. van der Deyster, 1725.

Lazius, Wolfgang. *Fragmentum vaticinii cuiusdam (ut conjicitur) Methodii, episcopi ecclesie Paterenis, et Martyris Christi . . . et vice Prognostici cuiusdam ad annos futuros.* Vienna: Johann Singriener the Elder heirs, 1547. VD16 ZV 9507.

Leidinger, Georg, ed. *Andreas von Regensburg: Sämtliche Werke.* Quellen und Erörterungen zur bayerischen Geschichte, n.s., 1. Munich: M. Rieger, 1903.

Leowitz, Cyprian. *De coniunctionibus magnis insignioribus superiorum planetarum, Solis defectionibus et Cometis, in quarta Monarchia, cum eorundem effectuum historica expositione.* Lauingen: Emanuel Saltzer, 1564. VD16 L 1268.

Leowitz, Cyprian. *Ephemeridum novum atque insigne opus ab anno domini 1556. usque in 1606. accuratissime supputatum: cui praeter alia omnia in caeteris editionibus addi solita, etiam haec accesserunt.* Augsburg: Philipp Ulhart the Elder, 1557. VD16 L 1263.

Leowitz, Cyprian, and Samuel Eisenmenger. *Prognosticon. Warhafftige weissagung der fürnemsten dingen so vom M. D. LXIIII. Jar biß auff das 1607. sich zůtragen werden / auß den Finsternussen und grossen Ephemeri des Hochgelerten Cypriani Leovicii / und auß dem Prognostico Samuelis Syderocratis / gezogen und zusamen gestalt.* Basel, 1568. VD16 ZV 25875.

Lichtenberger, Johannes. *Die weissagunge Johannis Lichtenbergers deudsch / zugericht mit vleys. Sampt einer nutzlichen vorrede und unterricht D. Martini Luthers / Wie man die selbige und der gleichen weissagunge vernemen sol.* Wittenberg: Hans Lufft, 1527. VD16 L 1597.

Luther, Martin. *D. Martin Luthers Werke: Kritische Gesamtausgabe.* Vol. 40. Weimar: Hermann Böhlaus Nachfolger, 1930.

Luther, Martin. *Dr. Martin Luther's Briefwechsel.* Edited by Ernst Ludwig Enders. Vol. 9. Calw and Stuttgart: Evangelischer Verein, 1903.

Luther, Martin. *Etliche warhafftige weissagung / und fürneme spruche des Ehrwirdigen Vaters / Hern Doctor Martini Luthers / des dritten Helie / vom trübsal / abfal / finsternissen / Oder aber verfelschungen reiner Lere / so Deudtschlandt künfftiglich nach seinem tode / widerfaren solle.* Edited by Johannes Timann. Magdeburg: Michael Lotter, 1552. VD16 L 3474.

Magirus, Ambrosius. *Prognostication oder Practica / nach Himlischer Influentz / auff das Jahr . . . M. D. LXVIII.* N.p: n.p., 1567. VD16 ZV 10243.

Nagel, Paul. *Himmels Zeichen. Grosse Coniunctiones Planetarum superiorum, und newer Wunderstern / so Anno 1604. den 29. Septembris erschienen: Was sie bedeuten / und wie wunderbar es in der Welt / vor dem Tage deß grossen Richters Jesu Christi / die zeit uber wird zugehen / beschrieben.* Halle (Saale): Joachim Krusecke for Erasmus Hynitzsch, 1605. VD17 3:002506P.

Neuheuser, Wilhelm Eon. *Victoria Christianorum verissimorum universalis; Das ist: Ein*

Gründtliche Beschreibung / welcher gestalt alle wahre Evangelische Christen von jetziger zeit an / uber und wider alle Widersacher Göttliches Worts / zu reinem Christlichen Glauben / Sieg und Uberwindung erhalten werden. Friedwegen [Salzburg]: Samuel Ehehafft, 1618. VD17 14:006754K.

Prognosticon. So mit vornehmer Astronomorum Calculation, auff das 1629. Jahr gerichtet / und der Römischen Key: May: zugesendet worden. N.p: n.p., 1629. VD17 23:332291K.

Propheceien und Weissagungen. Vergangne / Gegenwertige / und Künfftige ding / Geschichten unnd Zûfäll / aller Stende. Frankfurt am Main: Christian Egenolff, 1550. VD16 P 5068.

Prophecey Wunderbarlicher zûkünftiger ding die sich itzundt gewißlich erneüwen / und biß nach ende des Endtchrists erscheynen / und nach seiner sichtigklichen uffart / unnd nit ehe / ir ende erreichen werden. Oppenheim: Jakob Köbel, 1522. VD16 P 5064.

Schönfeld, Victorin. *Prognosticon astrologicum. Auff die vier Zeiten und andere bedeutung der Planeten / Auff das Jar 1575.* Wittenberg: Clemens Schleich and Anton Schöne, 1575. VD16 S 3718.

Schoppe, Andreas. *Christliche unnd Nötige Warnung für dem erdichten Lügen-Geist der falschen Propheten und fürwitzigen Leute / so die gewisse zeit des jüngsten Tages auszurechnen / zu nennen und zu Weissagen sich bemühen / und felschlich rühmen / gestellet.* Wittenberg: Johann Dörffer, 1596. VD16 S 3867.

Severus, Paul. *Newe Zeitunge / Von der bedeutung die da folgen werden / aus dem obgemelten Constellation / und der Finsternissen.* N.p.: n.p., 1563. VD16 ZV 14383.

Solikowski, Jan Dymitr. *Probi et Galliae ac Poloniae amantis viri, ad Gallos et Sarmatas oratio. Accessit insigne et pervetus vaticinium de liliorum et aquilae septemtrionalis coniunctione.* Basel: n.p., 1575. VD16 ZV 23084.

Virdung, Johann. *Practica von dem Entcrist und dem jüngsten tag auch was geschehen sal vor dem Ende der welt.* Speyer: Anastasius Nolt, 1525. VD16 V 1302.

Warhaffte und eigentliche Beschreibung / dern Historia / wie der König in Franckreich / dessen Nahmens der Dritt / Henrich von Valois als er belagerte die Statt Paris zu Pont S. Clou / von einem Jacobinen Oder Prediger Mönch / eilendt vom leben zum todt bracht / am Ersten tag Augusti. Anno 1589. Sampt einer Weissagung / so vor Hundert Jahren / von des Königs todt / geprophecetet ist worden. Cologne: Nikolaus Schreiber, 1589. VD16 W 470.

Winckler, Georg. *Summarische Practic Georgii Wincklers Forchemii / Fürstlichen Würtenbergischen bestelten Medici zu Bietikheim / auff das Jar M. D. LXXIIII.* Nuremberg: Valentin Fuhrmann, 1573. VD16 W 3428.

Wolf, Johann. *Johan. Wolfii J.C. lectionum memorabilium et reconditarum centenarii xvi. Habet hic Lector Doctorum Ecclesiae, Vatum, Politicorum, Philosophorum, Historicorum, aliorumque sapientum et eruditorum pia, gravia, mira, arcana, et stupenda; iucunda simul et utilia, dicta, scripta, atque facta; Vaticinia item, vota, omina, mysteria, Hieroglyphica, miracula, visiones, antiquitates, monumenta, testimonia, exempla virtutum, vitiorum, abusuum; typos insuper, picturas, atque imagines . . . Cum indice.* Lauingen: Leonhard Reinmichel, 1600. VD16 W 4210.

Works Cited

Balodis, Francis. *Vȧld och frihet: En lettisk universitetsprofessors minnen.* Stockholm: Hugo Gebers, 1941.

Barnes, Robin Bruce. *Prophecy and Gnosis: Apocalypticism in the Wake of the Lutheran Reformation.* Stanford: Stanford University Press, 1988.

Bauer, Barbara. "Die Rezeption mittelalterlicher Prophezeiungen im 17. und 18. Jahrhundert." In *Mittelalterliche Denk- und Schreibmodelle in der Deutschen Literatur der frühen Neuzeit*, edited by Wolfgang Harms and Jean Marie Valentin, 111–48. Chloe 16. Amsterdam: Rodopi, 1993.

Beyer, Jürgen. "George Reichard und Laurentius Matthaei: Schulmeister, Küster, Verfasser, Buchhändler und Verleger im letzten Jahrzent des Dreißigjährigen Krieges." In *Lesen und Schreiben in Europa 1500–1900: Vergleichende Perspektiven*, edited by Alfred Messerli and Roger Chartier, 299–333. Basel: Schwabe, 2000.

Bignami-Odier, Jeanne. *Études sur Jean de Roquetaillade (Johannes de Rupescissa)*. Paris: Vrin, 1952.

Bots, Hans, Ignaz Matthey, and Mathias Meyer. *Noordbrabantse studenten 1550–1750*. Tilburg: Stichting Zuidelijk Historisch Contact, 1979.

Broeckx, C. "Lettre a M. le docteur P. J. van Meerbeeck de Malines sur une publication de R. Dodoens inconnue des bibliophiles." *Annales de l'Académie d'archéologie de Belgique* 19 (1862): 5–18.

Bruin, C. C. de. *De Statenbijbel en zijn voorgangers*. Leiden: A. W. Sijthoff, 1937.

Bumke, Joachim. "The Fluid Text: Observations on the History of Transmission and Textual Criticism of the Thirteenth-Century Courtly Epic." In *Visual Culture and the German Middle Ages*, edited by Kathryn Starkey and Horst Wenzel, 99–113. New York: Palgrave Macmillan, 2005.

Burger, Combertus Pieter, and Ernst Wilhelm Moes. *De Amsterdamsche boekdrukkers en uitgevers in de zestiende eeuw*. Amsterdam: C. L. van Langenhuysen, 1900.

Chartier, Roger. *The Order of Books: Readers, Authors, and Libraries in Europe between the Fourteenth and Eighteenth Centuries*. Translated by Lydia G. Cochrane. Stanford: Stanford University Press, 1994.

Coote, Lesley. *Prophecy and Public Affairs in Later Medieval England*. Woodbridge, Suffolk: York Medieval Press in association with Boydell Press, 2000.

Deppermann, Klaus. *Melchior Hoffman: Social Unrest and Apocalyptic Visions in the Age of Reformation*. Edinburgh: T. and T. Clark, 1987.

Derksen, John D. *From Radicals to Survivors: Strasbourg's Religious Nonconformists over Two Generations, 1525–1570*. 't Goy-Houten: Hes en de Graaf, 2002.

DeVun, Leah. *Prophecy, Alchemy, and the End of Time: John of Rupescissa in the Late Middle Ages*. New York: Columbia University Press, 2009.

Diekmann-Dröge, Gabriele. "'Van den Eerwerdigen Meester Jan Goosens': Zur Bücherzensur in Antwerpen im 16. Jahrhundert." In *Franco-Saxonica: Münstersche Studien zur niederländischen und niederdeutschen Philologie; Jan Goossens zum 60. Geburtstag*, edited by Robert Damme, 361–75. Neumünster: Karl Wachholtz, 1990.

Dingel, Irene. "The Culture of Conflict in the Controversies Leading to the Formula of Concord (1548–1580)." In *Lutheran Ecclesiastical Culture, 1550–1675*, edited by Robert Kolb, 15–64. Leiden: Brill, 2008.

Dixon, C. Scott. "Popular Astrology and Lutheran Propaganda in Reformation Germany." *History* 84 (1999): 403–18.

Doedes, J. I. "Nieuw merkwaardigheden uit den oude-boeken-schat." *Studiën en bijdragen op 't gebied der historische theologie* 4 (1880): 207–42.

Duke, Alastair C. *Dissident Identities in the Early Modern Low Countries*. Edited by Judith Pollmann and Andrew Spicer. Burlington: Ashgate, 2009.

Dupont-Bouchat, Marie-Sylvie, Willem Frijhoff, and Robert Muchembled. *Prophètes et sorciers dans les Pays-Bas, XVIe–XVIIIe siècle*. Paris: Hachette, 1978.

Efron, Noah J. "Nature, Human Nature, and Jewish Nature in Early Modern Europe." *Science in Context* 15 (2002): 29–49.

Ehrstine, Glenn. *Theater, Culture, and Community in Reformation Bern, 1523–1555.* Leiden: Brill, 2002.

Englert, Anton. "Zu Fischarts bilderreimen." *Zeitschrift für deutsche Philologie* 34 (1903): 534–40; 35 (1904): 390–95.

Faems, An. "Deynde der werelt naket: Een eindtijdvoorspelling uit het begin van de zestiende eeuw." In *Kennis-maken: Een bloemlezing uit de Middelnederlandse artesliteratuur*, edited by Orlanda S. H. Lie and Lenny M. Veltman, 73–89. Hilversum: Verloren, 2008.

Ferrari, Barbara. "Le Vade mecum in tribulatione de Jean de Roquetaillade en moyen français (ms. BAV, Reg. lat. 1728)." In *Pour acquerir honneur et pris: Mélanges de moyen français offerts à Giuseppe Di Stefano*, edited by M. Colombo and C. Galderisi, 225–36. Montreal: Ceres, 2004.

Ferrari, Barbara. "Un 'petit traictié' extrait du 'Vade mecum in tribulatione' de Jean de Roquetaillade (1356): Édition du ms. BAV, Reg. lat. 1728." *Studi francesi* 55 (2011): 301–22.

Francois, Wim. "Jacob van Liesvelt, Martyr for the Evangelical Belief?" In *More than a Memory: The Discourse of Martyrdom and the Construction of Christian Identity in the History of Christianity*, edited by Johan Leemans, 341–69. Louvain: Peeters, 2005.

Frederiks, Johannes Godefridus, and Frans Josef Peter van den Branden. *Biographisch woordenboek der Noord- en Zuidnederlandsche letterkunde.* Amsterdam: L. J. Veen, 1888.

Freytag, Gustav. *Bilder aus der deutschen Vergangenheit.* 3 vols. Leipzig: S. Hirzel, 1896.

Frijhoff, Willem. *Embodied Belief: Ten Essays on Religious Culture in Dutch History.* Hilversum: Verloren, 2002.

Frijhoff, Willem. *Wegen van Evert Willemsz.: Een Hollands weeskind op zoek naar zichzelf, 1607–1647.* Nijmegen: SUN, 1995.

Führer, Jochen. *Die Kirchen- und die antireformatorische Religionspolitik Kaiser Karls V. in den siebzehn Provinzen der Niederlande, 1515–1555.* Leiden: Brill, 2004.

Gelderen, Martin van. *The Political Thought of the Dutch Revolt, 1555–1590.* Cambridge: Cambridge University Press, 2002.

Gillespie, Gerald Ernest Paul. *Echoland: Readings from Humanism to Postmodernism.* New York: Peter Lang, 2006.

Grange, Antoine Rivet de la. *Histoire littéraire de la France.* Vol. 41. Paris: Imprimerie nationale, 1981.

Green, Jonathan. *Printing and Prophecy: Prognostication and Media Change 1450–1550.* Cultures of Knowledge in the Early Modern World. Ann Arbor: University of Michigan Press, 2012.

Green, Jonathan. "Printing the Future: The Origin and Development of the Practica Teütsch to 1620." *Archiv für Geschichte des Buchwesens* 67 (2013): 1–18.

Greetham, David C. *Textual Scholarship: An Introduction.* New York: Garland, 1992

Halbronn, Jacques. *Le texte prophétique en France: Formation et fortune.* 3 vols. Villeneuve-d'Ascq: Presses universitaires du Septentrion, 1999.

Harms, Wolfgang, and Michael Schilling. *Die Sammlung der Zentralbibliothek Zürich: Kommentierte Ausgabe.* Vols. 6–7. Deutsche illustrierte Flugblätter des 16. und 17. Jahrhunderts. Tübingen: Niemeyer, 1997.

Hartmann, Martina. *Humanismus und Kirchenkritik: Matthias Flacius Illyricus als Erforscher des Mittelalters.* Stuttgart: Jan Thorbecke, 2001.

Hauffen, Adolf. "Die Verdeutschungen politischer Flugschriften aus Frankreich, den Niederlanden und der Schweiz." *Euphorion* 8 (1901): 529–71.

Hauffen, Adolf. "Die Verdeutschungen politischer Flugschriften aus Frankreich, der Schweiz und den Niederlanden." *Euphorion* 9 (1902): 637–56.

Hauffen, Adolf. "Fischarts Bildungsreise und seine philosophischen Studien in Paris und Straßburg." *Euphorion* 20 (1913): 332–56, 589–606.

Hauffen, Adolf. *Neue Fischart-Studien.* Euphorion Ergänzungsheft 7. Leipzig: Carl Fromme, 1908.

Heinemann, Otto. *Kataloge der Herzog-August-Bibliothek Wolfenbüttel.* Alte Reihe, Nachdruck der Ausgabe 1884–1913, 5 (Die Augusteischen Handschriften 2). Frankfurt am Main: Vittorio Klostermann, 1966.

Herkommer, Hubert. "Johannes de Rupescissa (Jean de Roquetaillade)." In *VL²* 4:724–29.

Heyer, Alfons. "Zweite Nachlese zu Weller: Die ersten deutschen Zeitungen." *Zentralblatt für Bibliothekswesen* 5 (1888): 214–25, 272–83.

Hoffmann, Christian. "Bücher und Autographen von Johann Fischart." *Daphnis* 25 (1996): 489–579.

Hoffmann-Krayer, Eduard, and Hanns Baechtold-Staeubli. *Handwörterbuch des deutschen Aberglaubens.* Berlin: de Gruyter, 1974.

Hofman, E. "De Antwerpse drukker Frans Fraeten: De verhouding tussen de vroegste gereformeerde en doopsgezinde liedboeken." *Doopsgezinde Bijdragen,* n.s., 20 (1994): 71–82.

Hofman, E. "Liederen en refreinen van Frans Fraet?" *Spiegel der Letteren* 42 (2000): 227–58.

Hofmann, Hans-Ulrich. *Luther und die Johannes-Apokalypse: Dargestellt im Rahmen der Auslegungsgeschichte des letzten Buches der Bibel und im Zusammenhang der theologischen Entwicklung des Reformators.* Tübingen: J. C. B. Mohr (Paul Siebeck), 1982.

Honegger, Peter. *Die Schiltburgerchronik und ihr Verfasser Johann Fischart.* Hamburg: E. Hauswedell, 1982.

Honemann, Volker. "Ferrer, Vincenz." In *VL²* 2:726–27.

Hotson, Howard. *Paradise Postponed: Johann Heinrich Alsted and the Birth of Calvinist Millenarianism.* Dordrecht: Kluwer, 2000.

Howorth, Henry Hoyle. *History of the Mongols: From the 9th to the 19th Century.* London: Longmans, Green 1830.

Jaspers, Gerardus Johannes. *Savonarola (1452–1498) in de Nederlanden: Een bibliografie van zijn gedrukte werken met inleidende notities omtrent zijn leven, zijn plaats in de geschiedenis en de drukkers/uitgevers van zijn werken.* Amsterdam: Buitenkant, 1998.

Kampen, Hinke van, et al. *Het zal koud zijn in 't water als 't vriest: Zestiende-eeuwse parodiën op gedrukte jaarvoorspellingen.* The Hague: Nijhoff, 1980.

Kleinschmidt, Erich. "Gelehrtentum und Volkssprache in der frühneuzeitlichen Stadt: Zur literaturgesellschaftlichen Funktion Johann Fischarts in Strassburg." *Zeitschrift für Literaturwissenschaft und Linguistik* 37 (1980): 128–51.

Kossmann, Ernst Heinrich, and E. H. Mellink. *Texts concerning the Revolt of the Netherlands.* Cambridge: Cambridge University Press, 1974.

Kronenberg, Maria Elizabeth. *Verboden boeken en opstandige drukkers in de Hervormingstijd.* Amsterdam: P. N. van Kampen, 1948.

Kühlmann, Wilhelm. "Johann Fischart." In *Deutsche Dichter der frühen Neuzeit,* 589–612. Berlin: Schmidt, 1993.

Kurze, Dietrich. "Johann von Wünschelburg." In *VL²* 5:770–76.

Kurze, Dietrich. *Johannes Lichtenberger (†1503): Eine Studie zur Geschichte der Prophetie und Astrologie.* Lübeck: Matthiesen, 1960.

Kuttner, Erich. *Het hongerjaar 1566.* Amsterdam: Amsterdamsche Boek- en Courant-maatschappij, 1949.

Lecanu, Auguste-François. *Dictionnaire des prophéties et des miracles.* 2 vols. Paris: J.-P. Migne, 1852–54.

Leppin, Volker. *Antichrist und Jüngster Tag: Das Profil apokalyptischer Flugschriftenpublizistik im deutschen Luthertum 1548–1618.* Gütersloh: Gütersloher Verlagshaus, 1999.

Lerner, Robert. Introduction to *Liber secretorum eventuum,* by Johannes de Rupescissa. Edited and translated by Robert E. Lerner and Christine Morerod-Fattebert. Fribourg: Editions Universitaires Fribourg Suisse, 1994.

Lerner, Robert. "'Popular Justice': Rupescissa in Hussite Bohemia." In *Eschatologie und Hussitismus: Internationales Kolloquium, Prag 1.–4. September 1993,* edited by Alexander Patschovsky, František Šmahel, and Antonín Hrubý, 39–51. Prague: Historický Ústav, 1996.

Lerner, Robert. *The Powers of Prophecy: The Cedar of Lebanon Vision from the Mongol Onslaught to the Dawn of the Enlightenment.* Berkeley: University of California Press, 1983.

Loosjes, Jakob. *Geschiedenis der Luthersche kerk in de Nederlanden.* The Hague: Nijhoff, 1921.

Maas, Paul. *Textual Criticism.* Translated by Barbara Flower. Oxford: Clarendon, 1958.

Marnef, Guido. *Antwerp in the Age of Reformation: Underground Protestantism in a Commercial Metropolis, 1550–1577.* Baltimore: Johns Hopkins University Press, 1996.

Mauer, Benedikt, and Theresia Hörmann. *Medien und Weltbilder im Wandel der frühen Neuzeit.* Augsburg: Wissner, 2000.

McGinn, Bernard. *Antichrist: Two Thousand Years of the Human Fascination with Evil.* New York: Columbia University Press, 2000.

Mentgen, Gerd. *Astrologie und Öffentlichkeit im Mittelalter.* Stuttgart: Hiersemann, 2005.

Meusebach, Karl. *Fischartstudien des freiherrn Karl Hartwig Gregor von Meusebach, mit einer Skizze seiner literarischen Bestrebungen.* Halle (Saale): Niemeyer, 1879.

Möhring, Hannes. *Der Weltkaiser der Endzeit: Entstehung, Wandel und Wirkung einer tausendjährigen Weissagung.* Stuttgart: Jan Thorbecke, 2000.

Moldaenke, Günter. "Flacius Illyricus, Matthias." In *Neue Deutsche Biographie,* 5:220–22. Berlin: Duncker und Humblot, 1961.

Montag, Ulrich. *Das Werk der heiligen Birgitta von Schweden in oberdeutscher Überlieferung: Texte und Untersuchungen.* Munich: Beck, 1968.

Moser, Virgil. "Sprachliche Studien zu Fischart." *Beiträge zur Geschichte der deutschen Sprache und Literatur* 36 (1910): 102–219.

Moynihan, Robert. "The Development of the 'Pseudo-Joachim' Commentary 'Super Hieremiam': New Manuscript Evidence." *Mélanges de l'Ecole française de Rome: Moyen-Age, Temps modernes* 98 (1986): 109–42.

Müller, Beate. "Zensurforschung: Paradigmen, Konzepte, Theorien." In *Buchwissenschaft in Deutschland: Ein Handbuch,* edited by Ursula Rautenberg, Monika Estermann, and Volker Titel, 1:321–60. Berlin: de Gruyter, 2010.

Müller, Jan-Dirk. "Texte aus Texten: Zu intertextuellen Verfahren in frühneuzeitlicher Literatur, am Beispiel von Fischarts 'Ehzuchtbüchlein' und 'Geschichtklitterung.'" In *Intertextualität in der Frühen Neuzeit: Studien zu ihren theoretischen und praktischen Perspektiven,* edited by Wilhelm Kühlmann and Wolfgang Neuber, 63–109. Frankfurt am Main: Peter Lang, 1994.

Niccoli, Ottavia. *Prophecy and People in Renaissance Italy.* Translated by Lydia G. Cochrane. Princeton: Princeton University Press, 1990.

Nierop, Henk van. "Censorship and Illicit Printing and the Revolt of the Netherlands." In *Too Mighty to Be Free: Censorship and the Press in Britain and the Netherlands,* edited by Alastair C. Duke and C. A. Tamse, 29–44. Zutphen: Walburg, 1987.

Nischan, Bodo. "Confessionalism and Absolutism: The Case of Brandenburg." In *Calvinism in Europe, 1540–1620,* edited by Andrew Pettegree, Alastair C. Duke, and Gillian Lewis, 181–204. Cambridge: Cambridge University Press, 1994.

Nischan, Bodo. "Germany after 1550." In *The Reformation World,* edited by Andrew Pettegree, 387–409. London: Routledge, 2000.

Nischan, Bodo. *Lutherans and Calvinists in the Age of Confessionalism.* Aldershot: Ashgate, 1999.

Oestmann, Günther. *Die astronomische Uhr des Strassburger Münsters: Funktion und Bedeutung eines Kosmos-Modells des 16. Jahrhunderts.* Stuttgart: Verlag für Geschichte der Naturwissenschaften und der Technik, 1993.

Olson, Oliver E. "Matthias Flacius Faces the Netherlands Revolt." In *Caritas et Reformatio: Essays on Church and Society in Honor of Carter Lindberg,* edited by David M. Whitford, 103–12. St. Louis: Concordia 2002.

Olthoff, Frans. *De boekdrukkers, boekverkoopers en uitgevers in Antwerpen sedert de uitvinding der boekdrukkunst tot op onze dagen.* Antwerp: Buschmann, 1891.

Penman, Leigh T.I. "Climbing Jacob's Ladder: Crisis, Chiliasm, and Transcendence in the Thought of Paul Nagel (†1624), a Lutheran Dissident During the Time of the Thirty Years' War." *Intellectual History Review* 20 (2010): 201–26.

Penman, Leigh T. I. "'Repulsive Blasphemies': Paul Nagel's Appropriation of Unprinted Works of Jakob Böhme and Valentin Weigel in His *Prodromus Astronomiae Apocalypticae* (1620)." *Daphnis* 38 (2009): 597–620.

Petersen, Rodney. *Preaching in the Last Days: The Theme of "Two Witnesses" in the Sixteenth and Seventeenth Centuries.* New York: Oxford University Press, 1993.

Pettegree, Andrew. *The Book in the Renaissance.* New Haven: Yale University Press, 2010.

Pettegree, Andrew. *Emden and the Dutch Revolt: Exile and the Development of Reformed Protestantism.* Oxford: Clarendon, 1992.

Preger, Wilhelm. "Flacius Illyricus, Matthias." In *Allgemeine Deutsche Biographie,* 7:88–101. Leipzig: Duncker und Humblot, 1878.

Putnam, Ruth. *William the Silent, Prince of Orange (1533–1584), and the Revolt of the Netherlands.* New York: Putnam, 1911.

Rathgeber, Julius. *Strassburg im sechzehnten Jahrhundert, 1500–1598: Reformationsgeschichte der Stadt Strassburg.* Stuttgart: J. F. Steinkopf, 1871.

Reeves, Marjorie. *The Influence of Prophecy in the Later Middle Ages: A Study in Joachimism.* Oxford: Clarendon, 1969.

Reske, Christoph, and Josef Benzing. *Die Buchdrucker des 16. und 17. Jahrhunderts im deutschen Sprachgebiet.* Wiesbaden: Harrassowitz, 2007.

Rohr, F. *Die Prophezeiung von der Entscheidungsschlacht des Europäischen Krieges am Birkenbaum und andere Kriegsprophezeiungen: Neue Beiträge zu ihrer Deutung und zur Untersuchung ihres Wahrheitsgehalts.* Bocholt: Temming, 1917.

Roose, L. "De Antwerpse hervormingsgezinde rederijker Frans Fraet." *Jaarboek de Fonteine* 1 (1969–70): 95–107.

Rührmund, Ernst. *Johann Fischart als Protestant.* Anklam: Poettcke, 1916.

Sandblad, Henrik. *De eskatologiska föreställningarna i Sverige under reformation och motreformation.* Uppsala: Almqvist och Wiksell, 1942.

Schade, Richard Erich. "Kunst, Literatur und die Straßburger Uhr." In *Tobias Stimmer, 1539–1584: Spätrenaissance am Oberrhein; Ausstellung im Kunstmuseum Basel, 23. September-9. Dezember 1984*, edited by Dieter Koepplin, 112–17. Basel: Kunstmuseum Basel, 1984.

Schanze, Frieder. "Der Buchdruck eine Medienrevolution?" In *Mittelalter und frühe Neuzeit: Übergänge, Umbrüche und Neuansätze*, edited by Walter Haug, 286–311. Tübingen: Niemeyer, 1999.

Schindling, Anton. *Humanistische Hochschule und freie Reichsstadt: Gymnasium und Akademie in Strassburg 1538–1621*. Wiesbaden: Steiner, 1977.

Schmieder, Felicitas. "Letteratura profetica, oracolare e sibillina fra XIII e XV secolo." *Oliviana* 3 (2009). http://oliviana.revues.org/index343.html.

Schmitt, Wolfram. "Bruder Dietrich (von Zengg)." In *VL*² 2:102.

Schmolinsky, Sabine. "Prophetia in der Bibliothek: Die Lectiones memorabiles des Johannes Wolf." In *Zukunftsvoraussagen in der Renaissance*, edited by Klaus Bergdolt and Walther Ludwig, 89–130. Wiesbaden: Harrassowitz, 2005.

Schottenloher, Karl. "Untergang des Hauses Habsburg, von Wilhelm Misocacus aus den Gestirnen für das Jahr 1583 vorhergesagt: Eine verkappte politische Flugschrift." *Gutenberg-Jahrbuch* 26 (1951): 127–33.

Schuler, Théophile. *Das Strassburger Münster*. Strasbourg: Schuler, 1817.

Scott, James C. *Domination and the Arts of Resistance: Hidden Transcripts*. New Haven: Yale University Press, 1990.

Seebaß, Gottfried. "Die Bedeutung der Apokalyptik für die Geschichte des Protestantismus." *Una Sancta* 43 (1988): 101–11.

Seelbach, Ulrich. "Fremde Federn: Die Quellen Johann Fischarts und die Prätexte seines idealen Lesers in der Forschung." *Daphnis* 29 (2000): 465–583.

Smit, W. A. P. *Kalliope in de Nederlanden: Het Renaissancistisch-klassicistische epos van 1550 tot 1850*. 2 vols. Assen: van Gorcum, 1975.

Smoller, Laura. *History, Prophecy, and the Stars: The Christian Astrology of Pierre D'Ailly, 1350–1420*. Princeton: Princeton University Press, 1994.

Someren, J. F. van. *Pamfletten niet voorkomende in afzonderlijk gedrukte catalogi der verzamelingen in andere openbare nederlandsche bibliotheken*. Utrecht: A. Oosthoek, 1915.

Stöllinger-Löser, Christine. "Vaticinia de summis pontificibus." In *VL*² 2:1595–1600.

Talkenberger, Heike. *Sintflut: Prophetie und Zeitgeschehen in Texten und Holzschnitten astrologischer Flugschriften, 1488–1528*. Tübingen: Niemeyer, 1990.

Taylor, Rupert. *The Political Prophecy in England*. New York: Columbia University Press, 1911.

Thorndike, Lynn. *A History of Magic and Experimental Science*. 8 vols. New York: Macmillan, 1923.

Valkema Blouw, Paul. *Typographia Batava, 1541–1600: Repertorium van boeken gedrukt in Nederland tussen 1541 en 1600*. Nieuwkoop: de Graaf, 1998.

Valkema Blouw, Paul. "The Van Oldenborch and Vanden Merberghe Pseudonyms, or Why Frans Fraet Had to Die." *Quaerendo* 22 (1992): 165–90, 245–72.

Vauchez, André. "Jean de Roquetaillade († 1366 ca.): Bilan des recherches et état de la question." In *Eschatologie und Hussitismus: Internationales Kolloquium, Prag 1.—4. September 1993*, edited by Alexander Patschovsky, František Šmahel, and Antonín Hrubý, 25–37. Prague: Historický Ústav, 1996.

Waite, Gary K. *Reformers on Stage: Popular Drama and Religious Propaganda in the Low Countries of Charles V, 1515–1556*. Toronto: University of Toronto Press, 2000.

Wander, K. F. W., ed. *Deutsches Sprichwörter-Lexikon.* 5 vols. Leipzig: F. A. Brockhaus, 1873.

Warburg, Aby. *Heidnisch-antike Weissagung in Wort und Bild zu Luthers Zeiten.* Sitzungsberichte der Heidelberger Akademie der Wissenschaften, Philosophisch-historische Klasse 10. Heidelberg: Carl Winter, 1920.

Weber, Bruno. "'Die Welt begeret allezeit Wunder': Versuch einer Bibliographie der Einblattdrucke von Bernhard Jobin in Strassburg." *Gutenberg-Jahrbuch* 51 (1976): 270–90.

Weichenhan, Michael. *"Ergo perit coelum . . .": Die Supernova des Jahres 1572 und die Überwindung der aristotelischen Kosmologie.* Stuttgart: Franz Steiner, 2004.

Weller, Emil. *Die ersten deutschen Zeitungen.* Tübingen: Litterarischer Verein in Stuttgart, 1872.

Weller, Emil. "Zur Fischart-Literatur." *Anzeiger für Kunde der deutschen Vorzeit,* n.s., 4 (1857): 8–11.

Wieder, Frederik Caspar. *De Schriftuurlijke liedekens: De liederen der Nederlandsche Hervormden tot op het jaar 1566, inhoudsbeschrijving en bibliographie.* The Hague: Nijhoff, 1900.

Zedler, Gottfried. "Die Sibyllenweissagung: Eine in Thüringen entstandene Dichtung aus dem Jahre 1361." *Zeitschrift für deutsche Philologie* 61 (1936): 136–66, 274–88.

Zinner, Ernst. *Geschichte und Bibliographie der astronomischen Literatur in Deutschland zur Zeit der Renaissance.* 2nd ed. Stuttgart: Hiersemann, 1964.

Zinner, Ernst. *Leben und Wirken des Johannes Müller von Königsberg, genannt Regiomontanus.* Munich: Beck, 1938.

Index